The Executioner's
Toll, 2010

The Executioner's Toll, 2010

The Crimes, Arrests, Trials, Appeals, Last Meals, Final Words and Executions of 46 Persons in the United States

MATTHEW T. MANGINO

McFarland & Company, Inc., Publishers
Jefferson, North Carolina

LIBRARY OF CONGRESS CATALOGUING-IN-PUBLICATION DATA

Mangino, Matthew T., 1962–
The executioner's toll, 2010 : the crimes, arrests, trials,
appeals, last meals, final words and executions of
46 persons in the United States / Matthew T. Mangino.
p.   cm.
Includes bibliographical references and index.

ISBN 978-0-7864-7979-5 (softcover : acid free paper) ∞
ISBN 978-1-4766-1604-9 (ebook)

1. Capital punishment—United States—Case studies.
2. Executions and executioners—United States—Case studies.
3. Death row inmates—United States—Case studies.
4. Death row—United States—Case studies.   I. Title.
HV8699.U5M345 2014   364.66092'273—dc23   2014007734

BRITISH LIBRARY CATALOGUING DATA ARE AVAILABLE

Cover image © Mark Goddard/iStock/Thinkstock

Printed in the United States of America

*McFarland & Company, Inc., Publishers
Box 611, Jefferson, North Carolina 28640
www.mcfarlandpub.com*

To my wife, Juliann,
and our children, Mark and Melina,
thank you—I love you and couldn't have
done it without you.

Table of Contents

Preface

This book will introduce you to every condemned killer who was executed in 2010. It provides the details of each killing that brought about a sentence of death—details revealed only through court documents. The tragic circumstances that belie the victims will be exposed as each chapter profiles at least two deaths: a murder and an execution.

Why 2010? The book could have covered any year in the modern era of the death penalty, but had to include one year from beginning to end. A single calendar year provides a true picture of the death penalty, executions and the anguish of victims.

This book is not a collection of high-profile executions or a review of the difficult, sensational or blood-curdling cases. This book could have examined 1997 or 2007—it is a straightforward profile of every condemned killer executed in a single year—the defiant, the remorseful and the indifferent.

Each chapter will explore the crime, the trial, the appellate review, the offender's time on death row and the execution. As the pages turn, you will hear directly from the offender, the prosecutors who tried the cases, at times the judges, the corrections officials and of course the family of the victims. What did the offender eat for a final meal? What were the offender's final words? How did the family and supporters of the victims react? How does the death penalty work? How has the death penalty evolved? The answers are all within these pages.

In 2010, the death penalty slowed in its application, method and consummation. There were 46 executions in 2010 as compared with 52 in 2009. The number fell to 43 in both 2011 and 2012.

There were 114 death sentences imposed by juries in 2010. In 2009, there were 112. Those numbers are dwarfed by the most prolific years of the death penalty. In 1999, 98 men and women were executed. There were 315 men and women sentenced to death in 1996.

A close look at the death penalty in 2010 provides some perspective for the future of capital punishment in America.

Twelve states carried out executions in 2010. Texas led the way with 17. Ohio was second with eight, the most there since the death penalty was reinstated in 1999. Alabama carried out five, the third most nationwide.

In 2010, the average age of the condemned at the time of execution was 43.93 years of age. The youngest person executed was 28-year-old Michael James Perry, who killed three people in 2001. The oldest was 72-year-old Gerald Holland, who raped and killed a 15-year-old girl in 1986.

The average age at the time of the offense was 27.45 years of age. The youngest was Peter Catu, who was 18 years and one month when he and fellow gang members raped and murdered two young girls near Houston in 1993. The oldest was Holland, who was 49 when he committed rape and murder.

The average time between offense and execution, much of which is spent on death row, was 16.7 years. The longest time spent on death row was 32 years by David Lee Powell, who murdered a police officer with an AK-47 during a traffic stop. He was one of the longest-imprisoned death row inmates in the country. In 2008, a prisoner in Georgia was executed after spending more than 33 years on death row. The shortest time on death row was spent by Gerald Bordelon. He sexually assaulted and murdered his girlfriend's 12-year-old daughter. He spent only seven years and three months on death row because he waived his appeal rights and volunteered to be executed.

The racial make up of offenders included 27 white men, one white woman, 13 black men and five Hispanic men. Although there were 46 killers, there were 63 victims as a result of multiple killings by some offenders. A racial breakdown of victims looks like this: 39 white, 15 black, eight Hispanic and one Asian. Forty-five of the 46 offenders executed were men. However, 29 out of 63 victims were women. Twenty-seven, more than half of the killers, did not know their victim.

The method of execution has had the most significant impact on the declining number of executions across the country. In 2008, legal challenges to lethal injection limited the number of executions to 37. A challenge to lethal injection in the state of Kentucky made its way to the U.S. Supreme Court. In *Baze v. Rees*,[1] the court ruled that lethal injection did not violate the Eighth Amendment ban against cruel and unusual punishment.

A nationwide shortage of one of the drugs, sodium thiopental, used in all 34 death penalty states in 2010 required executions to be postponed or cancelled in Arkansas, California, Oklahoma, Tennessee and Kentucky.

Arizona was able to carry out an execution by importing sodium thiopental from the U.K. The British government later intervened and now restricts further export of the drug for purposes of executions.

California built a state-of-the-art execution chamber, but the state Supreme Court subsequently ruled that more time is needed to review the state's execution protocol established by the Department of Corrections.

Oklahoma received federal court approval to use pentobarbital, a drug used to euthanize animals, to replace sodium thiopental. On December 16, 2010, Oklahoma became the first state in the country to use pentobarbital when the state executed John David Duty. Nearly ten years before his execution, Duty was convicted of strangling to death his cellmate in an Oklahoma prison.

A number of states, led by Oklahoma, Ohio and Washington, have moved away from the three-drug protocol traditionally used by states with the death penalty to a single-drug protocol. Those states have successfully carried out executions using only a lethal dose of sodium thiopental. In March of 2011, Ohio moved to a single lethal dose of pentobarbital for all executions. As of 2013, 11 states are using a single-drug protocol.

Those who faced death in 2010 reacted to it in many different ways. Thirteen offenders chose to say nothing when offered the customary opportunity to make a final statement. Seventeen offenders apologized; 12 invoked religion in some way; only three cried and 14 remained defiant to the end.

Nearly one-third of offenders facing imminent death, often with overwhelming evidence supporting their conviction, would not apologize, ask for forgiveness or admit their crime. Julius Ricardo Young went to his grave saying, "I'm an innocent man, this is a miscarriage of justice, my attorney failed me, it's a tragedy."

Gary Johnson, who blamed his brothers who turned him in, declared, "What they did was wrong ... I never did anything in my life to anybody." Lawrence Reynolds wanted to bring some attention to the death penalty; "I have tried to bring attention to the futility and flagrantly flawed system we have today."

Michael Perry wanted to ease the conscience of those involved in his soon-to-be death by declaring, "I want to start off by saying I want everyone to know that's involved in this atrocity that they are forgiven by me."

As you read through this book, you will have adequate information to make your own decision about the legitimacy of these final words.

I'm not sure that anyone can truly make sense of some of the words that came out of the mouths of condemned killers moments from death. One prisoner from Arizona gave a cheer for his favorite college sports team: "Boomer Sooner!" One Texas man's last words were "OK warden do it" and another from Texas quipped, "Warden, let her rip."

A Washington man compared himself to the Green River Killer, who was responsible for at least 48 murders and received life in prison. He stated, "I only killed one person. I cannot really see that there is true justice." Commenting on the lethal injection process as he faded into death a Texas man observed, "I thought it was going to be harder than this." A Virginia man facing imminent death chose to complain about the procedure, "Last words being: I don't think y'all done this right, took too long to hook it up. You can print that." Five men ended on a common theme: "That's it."

All but two executions had supporters present on behalf of the victims. Those supporters consisted of family, friends and even the prosecutors who sought and won the death penalty convictions. Supporters present for eleven executions refused to make any public comment. Following at least ten executions, supporters thought death by lethal injection was too easy or too humane. Following nine executions the supporters present felt that justice had been served.

Some victim supporters complained about delay; others lamented that the process would not bring closure. Some victim supporters were downright indignant. Following an Ohio execution someone said, "The son of a bitch is dead." In Georgia, "I hope he burns 70 times in hell." In Texas, as the execution approached, someone remarked, "I can't wait for that bastard to take his last breath." Also, in Texas, a victim's supporter commented, "They should have hung him."

In Texas there was also forgiveness; "I have forgiven him," was heard after an execution. In Oklahoma, a woman who lost her son asked the court for a sentence of life in prison. Many supporters were simply satisfied that the offender would not hurt anyone else.

This book provides an inside look at, as U.S. Supreme Court Justice Harry A. Blackmun described it, "the machinery of death." After you have read about the 46 executions of 2010 you will have the ability to make a more informed decision about the future of the death penalty in America.

Introduction

Although the death penalty in America inflames passions on both sides of the issue—capital punishment is sparingly sought, rarely imposed, and the act of carrying it out has become so rare that its significance in American jurisprudence is in question.

The death penalty has evolved from a term of art utilized in the criminal justice system to cultural buzzwords used to reveal a philosophy on issues of law and order.

The death penalty has become, in many ways, a symbolic political term that lends itself to the illusion of toughness if you support the death penalty; and to the illusion of weakness if you do not support the death penalty.

The idea that a political candidate can establish her law and order bona fides by being pro–death penalty has enhanced the significance of the death penalty in American politics. As capital punishment has evolved into a political symbol, "Joe Six-Pack" at the corner bar can also confirm his tough, red-blooded, law-abiding persona through his support of the death penalty.

The death penalty has morphed into a hot-button political issue right up there with abortion, guns and taxes. The death penalty has taken its place with single issue voters: "You're either with us or against us." If you support the execution of men and women who have been convicted of premeditated murder, then you're a law-and-order guy. If you don't, well, you're a bleeding heart, and an enabler of crime and violence.

An examination of each execution carried out in 2010 puts a face—hundreds of faces—on the whole process of state-mandated death. A glimpse at the victims and the tragic loss of life, as well as the ripple effect of violent death, can be provocative.

The heinous things that human beings do to one another are both alarming and astonishing. A close look at the cold, callous and frightening conduct of convicted killers makes it clear why 32 states have the death penalty and makes one wonder why the other 18 states are reluctant to provide for the execution of some convicted killers.

Killers, and their families often mortified by their conduct, deserve unfiltered scrutiny as well. Killers have stories to tell, and those stories can be compelling. The almost surreal circumstances that come with pre-determined death is, for most, difficult to comprehend. Have the condemned reflected upon their conduct, have they thought about the pain they've caused, have they addressed it—do they appreciate that the end is inevitable and immediate?

The death penalty, and to whom it applies, should be more than a philosophical debate about good and bad, right and wrong or just desserts. The death penalty should provide some insight into human behavior and why some people engage in conduct that impacts others in such a violent way.

After a closer look at each execution, one begins to understand the anguish that the process creates for those touched by the process. The years that pass from verdict to execution takes a toll on the family of victims. The constant appeals, the new trials, the new sentence hearings, and the post-conviction procedures all fuel frustration with the criminal justice system.

The resignation, evident in the words and actions of the family of victims—some of whom have been summoned to the death chamber in the past only to be turned away by last-minute court intervention, is palpable. The families of the condemned, who in most instances continue to openly display their love and devotion, also suffer from the prolonged process of death.

All too often in this process, the human element is left out. The death penalty debate has taken on an almost Kafkaesque tone. The death penalty is not an intellectual exercise. In fact, a close look at the machinations of the death penalty reveals that there is little, if anything, intellectually honest about the entire process.

The method for carrying out nearly every modern execution is lethal injection. In 2010, there were 46 executions in the United States. Forty-four were by lethal injection, one by electrocution and one by firing squad, yet lethal injection has been the source of a great deal of consternation.

Some are confounded by the concept that an individual, who violently ended an innocent person's life, should be protected from enduring pain and suffering during death. Most notably are the families of victims. The coming chapters will reveal a common sentiment among families that witness the death of their loved ones' killers: death by lethal injection is too easy. Lethal injection was introduced by Oklahoma prison officials in 1977. Drug-induced death was thought to be a more humane method of execution intended to replace the noose, electrocution, gas and the bullet. Texas, the most prolific state in terms of capital punishment, was the first state to actually use lethal injection, and use it they did. Texas has carried out more than 500 executions since 1976. Texas is responsible for nearly 40 percent of all executions carried out in the United States since the death penalty was reinstated.

In spite of the universal use of drugs in executions, the challenges to lethal injection continue. In 2010, some states acknowledged a shortage of one of the three drugs, sodium thiopental, used for execution. Arizona and California sought to obtain sodium thiopental from the U.K. Arizona used imported sodium thiopental to carry out an execution.

Oklahoma sought, and was granted permission by the federal court, to use pentobarbital for the execution of John David Duty, the last execution carried out nationwide in 2010. Supporters on both sides argue whether lethal injection is humane. The U.S. Supreme Court has answered the question, but it is raised again and again. Lethal injection does not violate the Eighth Amendment ban against cruel and unusual punishment. However, in the final months of 2010, questions were raised. What if one of the drugs used for lethal injection was shipped into the U.S. from overseas? Would that violate the Eighth Amendment? The argument continued unabated by rulings in other states, the federal courts or even the U.S. Supreme Court.

The lethal injection issue is one of many issues that have been twisted and manipulated to cloud the fundamental question regarding the death penalty: Is the act of carrying out state-sponsored death a morally responsible act?

In the last decade, the U.S. Supreme Court has banned the execution of offenders who committed murder as juveniles, as well as those offenders who have a mental disability. The Court cited evolving standards of decency and a national consensus against the execution of juveniles and the mentally disabled. However, in 2009 the Court outlawed capital punishment for any crime but murder. The Court specifically banned the death penalty for child rape even though the national consensus seemed to be going in the direction of supporting capital punishment for child rapists.

Today, as state budgets have tightened, the issue is cost. Does it cost more to sentence a person to death or life in prison without the possibility of parole? Should cost be a factor? If the cost of the death penalty increases because of endless appeals, should the system reward killers by wiping out the death penalty because it costs too much?

That argument invokes the apocryphal story attributed to then-attorney Abraham Lincoln who said that he once represented a kid who killed his parents and wanted Lincoln to ask the court for mercy because the kid was now an orphan.

The arguments that have been raised with regard to capital punishment are, at times, as bizarre as Lincoln's argument and equally repugnant.

The issue of race is frequently raised in the death penalty debate. The arguments opposing the death penalty, based on racial bias, are not what one might assume. The issue is not that a disproportionate number of minorities are on death row or executed for that matter. The concern regarding race is that a killer is more likely to be sentenced to death if the victim is white as opposed to being a person of color—that is an interesting argument. However, in light of the fact that 94 percent of black men are killed by other black men, sentencing more killers of minorities to death would inevitably increase the number of minorities on death row and in the death chamber.

Exonerations have also garnered attention on both sides of the death penalty issue. As of the end of 2010, there have been 139 men and women released from death row. Some of those, 17 to be exact,[1] are factually innocent, exonerated through DNA testing. With regard to the other 122 former death row inmates, the issue is not so clear. There are a number of reasons why those inmates were removed from death row. The most prominent reasons are they were awarded a new trial as the result of a successful appeal, and the prosecution chose not to retry the case, or the former inmate was found not guilty at a subsequent trial. In the criminal justice system, "not guilty" is not the same as innocent.

Over the years, there have been suggestions that innocent men have been executed. In each instance those suggestions have been refuted. Some of those debunked cases have caused a great deal of embarrassment and have been a challenge to the credibility of some groups opposing capital punishment.

Today, there are two cases from Texas that have, once again, raised the issue of wrongful execution. Cameron Todd Willingham was executed for an arson that resulted in the death of his children. The forensic science used to solve the arson is now in question. In a separate case, Claude Jones was executed ten years ago for the murder of a shopkeeper. Recently conducted DNA testing of a single hair found at the crime scene was determined not to belong to Jones.

This book is an effort to put capital punishment in the hands of ordinary citizens, not just in theory, but in practice. Each chapter begins with death and ends with death. This book will unmask the superficial dogma of toughness versus weakness and will expose the transparency of arguments about the means of execution: the cost, race, politics and the many other claims that exist on the periphery of the fundamental issue—morality.

It is my hope that this book will help build a better understanding and appreciation for the most contentious act that any government can carry out, the imposition of a sanction that results in the end of life.

CHAPTER 1

Vernon Lamont Smith, a.k.a. Abdullah Sharif Kaazim Mahdi, Ohio. Executed January 7

Vernon Smith died on January 7, 2010. The medical staff at Southern Ohio Correctional Facility in Lucasville, Ohio, recorded the time of death as 10:28 a.m. He was the first man in the United States executed in 2010. Smith's life ended at age 37. However, the event that brought about his death occurred 16 years earlier at the counter of the Woodstock Market, in Toledo, Ohio.

On May 26, 1993, Smith fatally shot Sohail Darwish, a 28-year-old immigrant from Saudi Arabia. Darwish owned the Woodstock Market, a small convenience store. Smith, and a friend, entered the store to steal money and beer. Smith pulled out a gun and ordered Darwish to empty the cash register and hand over his wallet. Darwish reached for the money, and Smith shot him in the chest.

Earlier that afternoon, Smith met up with Herbert Bryson and Lamont Layson at a Toledo park located near Highland and Maplewood streets. According to court records,[1] the trio discussed "hitting a lick," street slang for committing a robbery. The three got in Bryson's car. Smith told Bryson to drive to the corner of Woodstock and Avondale, near the Woodstock Market. Layson stayed in the car while Smith and Bryson entered the market.

When Bryson and Smith entered the store, there were two people, Darwish and a former employee, Osand Tahboub, behind the counter. Bryson asked for beer, and Darwish came around the counter and walked over to the cooler to help him. Darwish grabbed a forty-ounce beer from the cooler and placed it on the counter. Bryson did the same. As Darwish rang up the sale, Smith pulled out a black handgun and ordered him to "open the cash register, motherfucker."

Darwish, who was standing next to Bryson, put his hands up in the air and did not resist. Bryson went behind the counter and hit several buttons on the cash register, trying to open it. Bryson ordered Darwish to open the cash register, which he did. Darwish then put his hands back up in the air.

Tahboub, who was visiting his former employer, said that Smith told Darwish to "move and empty your wallet, motherfucker." As Darwish reached for his wallet, Smith fired a single shot, hitting Darwish in the chest. Smith then ordered Tahboub to empty his wallet as well, and the two ran out of the store. Darwish was able to push the alarm button before he fell to the floor. He was shot in the upper left side of the chest—he bled to death on the market floor.

After Smith and Bryson left the store, Layson, who was still waiting in the car, noticed

Smith holding a gun in his hand when he and Bryson climbed back into the car. Smith said, "Dang, I forgot the beer." When Bryson asked Smith why he shot Darwish, Smith said that he shot him in the arm because he moved too slowly and that "he took too long ... opening the cash register."

Smith then said, "Fuck him, he is in our neighborhood anyway. He shouldn't be in our neighborhood with a store, no way." Later, Smith and Bryson split the $400 taken during the robbery. They also gave Layson all the stolen food stamps and another $50.

About two weeks after the murder, police detectives received information that Bryson and Smith were incarcerated in the Sandusky County Jail near Cedar Point Amusement Park in northwest Ohio. Based on this and other information received from sources, the police made up an eight-man photo array, including a photo of Herbert Bryson, to show to Tahboub. The next day, Tahboub pointed to Bryson's photo as "not the guy with the gun, but the other guy." Based on Tahboub's identification and the fact that Smith and Bryson were known to hang out, the police compiled a second photo array that included a picture of Smith. The police showed Tahboub the second array, and Tahboub immediately pointed out Smith as the gunman.

By the time the trial rolled around, Smith had converted to Islam and changed his name to Abdullah Sharif Kaazim Mahdi. He presented no evidence during the guilt phase of the trial. He was convicted of aggravated felony-murder and three counts of aggravated robbery.

* * *

At the subsequent penalty phase hearing, Mahdi's presentation included testimony of a Muslim counselor regarding Mahdi's conversion to Islam while awaiting trial; additionally Mahdi now counseled other prisoners. The counselor also testified that Mahdi told him that the shooting was unintentional, that he was nervous and scared and that the trigger had just gone off. Mahdi's wife testified that Mahdi had been upset and nervous the evening of the shooting and for days afterward. She further testified that when he heard news that Darwish was dead, Mahdi sat down, cried and told her that the murder had been an accident. Moreover, Mahdi's wife testified that, on the afternoon before the crime, she and her husband went to see the film *Menace II Society*, whose opening scene depicted an interracial crime in which a black man had words with a store owner and angrily shot him.

A psychologist also testified during the penalty phase and noted the striking parallels between the film and the crime, believing that it could not have been a coincidence that Mahdi later committed a crime so similar to the one he witnessed in the film. In addition, the psychologist testified to the effects of various social and cultural factors on Mahdi, all of which, he believed, impaired Mahdi's ability to conform his conduct to the law. The psychologist testified that these factors, combined with Mahdi's difficult childhood, caused a mental illness. The psychologist was unable to identify the illness with specificity due to Mahdi's lack of cooperation during the interview process.

The jury returned with a death sentence; in turn, the trial court sentenced Mahdi to death and to a consecutive term of 18 to 53 years in prison.

On direct appeal, the state court of appeals upheld the convictions and sentences. The Ohio Supreme Court affirmed the court's decision.[2] Mahdi exhausted all of his state post-conviction remedies.

In 2002, Mahdi filed a federal habeas corpus petition that included ten claims. Because the claims presented were adjudicated on the merits by the Supreme Court of Ohio and the decision was not contrary to clearly established federal law, the federal district court denied Mahdi's petition for a writ of habeas corpus. The Sixth Circuit Court of Appeals affirmed the district court's decision.[3] The U.S. Supreme Court refused to hear Mahdi's appeal.

* * *

There is no question that Mahdi shot Darwish. Assistant State Public Defender Kimberly Rigby, one of the Mahdi's attorneys, explained the shooting as an intentional act to wound.

"What happened was obviously tragic, but Mahdi did not mean to carry out murder," she said.

"He shot Mr. Darwish in what he thought was the arm, although it was really the upper chest under the collar bone. He only shot him one time. He did not harm the witness. He did not shoot Mr. Darwish again when he got up to trigger the alarm. [A doctor for the defense] who looked at the coroner's report noted that a shot in this area is typically not fatal. A little to the left or right and Mr. Darwish would have survived."[4]

Assistant County Prosecutor J. Christopher Anderson had a different take. Anderson was one of the two prosecutors who represented the state of Ohio at trial. Anderson said even the passing years could not erase the evidence that remained vivid in his memory. "He shot him at point-blank range right in the chest. What do you intend when you do that?" he said. "If you shoot somebody in the chest from a foot away, you intend to kill him."[5]

Mr. Anderson also suggested that of the three men who rolled up on the Woodstock Market that day, only Mahdi knew where the market was located. Mahdi directed his accomplices to the corner of Avondale and Woodstock avenues.

Mahdi's accomplices Bryson and Layson are cousins. They reached plea agreements in exchange for their testimony against Mahdi. Bryson, who entered the store with Mahdi, was sentenced to 10 to 25 years for involuntary manslaughter and was eligible for parole consideration in 2011. The driver, Layson, was sentenced to seven to 25 years for aggravated robbery; he was paroled 2003.[6]

* * *

Mahdi was the 34th person executed in Ohio since the death penalty was reinstated in 1999. When Wilford Berry was executed in 1999, the first execution in the modern era of Ohio's death penalty, it had been 36 years since the state executed a condemned prisoner.

Mahdi's execution was Ohio's second using a single-drug method. Ohio, like every other states with the death penalty, required a three-drug protocol be administered to carry out executions by lethal injection. Kenneth Biros was the first person to be put to death, in December 2009, using only a lethal dose of sodium thiopental. Biros' execution was the first in Ohio since September 2009 when Ohio Governor Ted Strickland halted all executions after a botched attempt to execute another prisoner, Romell Broom. The prison staff could not locate a vein to accommodate Broom's three-drug lethal injections. Broom's execution was halted after about two hours.[7]

The one-drug method used on Biros had never been tried on a U.S. death row inmate.

The eyes of the nation were on Ohio to see if the new method worked. It did. Ironically, Biros had delayed his execution by challenging the three-drug method as cruel and unusual punishment. When his challenge was dismissed, he became the first man in America executed through a single-drug method.

Mahdi arrived at the Southern Ohio Correctional Facility at Lucasville at 9:45 a.m. the day before his execution. He fasted from sunrise to sunset before eating a meal of whole and chopped dates and hot tea with lemon and honey. He also received olive oil to groom his beard and a "miswak" stick, a twig from the Peelu tree commonly used in Muslim countries to clean teeth.[8]

As Mahdi's execution approached, he never showed remorse over the murder and refused to cooperate during clemency hearings. In spite of Mahdi's apparent disinterest in clemency, two of the seven state parole board members recommended clemency to Governor Strickland. The governor admitted that he wrestled with Mahdi's clemency request. However, he did not intervene to commute Mahdi's sentence. He notified Mahdi's legal team of his decision the afternoon before the scheduled execution.[9]

*   *   *

Darwish's two teenage daughters, both dressed in black, witnessed the execution along with their mother, Charlotte. Darwish and Charlotte had a one-year-old, Dolly, and Charlotte was pregnant with their second daughter, Mona, at the time of the murder. Sixteen-year-old Mona is believed to be the youngest person ever to witness an execution in Ohio.

"When I look back on that day, I just see a white wall. I just see white because I lost all grip of reality.... It was blank, empty, cold," recalled Charlotte.[10]

"[This execution] is going to open up a whole new chapter. I'm now not only the widow of the murdered man, but I'm the widow of the murdered man whose killer was executed," she said. "It's going to bother me and pester my soul. Now there are two lives down the drain, all because of the actions of Vernon Smith."[11]

Darwish's widow never sold the store. She sold or donated the contents and locked the door. "I couldn't do it," she said. "I couldn't put a price on the literally blood, sweat and tears he invested."[12]

"I feel very bad for his family," Charlotte said of Mahdi as his execution approached. "My heart aches for them for what they're about to go through and endure, what we've been through these past 16 years."[13]

"All you have to live with is memories, but you can't touch a memory, you can't have a conversation with a memory. You may get a little solace out of it, but in the end it's empty because there's nothing there," said Charlotte.[14]

"Pictures are amazing things, but they're also horrible things as well," she added. "You've got that picture as a memory, but that image haunts you. You just stare at that picture, but that picture doesn't talk back to you. It can't help you, it can't laugh with you when you're happy, it can't cry with you when you're sad."

"My thoughts haven't changed," Charlotte continued. "Vernon Smith [Mahdi]—he lives, he dies. It's not going to bring my husband back."[15]

As a child Darwish would play market with his sisters in his home of Saudi Arabia.[16] Even as a young man he dreamed of owning his own store. Soon after his marriage to Charlotte he fulfilled his dream in Toledo, Ohio. "He actually accomplished his dream," Charlotte said. "And he was such a help to the community in that area. He had customers that he knew didn't have money and who had kids, so he'd give them food. That's the kind of person he was."[17]

Darwish moved to the United States after he was told by Saudi Arabian officials that he could only attend an agricultural school. Once in the U.S. he pursued an education at the University of Toledo.

* * *

The execution chamber is a solemn place. The condemned face imminent death often only with the companionship of aloof, detached prison officials who are employed to ensure that death is as swift and humane as possible. In every state that carries out executions, there are at least two rooms adjacent to the execution chamber. Both have windows that overlook the chamber. One room houses the family of the murder victims; the other the family, friends and lawyers of the condemned.

During those final moments there is anguish in both of those rooms. The victim's family is flushed with emotion. While some family members may be happy that the killer of their loved one will soon be dead, all are tormented by the fact that this event will not bring their loved one back and may not even bring much anticipated closure.

The condemned inmate's family is in anguish. They will witness what few people have and absolutely no one wants to—the sudden death of an otherwise healthy family member. In those final moments, prison personnel will invite the condemned to make a final statement.

Some inmates, facing death in a matter of minutes, will say nothing. Some will pray. Some will apologize or ask for forgiveness.

In Mahdi's case the execution process lasted 28 minutes. The prison execution team had little trouble finding useable veins through which the lethal anesthetic could flow. Fourteen minutes into the process, Mahdi made the 17 step walk from the holding cell to the execution chamber. He made eye contact with his imam, Atef Hamed, as he entered the room, but after he was strapped to the gurney, he stared only at the ceiling or closed his eyes as he appeared to silently mouth Islamic prayers.[18]

When the warden asked him if he had a final statement, he audibly repeated a prayer four times in Arabic, "There is no God but God, and Mohammed is his prophet." He then returned to mouthing it silently. It was Darwish's wife Charlotte who told others in the room, including media witnesses, what he was saying.[19]

He never looked at or addressed the Darwish family. He went to his death without apologizing for the despicable act he committed some 16 years earlier.

At 10:21 a.m., strapped to a gurney in the death house at Lucasville, Mahdi fell silent as his lips slowed. His mouth opened wide, as though he were yawning, then his head jerked back. He twitched for a moment, but it appeared he simply fell asleep. He stopped breathing two minutes later.[20]

At 10:28 a.m., a member of the medical team checked for a heartbeat. A curtain blocked the view of the room as the coroner examined Mahdi. The curtain was reopened at 10:30 a.m., eight minutes after the drug was injected—he was dead.

Mahdi was the first person in Ohio, and the first person nationwide, to be executed in 2010. It is worth noting that approximately 189 killers were sentenced to death in Ohio prior to Mahdi receiving a death sentence. Some of those death sentences were overturned and some of those death row inmates died of natural causes. Thirty-one Ohio inmates were executed before Mahdi.

Chapter 2

Kenneth Mosley, Texas. Executed January 7

Kenneth Mosley was wearing his black framed glasses as he lay motionless, his arms and chest strapped to a gurney.[1] Mosley was inside the death chamber of Texas State Penitentiary at Huntsville, Texas' oldest prison, built in 1849. He had a three-drug cocktail of sodium thiopental, pancuronium and potassium chloride circulating through his veins. He was dead.

Mosley was a native of Flint, Michigan.[2] He grew up in rural Arkansas and had an extensive criminal record. Mosley's supporters described his upbringing as poverty-stricken and abusive in a family of poor farm workers. They complained that his exposure to toxic pesticides as a child, possible brain damage and his use of cocaine to self-medicate for depression were all kept from the jury.[3] He blamed his legal problems on drug addiction.

However, his criminal record included sexual assault and arrests for possession of marijuana, illegal knives and for stealing items from a Home Depot only to return them for cash refunds.[4]

At the time of the shooting, he was wanted for robbery at a fast-food restaurant five days earlier in nearby Mesquite. He had recently been fired from his job with a Coca-Cola bottler for testing positive for cocaine.[5]

Mosley was pronounced dead at 6:16 p.m. on January 7, 2010. He was the second man executed in 2010. He was the first executed in Texas in 2010. The year before, Texas was responsible for 24 of 52 executions nationwide.[6]

Texas has been extremely prolific when it comes to executions. Mosley was the 448th person executed in Texas—far more than any other state. Nationwide, Mosley was the 1,190th person executed since the reinstatement of the death penalty.

* * *

Mosley's execution was the final chapter in a real-life tragedy that was nearly 13 years in the making. It was an unseasonably warm Saturday morning in Garland, Texas, on February 15, 1997. Garland Police Officer Michael Moore, a 10-year veteran and a father of three, was having lunch with a couple other police officers at a diner not far from a Bank One branch on Centerville Road in Garland.

A dispatch came over the police radio—a 9-1-1 call had been received from a nearby Bank One branch about a possible robbery in progress. The three officers left their lunches and headed directly for the bank.

Mosley entered the bank about noon. He was wearing long dark clothing and a dark toboggan-style cap.[7] The warm weather and unusual clothing piqued the interest of some of the bank employees. As Mosley waited in line, a bank teller recognized Mosley. She was certain that Mosley was the guy who robbed the bank about a month earlier. The bank manager hit the silent alarm and called 9–1–1.

Mosley was still waiting in line to see a teller when the police arrived. Several witnesses watched as Officer Moore entered the bank and approached Mosley. The officer tapped the suspect on the back and said, "I would like to speak with you."[8] Mosley resisted Moore's request, and the two men began to struggle. Mosley then pulled a gun from underneath his shirt. Several shots rang out, and Moore shoved Mosley through a nearby window. They fell to the ground into one of the drive-through lanes. A witness from across the street saw Mosley pause to look around, point his gun at Officer Moore and shoot him.[9] Mosley shot Moore four times. One bullet struck him over the top edge of his protective vest and penetrated his heart.

Fellow officers administered CPR, paramedics arrived at the scene within minutes, and Moore was flown by helicopter to Baylor University Medical Center. He was pronounced dead only hours after the shooting.[10]

Mosley began to walk away from the bank but was spotted by another police officer who ordered Mosley to stop, drop the gun and get on the ground. Mosley turned to shoot. The officer shot him once in the wrist, and Mosley dropped the gun. Mosley then complied with the officer's directive to get on the ground. He was handcuffed. Authorities later found he was carrying a holdup note.[11]

*　*　*

Mosley was arrested. On March 18, 1997, a Dallas County grand jury indicted Kenneth Mosley for capital murder in the death of Officer Moore. Less than seven months later, a Dallas County jury found Mosley guilty of murder.

During trial, Mosley only contested the issue of intent. He claimed the gun fired by accident according to his trial testimony, which the district court summarized: "in essence, Mosley testified that as he attempted to surrender his gun to Officer Moore, he accidentally discharged it five times, hitting Officer Moore four times and killing him." "I never knew that gun had went off," Mosley testified.[12]

On October 16, 1997, during a separate penalty-phase hearing, Mosley concluded his testimony with an outburst that included extremely profane and graphic comments to the Moore family and the jury. He chastised the jury for finding him guilty of capital murder and attacked the Moore family by bitterly exclaiming, "The Moore family, all they wanted is somebody they think slaughtered their loved one to die. All they wanted was a conviction." The judge ordered his removal from the courtroom.[13]

According to court records,[14] Mosley appealed to the Texas Court of Criminal Appeals, which affirmed the conviction and sentence in the spring of 2000. Mosley filed a motion for rehearing, which was granted. On rehearing the court reaffirmed its prior decision.

Along with his direct appeal, Mosley filed an application for writ of habeas corpus in the trial court on July 17, 2000. The trial court filed findings of fact and conclusions of law recommending that Mosley's writ be denied, and the Texas Court of Criminal Appeals adopted those findings and conclusions, with a few noted exceptions, denying habeas relief in 2003.

Mosley then filed a petition for writ of certiorari with the United States Supreme Court, which was denied on February 23, 2004.

Mosley filed a federal petition for a writ of habeas corpus in a Dallas federal district court in 2005.[15] Two years later, a federal magistrate recommended that the district court deny Mosley's petition. Mosley filed yet another petition for writ of certiorari in the U.S. Supreme Court in April of 2009, and later a motion for a stay of execution.

On September 23, 2009, the U.S. Supreme Court granted a stay of execution pending its disposition of Mosley's petition for a writ of certiorari.[16] The Supreme Court denied Mosley's petition for a writ of certiorari in October and lifted the previously-imposed stay of execution. The trial court subsequently entered an order rescheduling the execution for January 7, 2010.

Mosley's legal team spent nearly 13 years going through the appeals process. His execution was postponed twice in the year leading up to his execution. However, shortly before 6 p.m. on January 7, his appeals were declared exhausted, allowing his execution to move forward.[17]

Mosley was placed on "death watch," a 72-hour period during which he was monitored every 15 minutes by prison guards. According to prison officials, Mosley spent his last 72-hours sleeping, reading, pacing his cell and showering. He saw his last visitor two days before his execution. The unidentified visitor spent about five hours with Mosley and the two shared a meal together.[18]

Mosley's last meal, served at 4 p.m. was an assortment of fried foods including three pieces of chicken, two pork chops, a cheeseburger, 10 pieces of bacon, French fries, okra, green tomatoes and apple cobbler.[19]

* * *

Sheila Moore knew nothing about her husband's lethal injuries as she and a friend were on their way to the Garland Police Department. They had intended to leave the Moores' 9-month-old son, Zachary, with his father at the end of his shift. The women were planning a late lunch.[20]

Sheila first learned that something was wrong as she drove to the station to meet her husband. A neighbor called to say that there were police officers outside the Moores' home. A police officer got on the phone and told Sheila that there had been an accident.

When Sheila got to the police station, a crowd was waiting for her, including her son's daycare provider, whom the police had called to come and get the baby. "I knew it was serious then," she recalled. "They took me into a room and said David had been fatally wounded. It hit me like a ton of bricks."[21]

She was driven to the hospital, where the medical staff allowed her to see her husband's body. "One of the nurses gave me his hand, and I held it for a while," she said. "You expect him to squeeze your hand. It just didn't seem real."[22]

David Moore was buried at his family's farm in Kentucky. His body was moved to Kentucky after a funeral and vigil in Garland with full honors for an officer felled in the line of duty. Moore was only the second Garland officer to die in the line of duty.

* * *

Sheila was on the list to witness the execution. However, she went to Huntsville still undecided about whether she would witness Mosley's death. "A friend of mine told me I should give Mosley one last chance to ask for forgiveness for what he's done," Sheila said. "I don't know if he'll do it, but that's the reason I would be there."[23]

The decision wasn't an easy one.

Sheila had mixed feeling about the death penalty and that internal struggle became public after Mosley's trial, when she questioned whether the state should execute her husband's killer. The death penalty had not bothered her, she said, until it became personal. "When it's real close to home, you have to question it. Is it right? I don't know," she said after Mosley was sentenced to death. "Who are we to decide whether this man should live or die?"[24]

As Mosley's execution rolled around, Sheila Moore still had not decided whether she would witness the execution. "I know he is not a good person," she said of Mosley. "But I really have not decided if I can watch him die."[25]

When Mosley was asked if he wanted to make a statement to the people who gathered to witness his death, he shook his head and mouthed the word, "No." He never looked at the dozen or so people standing behind a transparent screen, a few feet from his face.[26]

As the lethal combination of drugs began taking effect, Mosley made what sounded like a few snores and a slight gasp then he was still. Nine minutes later, at 6:16 p.m. he was dead.

"While earthly justice was served, it does not change what happened almost 13 years ago," Sheila said in a statement read by her brother about 15 minutes after Mosley died. "There will always be an empty place in our hearts for our husband, father and friend. We pray for healing for everyone involved."[27]

Although Sheila had been hesitant about the death penalty, when the time came, she stood silently behind Garland Police Captain Bill Cortez and watched as the state carried out the execution by lethal injection.

"David believed in the death penalty," she said. "I know if it was reversed—and I was the one who died—David would be there in a heartbeat."[28]

"I've thought about this off and on over the years," Sheila said. "I knew we were getting to the point where the girls would be able to decide whether to go down there with me or not."[29]

Since both daughters were over 18, the minimum age to witness an execution in Texas, they debated whether to put their names on the list of five people who would watch the lethal injection. "It's hard," said Courtney, the eldest daughter. "There's a lot of mixed feelings."[30] The girls decided not to witness the execution.

Captain Cortez was not impressed by Mosley's execution, "It seemed just too easy, too easy of a punishment."[31]

A busload of police officers and family friends traveled to Huntsville with the Moore family. Moore's son Zachary was nine months old when his father was killed. Now in eighth grade, the 13-year-old could not witness the execution but was part of the vigil outside the prison.

"He was a baby when his father died, so he has no memories of everything that happened," Sheila Moore said. "At least, he can have this."[32]

Mosley was the first person executed in Texas in 2010. Texas courts sentenced 632 killers to death prior to Mosley receiving a death sentence. Texas is the most prolific of all states when it comes to the death penalty. Texas executed 447 death row inmates prior to executing Mosley.

CHAPTER 3

Gerald J. Bordelon, Louisiana.
Executed January 7

Gerald J. Bordelon wanted to die. In 2002, he was on parole for sexual assault when he raped and murdered a 12-year-old girl. He told authorities he would "commit the same crime again if ever given the chance."[1]

It took seven men to remove Bordelon's shackles and strap him to the black padded gurney in the prison death chamber at Angola, Louisiana. Bordelon was wearing a T-shirt and blue jeans. There was a curtain separating him from the witnesses who sat in rooms adjoining the death chamber.

Bordelon stared at the ceiling as prison officials closed the curtains for the insertion of the intravenous tubes that would circulate the lethal drugs through his veins. The curtains were reopened and the eyes of each witness were riveted on Bordelon. He spoke softly to Louisiana State Penitentiary Warden Burl Cain. Bordelon took several deep breaths as the drugs were administered.[2]

* * *

A little more than seven years passed between the murder of Courtney LeBlanc and Bordelon's scheduled execution. In the modern era of the death penalty, that is a remarkably swift date with death. In the two states that have carried out the most executions, the average length of time from crime to execution is 10.26 years in Texas and 12.68 years in Florida.[3] The average time between the murder and execution for the 46 offenders executed in 2010 was 16.7 years. In Louisiana more than half of those condemned to death have spent more than 10 years on death row.

The only reason that Bordelon's execution occurred quickly is that he was a volunteer, he wanted to die, and even that was a time-consuming struggle. The Louisiana Supreme Court ruled in October of 2009 that Bordelon was competent to waive his appeals in state and federal court, finding that testimony from psychiatrists who examined him excluded the possibility that his waiver was influenced by brain damage, mental disability or personality disorders that impair cognitive function.

Bordelon had a "diagnostic profile of sexual sadism" and psychiatrists found that his crimes involved an escalating pattern of violence. Bordelon pleaded guilty to sexual battery in 1982 and received a 10-year sentence. When he killed Courtney, he was on parole after serving 10 years of a 20-year sentence for forcible rape and two counts of aggravated crime against nature, which, in Louisiana, is sodomy by force, threat or the victim's diminished capacity.[4]

The testimony presented during Bordelon's hearing to waive his right to appeal also excluded the possibility that his decision was the product of despair and suicidal ideation. At the same time, the Supreme Court reviewed the death sentence, finding that it was not excessive because the jury found that his victim was killed during the commission of aggravated rape and second-degree kidnapping.

Bordelon was the third person executed in the United States in 2010. Executions in Louisiana have been infrequent. Bordelon was the 28th person executed for murder in Louisiana since executions resumed in 1983. Before Bordelon's execution, Louisiana's last execution occurred in May 2002.[5]

He was the eighth person in Louisiana executed by lethal injection and the first in modern times to die without exercising his constitutional right to appeal his conviction and sentence.

*   *   *

The investigation into Courtney's murder rapidly expanded to include the FBI. Although the crime occurred across two states, the FBI got involved because of an ongoing investigation into the Baton Rouge Serial Killer. The murder of seven women around Louisiana State University and Baton Rouge was ultimately determined to be the responsibility of Derrick Todd Lee.[6] Courtney's murder would go in a different direction.

According to court records,[7] in the course of the investigation, the police interviewed Bordelon several times. He also completed a questionnaire which FBI agents sent to the Bureau's Behavior Analysis Unit. The result of the analysis led the FBI to focus their investigation on Bordelon. On November 22, 2002, they placed him under surveillance, following him that night into Mississippi, where he visited a graveyard close to his parents' property in Gloster, but then losing contact with him in the darkness. He was on parole at the time he travelled to Mississippi and the officers knew that he had violated the terms of his parole by paying a visit to the graveyard. However, they did not take him into custody to avoid jeopardizing the ongoing investigation into Courtney's disappearance.

Within days, FBI Agent Glen Methvien asked Bordelon to come to the Denham Springs Police Department. He arrived in his own car which was impounded and searched, after his arrest. The agent also requested that Jennifer Kocke and Bordelon's sister Cindy come to the station house to confront Bordelon according to a script prepared by the FBI. The women followed the script and individually informed Bordelon that if he wanted to have anything to do with them again that he should disclose whatever he knew about Courtney's disappearance.

After the women left the station house, Bordelon met with Agent Methvien and FBI profiler Mary Ellen O'Toole. He told the agents that he wanted to talk with his sister Cindy again and that afterwards he would take them where they needed to go.

The agents placed the defendant under arrest for violating his probation and then drove him to his sister's house where he spoke to her from the back of a patrol unit while she stood at the opened window outside of the vehicle.

Finally, after approximately 20 minutes, Cindy Landry leaned inside the vehicle and hugged her brother goodbye. He then directed the agents to Courtney's body which was in the thick underbrush along the banks of the Amite River only minutes from his sister's home.

According to court records, Bordelon told the police that on November 15, 2002, he decided to drive over to the Highland Village trailer park to spend a few hours at his estranged wife Jennifer Kocke's trailer. He had been accused of molesting her children and was to have no contact with them.

He walked into the trailer through the back door and was surprised to find his stepdaughter Courtney alone and asleep on the couch. Bordelon went back outside, drove out of the trailer park and left his car on a side road. He then walked back through the woods to Kocke's trailer. He woke Courtney and told her to come with him. Bordelon took a large butcher knife from the kitchen when they left the trailer. He told Courtney he would kill her if she screamed or tried to run.

Bordelon then drove with the victim into Mississippi where he turned into the woods off a gravel road, forced Courtney out of the car and told her to take off her clothes. He then had Courtney kneel in front of him and perform oral sex on him, ejaculating in her mouth. When he was finished, Courtney put on her T-shirt and shorts but carried her underwear back to the car.

They left Mississippi around 9 a.m. and returned to Baton Rouge. He made Courtney walk down a dirt path near the Amite River, and Courtney asked, "Where are we going?" He told her they were going "to the river." When asked what Courtney's last words were, Bordelon said, "Why do you like the river?"

After reaching the banks of the river, Bordelon said he pushed Courtney down. She fell on her face and then rolled over. He straddled her and choked her with his hands. Courtney was able to bite Bordelon's left thumb hard enough to cause bleeding. Courtney's T-shirt came off as she fought, and the knife, which he had put in his back pocket when he got her out of his car, fell to the ground. After choking Courtney to death, Bordelon said he moved her body into a wooded area, concealed her with heavy underbrush, and then returned to his car.

When he left the scene, Bordelon discarded Courtney's underwear which had been lying on the floorboard of his car. In this statement, he repeatedly denied that he had raped his stepdaughter vaginally or anally, although, in a ride to Mississippi, he eventually admitted that he had rubbed Courtney in both places but never penetrated her.

He then called his sister and went to her home so he could wash his clothing. Both Bordelon's semen and Courtney's DNA were found in Bordelon's car.

The results of DNA testing was damaging for the defense. The report details several stains, other than blood with some sperm residue, found in Bordelon's car. According to the results, one of those stains contained both Bordelon and Courtney's DNA—mixed together.[8]

*   *   *

When he met Courtney's mother on the Internet, Bordelon was on parole for sexual assault. Bordelon married Kocke a year later. After they were married, Bordelon and Kocke moved from Louisiana to Mississippi and lived in a trailer owned by Bordelon's parents outside of Gloster, Mississippi. However, during the Christmas holidays in 2001, they separated after Courtney and her sister told their mother that Bordelon touched them inappropriately, but Kocke remained in contact with Bordelon after the split, according to court documents.[9]

The Louisiana Parole Board indicated that a parole agent informed Kocke before she married Bordelon that Bordelon was a convicted sex offender. He had received psychiatric treatment in 1979 after being accused of rape and kidnapping. He pleaded guilty to sexual battery in 1982 and was convicted of rape and crimes against nature in 1990.

In October 2003, after Courtney's death, Kocke was convicted of child abuse in Mississippi for failing to keep Bordelon away from her children. She received a suspended five-year sentence, with five years of probation.[10]

*   *   *

Three of Courtney's relatives watched the execution, including her uncle Damian Kocke, her sister Brittany Boudreaux and her mother Jennifer. Muffled crying could be heard from the victim's family seated in an observation room adjacent to the death chamber where they watched Bordelon die. After witnessing the execution, the family left Angola Prison without speaking to reporters.

Bordelon was far from silent in the time leading up to his execution as he lay strapped to the gurney. Warden Cain described Bordelon as "very upbeat, cheerful and very remorseful" throughout the day leading up to his execution. Bordelon spent the earlier part of his last day at Angola Prison visiting with family members until about 3 p.m. He ate his last meal of fried sac-a-lait, crawfish étouffée, a peanut butter and jelly sandwich and cookies at about 4 p.m.[11]

In the death chamber, when asked if he had any last words, Bordelon apologized to Courtney's mother, sister and uncle. "I'm sorry. I don't know if that brings any closure or peace. It should have never happened, but it did, and I'm sorry."[12]

In a written statement read by his attorney, Jill Craft, Bordelon said the murder "shouldn't have happened."

"Courtney's family suffered; my family has suffered. I feel like I am doing the right thing by standing up and taking responsibility," Bordelon wrote.[13]

Craft said Bordelon confessed to other criminal activities during her visits with him, but she said she was not at liberty to disclose them. Craft said she could not discuss the specifics of the crimes her client discussed with the FBI. "I can say that he really did the right thing to cleanse his soul," Craft said. Craft, of Baton Rouge, represented Bordelon for about three years as he sought to avoid having his 2006 conviction and sentence in Livingston Parish appealed to higher courts.[14]

After the execution, Warden Cain gave additional information about a telephone call Bordelon was allowed to make to two women the night before his execution. One of the women was a friend of Jennifer Kocke. She dropped off Courtney at Kocke's home the day before she was abducted.

Cain, who said he listened to the conversation on a telephone extension because the women were not on Bordelon's approved visitor list, said Bordelon absolved Kocke's friend of any blame for dropping Courtney off to stay alone at the trailer. "He said if it hadn't happened that day, when the lady dropped Courtney off, and nobody was at home because her mother was at the hospital, it would have been another day. It would have happened," Cain said.

"That was really important, I think, for the lady who dropped Courtney off," the warden added.

Without elaborating, Cain said Bordelon also "did the right thing to give one of those ladies a lot of peace about her own child."[15]

* * *

Against his white T-shirt Bordelon wore a gold cross given to him by his 19-year-old daughter, with whom he exchanged necklaces earlier in the day. He had given her a cross made by a fellow inmate. Bordelon's eyes were red-rimmed from crying, as he haltingly said his final words, "I'd like to apologize to my family and tell them that I love them."[16]

In the final moments before the lethal dose was administered, Bordelon again expressed his remorse and asked Cain to tell his daughter that he was not afraid.

After a quick examination, Bordelon was pronounced dead at 6:32 p.m. only minutes after being administered three drugs to put him to sleep, stop his breathing and stop his heart.

Warden Cain announced, "We now pronounce Gerald Bordelon dead. We've sent his soul for final judgment."[17]

CHAPTER 4

Gary James Johnson, Texas. Executed January 12

Gary Johnson did not leave this world with contrition. While awaiting execution, his final words dripped with defiance and disappointment. At the invitation of prison officials, Johnson said, "Just tell my family good-bye." But then, his voice choking with emotion, he urged relatives to tell other family members, "You tell the rest of them what they did was wrong for letting me take the fall for what they did. I never done [sic] anything in my life to anybody."[1]

Eleven minutes after Johnson's statement, he was dead. He was administered a lethal three-drug mixture at 6:15 p.m. The 59-year-old Johnson did not want to die. Earlier in the day, his lawyers asked the U.S. Supreme Court to stay his execution, saying he was nearly blind, in poor health and posed no danger to society if his life was spared. The court disagreed and rejected his plea for mercy.

Statements made under the belief of impending death have always been given special recognition under the law. In most states, rules of evidence permit the introduction of death statements in court as evidence over a hearsay objection.

However, Johnson is not the first killer to leave this life with a lie on his lips. In 2006, Virginia's outgoing Governor Mark Warner had issued an order requiring DNA testing on evidence in the case of rapist and murderer Roger K. Coleman. The unusual aspect about this case was that Coleman had been executed in 1992.

Prior to his execution, *Time* magazine put Coleman on its cover and Pope John Paul II tried to intervene on his behalf. The last words spoken by Coleman were, "An innocent man is going to be murdered tonight." Coleman was right, somewhere in Virginia an innocent man was killed that night, but it was not Coleman.

The governor-ordered DNA testing proved that Coleman did, in fact, murder his sister-in-law. It should not be a surprise that he thought nothing of lying to his supporters with his dying breath. He was also a pallbearer at his victim's funeral.

Jim McCloskey, executive director of Centurion Ministries, a nonprofit organization that works to free prisoners falsely accused of rape or murder, was on the receiving end of Coleman's eleventh-hour lie. He told the *Philadelphia Inquirer* that if Coleman's exoneration leads to the end of capital punishment, "[He] will not have died in vain."

Richard Dieter of the Death Penalty Information Center, an anti–death penalty group, suggested to *USA Today* that finding the execution of an innocent man would put a final nail through the pro–death penalty movement. Dieter's claim puts death penalty opponents in the unenviable position of actually hoping for what they are trying to prevent—the execution of an innocent person.

Coleman's case could not have turned out worse for the anti–death penalty movement. Not only did Coleman not provide the "death nail" that the movement hoped for, he provided death penalty supporters with a "poster child" for execution. Who wouldn't want to flip the switch on a guy who rapes and murders his sister-in-law, carries her coffin to its final resting place and leaves this world with a lie on his lips?

* * *

In 1986, James Hazelton and his brother-in-law, Peter Sparagana, were murdered. The two were gunned down while investigating a call from a neighbor who reported intruders had driven through a secured gate at Hazelton's Triple Creek Ranch about 10 miles west of Huntsville, the home of the Texas death chamber.

According to court records,[2] Bill and Shannon Ferguson were neighbors of the Triple Creek Ranch. On the evening of April 30, 1986, the Fergusons noticed a truck pulled over near a gate adjacent to the ranch. They saw someone get out of the truck, heard a chain rattle on the gate and saw the truck go through the gate and onto the ranch.

The truck's headlights were off, but Mrs. Ferguson noticed an unusual brake light pattern on the truck. Mrs. Ferguson went to her barn and called Jim Hazelton's home. She spoke to Hazelton's wife. Ferguson told her that a burglary might be taking place because a truck had entered the ranch with its lights off. Hazelton's wife told Ferguson that her husband would be right out.

About fifteen minutes later, the Fergusons saw Hazelton's truck appear at the same gate. Hazelton was unable to enter the ranch through that gate, so he backed up and entered the ranch from another location. Eventually the Fergusons heard Hazelton's truck stop. When they heard a gunshot, Mrs. Ferguson went back to the barn to call the police and Mrs. Hazelton.

Mr. Ferguson remained outside. Several minutes after the first gunshot, Mr. Ferguson heard several shots fired in rapid succession. After a brief silence, Mr. Ferguson heard someone plead for his life. The pleas were silenced by two more shots. Hazelton and his brother-in-law, Peter, were dead.

* * *

It took about two years for investigators to assemble their case against Johnson, who once worked at the ranch, and his brother, Terry Johnson. The brothers became suspects after Mrs. Ferguson described the distinctive brake lights she observed on the suspect's truck.

Three of Johnson's brothers—Tracey, Randy, and Ricky—testified against him at trial. Tracey testified that Johnson came to Missouri during the fall of 1986, returned Tracey's .44 caliber pistol and told Tracey to destroy it because the gun had been used in a double murder carried out by Johnson and their brother, Terry.

Ricky testified that, during Johnson's visit to Missouri, he was in possession of the .44 caliber pistol. He admitted killing one man with the gun, and said that he and Terry also killed a second man. A state firearms examiner later identified a bullet fragment retrieved from Hazelton's body as having been fired from the same .44 caliber pistol that Johnson returned to Tracey.

Randy testified that Johnson told him that he and Terry were out at the Triple Creek

Ranch to steal something when two men "got the drop on them." While Terry distracted them, Johnson shot one of the men. Johnson and Terry caught the other man, brought him back to the barn, made him kneel and tied his hands behind his back. While he pleaded for mercy, Johnson shoved the gun in his mouth. The medical examiner testified that Hazelton died from a contact bullet wound to the mouth. Randy testified that Johnson told him the two men were killed because "dead men don't talk."

Surprisingly, the defense called Johnson's brother, Terry, as a witness. Terry testified that Johnson killed both of the victims. Terry described the murders like this. Hazelton and Sparagana discovered Terry Johnson but didn't see Johnson, who opened fire with a .44-caliber Magnum pistol and shot Sparagana. Hazelton tried to run but was caught and shot by Johnson.

The defense also presented testimony from two inmates in the Walker County Jail that Terry Johnson confessed that he killed both of the victims. Johnson was convicted of first-degree murder.

The penalty phase of Johnson's trial, the point where the jury decides life and death, included dueling experts. Dr. James P. Grigson, a psychiatrist, testified, based on a hypothetical question, that Johnson would be a future danger to society. "Most certainly an individual with that type of history and behavior would continue to commit acts of violence," Grigson testified.[3]

Grigson was known as "Dr. Death" for his willingness to be a hired gun by prosecutors in death penalty cases. His opinion about Johnson's future dangerousness was based on Walker County District Attorney Frank Blazek's description of Johnson's one prior arrest and the two murders for which he was standing trial. Grigson admitted that he had never examined Johnson or his criminal history.

Johnson had been arrested 17 years prior to the murders for shooting a neighbor's dog and later paid $150 restitution to the dog owner, according to court testimony.

Testimony that Johnson had bragged to his brothers that he had killed Hazelton and Sparagana indicates that he "doesn't have any regard for human life," said Grigson, who had, at that time, testified in 186 capital murder cases.[4]

Dr. Wendell Lee Dickerson, a psychologist, testified on behalf of Johnson that the American Psychiatric Association (APA) holds that psychiatrists who, like Dr. Grigson, purport to predict future dangerousness with a high degree of certainty "are engaging in practice little short of quackery."[5]

Dr. James Marquart, a sociologist, also testified for the defense. He pointed out that the APA takes the position that it is impossible to make a future dangerousness assessment with 100 percent certainty. He testified that his study of cases in which a prosecution expert predicted future dangerousness showed that the expert was wrong two-thirds of the time.[6]

District Attorney Blazek had told jurors he thought the death penalty was the appropriate punishment for the "brutality, the cold-bloodedness, the viciousness of the killings."[7]

Johnson's attorney told jurors the death sentence would not be fair because Johnson's co-defendant, his brother, Terry, had been offered a plea bargain by authorities in exchange for testifying against his brother. Terry had pleaded guilty and was sentenced to 99 years in prison.

A jury of seven men and five women deliberated for about 35 minutes before they found that Johnson acted deliberately and with a reasonable expectation that death would result, and that it was probable that Johnson would commit future acts of criminal violence and, thus, was a continuing threat to society. The trial court sentenced Johnson to death.

Johnson covered his face with his hands and cried softly after the verdict was read.[8]

*   *   *

Hazelton's brother, George, was among those who watched Johnson die. He stood just a few feet away and watched through a glass window. He declined to meet with reporters following the execution.[9]

Although the victim's family did not want to talk, the district attorney did. "This was not their first nighttime burglary," recalled Frank Blazek. The D.A. went on to say, "He put the gun in Hazelton's mouth ... Hazelton begged for his life and people across the way, in the nearby pasture, couldn't see all this but could hear a man begging for his life."[10]

Blazek said investigators found the same slogan etched in concrete outside Johnson's home and on a T-shirt he was wearing in a photograph: "Kill them all and let God sort them out." "It indicated callousness about human life," he said.[11]

Shannon Ferguson, the neighbor who called Hazelton about the suspicious truck entering the ranch, said, as the execution approached, that she's always "felt kind of responsible" for the two men being murdered because they wouldn't have investigated if she hadn't called. However, Ferguson also believes that if she ignored the Johnson brothers' suspicious activity, "I think they probably would have gone on and murdered more people."[12]

*   *   *

Johnson never took responsibility for the killings. He initially appealed his case to the Court of Criminal Appeals. He argued that his trial counsel was ineffective for calling his brother as a witness because he testified that Johnson killed both men.

In 1992, the Court of Criminal Appeals affirmed Johnson's conviction and sentence. The following year, the United States Supreme Court denied Johnson's petition for a writ of certiorari.

In 2007, Johnson's federal writ of habeas corpus was denied. The Fifth Circuit Court of Appeals thereafter affirmed the federal district court's denial of habeas relief in 2009. The U.S. Supreme Court again refused to hear Johnson's appeal.

*   *   *

Johnson spent more than 20 years on death row. In that time he never spoke to reporters. He never told his story. He refused to make a final statement before he broke into his cryptic claim of innocence. In the hours leading up to his execution, he ate his final meal which consisted of a po-boy sandwich, milk chocolate, Dr. Pepper and a pastry.[13]

The U.S. Supreme Court refused to grant an eleventh-hour stay of execution, and Governor Rick Perry refused to commute Johnson's sentence to life in prison.

On January 7, 2010, prison personnel strapped Johnson's arms, chest and legs to a gurney. His IV had been inserted prior to walking into the death chamber at Huntsville prison, the same room where 448 other men and women, all condemned killers, took their final breath.

One of Johnson's brothers, Dell, and a daughter were among witnesses in a room adjacent to the victim's family. The drugs were pumped through Johnson's veins. As his breathing became shallow and his pulse slowed, the curtain separating the witness rooms and the death chamber was closed. Minutes later Johnson's body was displayed to the witnesses. He was dead. The time was 6:26 p.m.[14]

CHAPTER 5

Julius Ricardo Young, Oklahoma. Executed January 14

Alene Young sat behind the glass partition adjacent to the death chamber—she was sobbing. She asked if she could stand up to the glass to see her son, Julius Ricardo Young, up close, but one of the prison guards told her she had to remain seated. "I love you so much," the elderly woman said. "I love you. You'll see me in the morning, son. Goodnight."[1]

Ms. Young was in McAlester, Oklahoma, a town of about 18,000 people in southeast Oklahoma. The dusty little town known as "Little Dixie" is home to "Big Mac," the 1,200-bed Oklahoma State Penitentiary.

The penitentiary was built in 1908 soon after Oklahoma won statehood. Besides being the home of death row and the state's execution chamber, McAlester is also known as the home of Carl Albert, who served in congress as speaker of the house, the highest office ever held by a native of Oklahoma.

None of that mattered to Alene Young as she sat and watched her son, once an ordained minister, prepare to die. "I'm very sad," Alene said, wiping tears from her eyes. "I had three sons, and he [Julius] is the last one alive."[2]

*   *   *

Julius Ricardo Young, according to court records,[3] was convicted of murdering his girlfriend's daughter and six-year-old grandson. The murders occurred two days after his girlfriend, Joyslon Edwards, advised him that she wanted to cool their relationship and that he would not get a key to her new apartment.

Edwards did not give Young a key because she wanted her daughter and grandson to "feel safe" when they visited her new apartment. Her daughter and grandson did not like Young.

Young had a key to the apartment where Edwards' daughter, Joyland Morgan, and her grandson, Kewan Morgan, still lived. On the day before the murders, Edwards demanded the key from Young, but he did not return it.

Joyland and Kewan were beaten to death in their Tulsa apartment on October 1, 1993. Their wounds indicated the murder weapon was a blunt instrument similar to a baseball bat, but the murder weapon was never found. Twenty-year-old Joyland sustained defensive wounds to her hands and arms and at least 13 blows to her face and head. These blows broke her jaw, tore open her scalp and fractured her skull. She was found slumped against a living room wall. Six-year-old Kewan died in his bed. He sustained massive head fractures caused by two separate blows.

Every night before she went to bed Joyland secured her front door with two locks and a security chain. Young opened both locks with a key and pushed through the security chain, breaking it. A piece of the broken chain was missing from the apartment.

There were no eyewitnesses. However, a downstairs neighbor was awakened at 3:40 a.m. by a single loud thump from Morgan's apartment. Joyslon Edwards testified she saw a baseball bat in Young's car trunk the night before the murders, but the next day it was gone.

Young always drove Edwards to work, and on the day of the murders, he arrived at 4:15 a.m., earlier than usual. Edwards asked him for change so she could use the vending machines at work. When Young pulled out the contents of his pocket, Edwards saw a piece of security chain similar to the one she had installed on her daughter's door. Later that day when Edwards learned of the murders, she reported this evidence to the police.

The police obtained a warrant to search the home where Young lived with his mother at the time. Edwards told police what Young had worn the previous evening. The police recovered the shoes described by Edwards, and these bore a visible spot of blood. Young accompanied the police during the search. He volunteered that the drop was fish blood. DNA testing revealed the drop was human blood consistent with that of Joyland and Kewan. The police also recovered a freshly-laundered shirt which tested positive for blood.

*   *   *

Young's final words were defiant, devoid of remorse and anything but contrite. Final acts of defiance are nothing new for those who oversee executions in the death chamber at "Big Mac." Oklahoma has the highest rate of execution per capita in the United States. Only Texas and Virginia have executed more people since the death penalty was reinstituted in 1976. In fact, Oklahoma only reinstated the death penalty in 1990.

The Oklahoma death chamber has been used to execute 171 men and three women, all by lethal injection. Oklahoma was the first jurisdiction in the world to adopt lethal injection as a method to carry out executions.

On a windy and rainy January 14, 2010, Young ate his final meal of a sirloin steak, a baked potato, onion rings, a tossed salad and a Coke.[4]

Young spoke his final words as he lay strapped to a gurney awaiting the lethal drug concoction that would take his life, "I am an innocent man. This is a miscarriage of justice," Young said in a rambling final statement, in which he denied being at the scene of the 1993 killings and that he had been let down by the legal system. "I didn't take the lives of Joyland Morgan and her son Kewan. My attorney failed me. It's a tragedy. I'm an innocent man. To my family, I love you."[5]

He told the Oklahoma Pardon and Parole Board during a clemency hearing in December of 2009, "I cannot confess to something I did not do." The board voted 4–1 to deny clemency for Young, who had exhausted all of his appeals.[6]

Young's attorney, Steve Presson, said prosecutors used outdated blood testing to link Young to the killings and that the blood evidence was later destroyed when a freezer in the Tulsa Police Department's evidence room malfunctioned, prohibiting further testing. He also said Young had been an ideal inmate who had never been cited for misconduct and who had taught other inmates to read. "He is a person deserving of mercy," Presson said.[7]

State prosecutors argued the evidence against Young was strong, noting that the jury's verdict had been upheld by various appellate courts. "I would submit to you, this is not the flimsy circumstantial case they would have you believe," Assistant Attorney General Seth Branham said.[8]

Alene Young said her son's trial was unfair. She believed her son was innocent and suggested that his religious background as an ordained minister was indicative of his good character. In 1994, the *Tulsa World* reported that Young was the pastor of the African Methodist Episcopal Church in Boynton, Oklahoma.

* * *

For years, Oklahoma has been a hotbed of capital punishment, with the state consistently ranking near the top in the number of death row inmates and executions. While death sentences decreased nationally in 2009, the number of inmates executed increased from 37 to 52 due to a Supreme Court decision relating to lethal injection.

Oklahoma, which conducted three of those executions, ranked sixth in the number of people put to death compared to the 35 other states, at the time, that used the death penalty. Nationwide, the number of inmates sentenced to death in 2009 was at its lowest since the death penalty was reinstated. In the past decade, death sentences have decreased nationwide by 63 percent. In 2009, 106 people were sentenced to death, compared to 284 people in 1999.[9]

There are 81 inmates on death row in Oklahoma. The Department of Corrections estimated that it costs $20,000 per year to house the average inmate. Death row inmates are not average inmates. Due to increased supervision and segregation from other inmates, housing an inmate on death row can cost three times as much as other inmates.

Other states estimate that a single case, from arrest to execution, costs between $1 million and $3 million, and some estimates are as high as $7 million. By comparison, the cost for life imprisonment is approximately $500,000, according to a report prepared by the Death Penalty Information Center, an anti–death penalty group.[10]

Dudley Sharp, of Justice for All, a pro–death penalty organization, estimates that life without parole (LWOP) cases will cost $1.2 million to $3.6 million more than a death penalty case over the life time of the offender serving life in prison. Sharp wrote, "There is no question that the upfront costs of the death penalty are significantly higher than for equivalent LWOP cases. There also appears to be no question that, over time, equivalent LWOP cases are much more expensive than death penalty cases. Opponents ludicrously claim that the death penalty costs, over time, three to ten times more than LWOP."[11]

State Senator Connie Johnson of Oklahoma City, said she hopes the current economy will help garner support to abolish capital punishment because death sentences are placing an unnecessary financial burden on the state. Senator Johnson contends that the public needs to know about the cost of the death penalty and is committed to promoting an education campaign with the Oklahoma Coalition to Abolish the Death Penalty.[12]

* * *

After the U.S. Supreme Court denied Young's final appeal, Oklahoma Attorney General Drew Edmondson requested an execution. The execution was set for January 14, 2010.

As the execution neared, Joyslon Edwards said she supports the state's carrying out the execution, saying it ensures that Young will never be released from prison. "That was my only daughter and her only son," she said. Edwards told the Pardon and Parole Board that Young often became angry when he drank. "Julius had some mean streaks in him," she said.[13]

Edwards said the execution would bring closure. "Once this is over, I will never bring this up anymore," she told the *Tulsa World*. "It will be a closed book in my life."[14]

Deon Morgan described the life his family wanted for Kewan, who was six years old when he was killed. "He didn't get to grow up," he said after the execution. "There wasn't riding a bicycle, driving cars, swimming, a family pet. He didn't get to experience that."[15]

Sixteen family members and friends of the victims also attended the execution. Morgan's father, Willie Walker, 59, of Tulsa, took issue with Young's final words. Young should have asked for forgiveness instead of denying the murders, he said. Nevertheless, "justice has been served," he said.[16]

At 6:21 p.m. Young lay motionless in the death chamber as the lethal drugs began to flow through his veins. Young took a few last gasps of air and fell silent. He was dead six minutes after the lethal injection process began.[17]

CHAPTER 6

Mark Aaron Brown, Ohio.
Executed February 4

The 1993 urban drama *Menace II Society*, starring Samuel L. Jackson, begins with the killing of two store clerks. Two young black men go to a convenience store operated by Asian immigrants in a predominantly black neighborhood. One of the men shoots the owner as he crouches behind the counter; an employee is murdered in the back of the store.[1]

Mark Brown wanted to recreate that movie scene in real life. As a result, Brown and two innocent victims lost their lives.

According to court records,[2] on a cold winter evening in the rough and tumble town of Youngstown, Ohio, Brown and some friends went to a convenience store to purchase beer and wine. It was January 28, 1994.

They drove to the home of Allen "Boonie" Thomas' cousin to play cards. A group of juveniles were hanging out at the house that evening. Brown and Boonie drank wine mixed with a number of Valiums and smoked marijuana in "blunts," cigars that have been cut open, emptied of tobacco, and filled with marijuana. While playing cards, Brown pulled out a gun and put it back in his coat pocket. As the card game progressed, Brown brought up the movie *Menace II Society*.

Menace II Society also played a role in the conviction of Vernon Lamont Smith chronicled in Chapter 1.

Later that night, Brown went to the Midway Market in Youngstown to buy more drinks. Gary Thomas, Boonie's uncle, gave Brown and Boonie a ride. Thomas parked the car while Brown and Boonie entered the market.

A group of young guys who had been at the house earlier were standing just outside the store. Two of the guys, Marcus Clark and Myzelle Arrington, saw Brown and Boonie leave the store. They then saw Brown re-enter the store alone, wearing a mask or bandana around his neck. They told police that Boonie and Thomas were in the car. When they heard gunshots from inside the store, Clark and Arrington took off running.

Thomas verified the boys' account of what occurred, and told police that before re-entering the store, Brown said, "I forgot to do something." While Brown was in the store, Thomas heard gunshots. Thomas saw Brown casually walk away from the store and get back into the car. When Thomas asked what happened, Brown replied, "Oh, that wasn't nothing but some firecrackers."

Thomas drove Brown and Boonie back to the house where he saw Brown "messing with the gun." Thomas also noticed blood on Brown's hand and clothing. Both Clark and Arrington saw Brown wiping off a 9-mm black gun. Arrington also saw Brown counting money.

Around 9:55 that evening, Officer Timothy Morgan, Jr., of the Youngstown Police Department received a call that a robbery was in progress at the Midway Market. He and his partner arrived at the market and found that two Arab men had been shot. One man was found lying on the floor face up and the other was kneeling behind the counter. Both men were dead.

A "blunt" and a packet of marijuana were on the floor nearby. The victims were the store's owner, Isam Salman, and an employee, Hayder Al Turk. The Mahoning County coroner determined that the victims died as a result of gunshot wounds to the head.

Lieutenant David McKnight interviewed several witnesses and, on January 31, 1994, secured a warrant for Brown's arrest. Just four days later, on February 3, 1994, Brown was arrested in Warren, Ohio, and transported back to Youngstown. After advising him of his Miranda rights, which he waived in writing, police began questioning him. During the questioning, Brown admitted being at the Midway Market but claimed that Boonie was the shooter.

Although police knew that video cameras in the store were not operating during the murders, the lieutenant asked Brown whether he knew that there were video cameras in the store. Brown said that he didn't notice. Police told him that there were two video cameras in the store. Brown replied, "Well, I guess you know what happened there then." When the police answered, "Yes," Brown said, "Well, you've got me." He also said, "Then you know I did it." Brown then admitted to shooting one of the guys, but said he didn't recall shooting the other guy.

The police did not tell Brown that he was caught on tape; they simply asked Brown if he was aware that there were cameras in the store. The fact that the cameras were inoperable was not divulged to Brown. In a sense, the police were not deceptive because, according to the U.S. Supreme Court,[3] deception is a permissible interrogation technique.

When Brown was apprehended, police retrieved a 9-mm Glock semiautomatic firearm under the couch cushion in the front room. The firearm was later identified by Steve Jones, who said that Brown had robbed him of his car at gunpoint on December 15, 1993; Jones's Glock was in the car's trunk at the time.

A forensic scientist examined the Glock firearm. Nine cartridge casings had been recovered from the crime scene and four bullets had been retrieved from the victims. He concluded that all nine cartridges were fired from the Glock firearm. He further concluded that the bullets recovered from the victims indicated that they were fired from a Glock weapon; however, he could not confirm or eliminate the Glock retrieved from the appellant as the weapon from which they were fired.

At trial, Brown took the stand in his own defense. Brown admitted shooting one of the victims but not the other. He testified that Boonie was with him at the time of the shooting and, after the first victim was shot, Boonie took the gun. He stated that he did not steal any money from the store. Brown further testified that he was "messed up" when police interviewed him and that he requested an attorney two or three times but that this request was denied.

The jury convicted Brown of two counts of aggravated murder committed with prior calculation and design. In other words, Brown committed premeditated murder. He was acquitted of the specification that the murders were committed while committing aggravated robbery. The jury recommended that Brown receive the death penalty for the aggravated murder of Salman and life imprisonment for the aggravated murder of Al Turk.

* * *

Brown argued on appeal that he was intoxicated and under the influence of drugs when he confessed. He maintained that his signed waiver was invalid because he did not fully understand his rights. The testimony of the detectives who interviewed Brown contradicted his claim.[4]

Detective McKnight testified that Brown was cooperative and alert during the interview. He further testified that he did not smell alcohol and did not observe anything that would indicate Brown was under the influence of drugs or alcohol. Furthermore, at the suppression hearing, Detective Gerald Maietta, who also interviewed Brown, testified that he exhibited no signs of being intoxicated or on drugs; instead, Brown was "friendly, cognizant, appeared to understand what we were talking about." Neither officer remembered Brown telling them that he was under the influence of drugs or alcohol.

A videotaped interview would have gone a long way to limit Brown's claims. In the 17 years since Brown's arrest, the manner in which interviews are conducted has come under scrutiny. Why videotape interviews and interrogations in homicide cases? Roughly 25 percent of the 245 people freed from prison by DNA testing in the last 20 years gave false confessions.[5]

Videotaping interrogations benefits both sides in a murder investigation and ultimately a murder trial. Police are immunized from complaints of mistreatment or coercion. Frivolous claims like those submitted by Mark Brown can be quickly dismissed. Legitimate claims can be adjudicated with the best possible evidence—the statement itself. Judges and juries can see the entire interrogation, allowing them to reach informed conclusions about the truth of a confession. Guilty people look guilty on videotape.[6]

Brown also argued that because of his youth and lack of experience with the criminal justice system, he was incapable of making a voluntary statement. Brown was 21 years old at the time of the offense, had finished tenth grade, and could read and write. He did not lack the intelligence to understand what was being asked of him. Moreover, Brown had been charged with and was convicted of two prior felonies, both times he was advised of his Miranda rights and represented by counsel. The court concluded that Brown could not legitimately argue that he was unfamiliar with the criminal justice system.[7]

Finally, Brown argued that the trial court should have suppressed his confession because police ignored his request to have an attorney present. Under the Fifth Amendment, if an accused requested counsel during questioning, the interrogation must cease until an attorney is present, according to the U.S. Supreme Court decision in *Edwards v. Arizona*.[8] For the interrogation to cease, however, the accused must clearly invoke his constitutional right to counsel. In order to do this, an accused "must articulate his desire to have counsel present sufficiently clearly that a reasonable police officer under the circumstances would understand the statement to be a request for an attorney."[9] The questioning need not stop if the request is ambiguous.

Detective McKnight testified that he had no recollection that Brown requested a lawyer. At the suppression hearing, Brown testified as follows: "Before he asked me to understand my rights, he asked me do I have any questions, and I asked him, don't I supposed to have a lawyer present; and neither one of them answered." The Ohio court found that Brown's statements were, at best, ambiguous.[10]

*   *   *

Brown was transported from the Ohio State Penitentiary in Youngstown to the Southern Ohio Correctional Facility in Lucasville on Wednesday morning February 3, 2010, the night before his scheduled execution. He spent most of the afternoon and night talking on the phone with friends, his sister, his attorney and two of the mothers of his children. One call stretched from 2:14 a.m. until 4:49 a.m.[11]

He had contact visits with his brother, his spiritual adviser, and his attorney for several hours Wednesday evening. He became emotional at about 7 p.m. when he received word that Governor Ted Strickland had denied his request for clemency.[12]

Throughout the evening, he ate a special meal that included a bacon double cheeseburger, onion rings, orange soda and ice cream. He did not eat breakfast on the morning of the scheduled execution, nor did he touch the T-bone steak, cooked well-done, that he requested.[13]

He slept from just before 5 a.m. until 6:20 a.m. when he showered and had cell-front visits with his spiritual adviser and two attorneys. He completed those visits after 8:30 a.m. and turned over his personal belongings to his legal counsel. The U.S. Supreme Court turned down Brown's appeals just after 9 a.m., delaying the execution by about 20 minutes.[14]

Prison staff took less than ten minutes to insert the IVs into both of Brown's arms. He then made the lonely 17-step walk from his holding cell to the death chamber. He made no final statement. He did not ask for forgiveness or apologize to the families of his victims.

After the single dose of sodium thiopental was administered at 10:40 a.m. he blinked several times, closed and opened his eyes and swallowed once before shutting his eyes one last time. At 10:42 a.m. his chest heaved, he appeared to yawn; his chest rose and fell slightly several more times and then he fell still.[15]

Just a dozen feet away, separated by glass, sat three family members of Isam Salman. Terri Rasul, the victim's sister; Majdy Salman, his son; and Walid Salman, his brother, witnessed Brown's execution. They sat silently throughout the process. Rasul clutched a photograph of a man and a woman; she later declined to say whether it was her late brother.

The victim witnesses lingered a few minutes to watch Brown's body loaded into a hearse, perhaps seeking final proof he was gone. A few minutes later, Rasul told reporters, "As sad as this may be, justice has been served. I hope this is a lesson learned by young people today to not do what Mark Brown did to my brother."[16]

CHAPTER 7

Martin Edward Grossman, Florida.
Executed February 16

Harvard law professor Alan Dershowitz believed that Martin Grossman's execution should have been postponed for 60 days. Grossman committed a murder in 1984. Twenty-five years had passed and Grossman's supporters were pleading for 60 more days.

Dershowitz wrote a letter on behalf of a coalition of Jewish groups pleading for mercy. "Even those who strongly support capital punishment would limit it to recidivists or people who commit the most heinous of crimes. Martin Grossman fits neither of those categories." Dershowitz added that Grossman's crime was unplanned, impulsive and the "product of a serious mental illness."[1]

Florida authorities didn't see it that way. Grossman was executed for killing wildlife officer Margaret "Peggy" Park in December 1984 after she found him with a stolen gun in a secluded area of Pinellas County, one of several counties that comprise greater Tampa Bay.

Grossman committed a brutal murder because he did not want to return to prison for a probation violation.

* * *

According to court records,[2] 19-year-old Martin Grossman and a friend, Thayne Taylor, drove to a wooded area near the Gulf Coast of Pinellas County on the night of December 13, 1984. The two planned to shoot a handgun which Grossman had recently obtained through a burglary. Grossman lived with his mother in neighboring Pasco County and was on probation after spending time in prison.

Officer Park was patrolling the area in her state vehicle when she came upon the two men and became suspicious. Park got out of the car with the motor running and her lights and flashers on. Park asked for Grossman's handgun and driver's license.

Peggy Park always knew she wanted to work out of doors. She grew up in Ohio and went to Ohio State University, graduating with a degree in natural resources and wildlife management in 1981. The next year she graduated from wildlife officer training school and was assigned to Pinellas County.

Grossman pleaded with Park not to report to his probation officer that he had a weapon and was unlawfully out of Pasco County. Either situation, possession of a stolen gun or being outside the county without permission would have resulted in a probation violation and his return to jail. Grossman was facing six to 12 months in prison.

Park refused the plea, and Grossman decided her life was expendable. Grossman traded her life for a year locked up as a probation violator.

As Park opened the driver's door to her vehicle and leaned in to pick up the radio microphone to call the sheriff's office, Grossman grabbed the large flashlight from her belt and struck her repeatedly on the head and shoulders, forcing her upper body into her vehicle.

Park shouted, "I'm hit" over the radio and screamed. Grossman continued the attack, and called for help from Taylor, who joined in the assault. Officer Park managed to draw her service revolver, a .357 magnum, and fired a wild shot within the vehicle. Simultaneously, she disabled Taylor by kicking him in the groin. Grossman wrestled the officer's gun away and fired a fatal shot into the back of her head. Grossman was six feet four inches tall and weighed 225 pounds. Park was five feet five inches tall and weighed 115 pounds. He broke his fingers wrenching the .357 away from Park.

The spent slug exited her head in front and fell into a drinking cup inside the vehicle. Grossman and Taylor retrieved the stolen gun and driver's license and fled with Park's weapon. Grossman would boast about his "feat" of violence and death on three separate occasions.

Immediately after the murder, they returned to Grossman's house. First, he and Taylor told the story of the killing to Brian Hancock, a friend who lived with Grossman and his mother. Hancock and Taylor buried the two weapons nearby.

Grossman was covered with blood and attempted, unsuccessfully, to burn his clothes and shoes which Taylor later disposed of in a nearby lake. Approximately a week later, Grossman and Taylor told their story to another friend, Brian Allan. Then 11 days after the murder, Hancock went to the police and Grossman and Taylor were arrested.

* * *

Taylor confessed to his involvement in the murder to a policeman and, later, Grossman made a jailhouse confession to a cellmate, Charles Brewer. The court ordered that Grossman and Taylor be tried together. Grossman opposed the consolidation of trials, knowing that Taylor's confession might have an influence on jurors regarding his own guilt.

At trial, Hancock, Allan and Brewer all testified against Grossman. The state also introduced Taylor's statement to the police. The jury was instructed that Taylor's admissions to the police could only be used against Taylor, not Grossman, pursuant to the landmark U.S. Supreme Court decision in *Bruton v. United States*.[3]

In addition, the state introduced the charred shoes, the two weapons, prints taken from Park's vehicle and testimony from a neighbor who observed the attempted burning of Grossman's clothes. The jury also heard about Grossman cleaning his van and changing the tires.

The State also presented expert testimony as to the cause of death and the significance of blood splatter evidence. The jury was instructed on premeditation and felony murder based on robbery, burglary and escape. Exactly one year after the murder December 13, 1985, Grossman was found guilty of first-degree murder and sentenced to death. Taylor was found guilty of third-degree murder and received a seven-year sentence and served only two years and ten months.

Grossman's direct appeal to the Florida Supreme Court was denied in 1988. The U.S. Supreme Court refused to hear Grossman's appeal in 1989. Over the next 20 years, Grossman filed multiple Writs of Habeas Corpus in state and federal court. All were dismissed. His request for clemency was denied in October of 2009.

*   *   *

Grossman didn't request a last meal before the execution. Instead, he had a chicken sandwich, can of fruit punch, and banana cream and peanut butter cookies that he bought from the prison canteen.[4]

His final visit began at 8:30 a.m. on the day of his execution. Grossman met with his aunt, Rosal Melton, and two female friends, Sharon Lion and Francine Whitehouse. The first two hours, a visitor's window separated him from his visitors and the last hour was a contact visit.[5]

Grossman's religious adviser, Rabbi Menachem Katz, was with him in his cell throughout the day. In preparation for his 6 p.m. execution, he showered at about 4 p.m. "He is calm, compliant and resolved to the fact his execution is going to happen," a prison spokesperson told the media before Grossman was walked to the death chamber.[6]

In a final statement, Grossman expressed remorse to the family of Peggy Park. "I would like to extend my heartfelt remorse to the victim's family," Grossman said. "I fully regret everything that happened that night, everything that was done, whether I remember everything or not. I accept responsibility."[7]

"I would like to say a prayer," the 45-year-old man added, then, lying on a gurney, hands strapped to arm boards. With needles in both arms, he began reciting a Jewish prayer called the Shema. It is the most sacred prayer in Judaism and the first prayer that Jewish children learn. Among its verses: "The Lord is our God; God is one."

*   *   *

Park's brother, sister and mother were among the 20 witnesses to the execution. They were seated directly in front of Grossman, who was visible through a window.

During the rather antiseptic execution, Park's mother stared at her daughter's killer who was just ten feet away. Afterwards, Margaret Park said she was thinking of the children of Haiti who were buried under concrete and died a horrible, scary death. Park was referring to the massive earthquake that struck the nation of Haiti on January 12, 2010.

As far as Park was concerned Grossman had it easy. When it came to Grossman's death by lethal injection Park said, "I think he had an easy one."[8]

Park's sister Betsy felt those 25 years were an excruciatingly long time to have to wait. They had to relive the trauma of her death over and over through the years. Betsy Park was sad her father didn't live to see the day the killer died. Park said she was upset with some opponents of the execution including the Pope for stepping in and with some Jewish groups which she said went too far. According to Park, the family was harassed over the past week and she thinks it is reprehensible. However, Park said she is glad that Grossman took responsibility, but said it was long overdue.[9]

"I don't take any pleasure in an execution, but it's time," said Peggy's mother Margaret. "He had very good representation all the way through. I think he's been treated very fairly by the state of Florida," she said. "It's long overdue." Margaret also said, "Every time something has come up, it has been like a wave coming up and knocking you back down, and you go over all the emotions again. We just need to have an end to this coming back and hitting us again."[10]

Margaret also said the execution wouldn't "bring closure," but it would "prevent him from ever, under any circumstances, being released and injuring other people. I spent twenty-five years teaching kids that they had to take responsibility for their actions," she said, "and I think he needs to be held accountable for what he did."[11]

The victim's younger sister, Betsy, told the *St. Petersburg Times* that Grossman's execution is not about vengeance. "It's to see it finished," she said. "He had a chance to make choices. And he made the wrong ones."

*   *   *

Not everyone wanted to see Grossman die. In fact, he had a lot of support nationwide and a few influential supporters as well.

An Internet petition drive to save Grossman netted more than 33,000 signatures and Governor Charlie Crist received thousands of phone calls and e-mail messages about the case. More than 110 rabbis wrote Crist to urge a stay of execution for a clemency hearing. A spokesperson for the governor announced that since the date the death warrant was signed, the governor's office had received about 49,000 letters, telephone calls or e-mails.[12]

The Vatican had also asked for Grossman's life to be spared in a letter written by Archbishop Fernando Filoni on behalf of Pope Benedict XVI. The letter said Grossman had "repented and is now a changed person, having become a man of faith." Even Holocaust survivor and Nobel laureate Elie Wiesel, wrote on behalf of Grossman; "These days, death is winning too many battles and life imprisonment is a harsh enough punishment."[13]

The execution brought about 30 protesters to a field across from the prison. While the protesters typically include members of Catholic churches, they were joined by Jewish participants, including Rabbi Stanley Howard Schwartz of Daytona Beach. He said protests should not be about Grossman's faith, but rather about the Biblical prohibition against killing. "The state of Florida should not commit murder," he said.[14]

The efforts to save Grossman were to no avail.

*   *   *

Witnesses were led into observation rooms adjacent to the death chamber at about 5:45 p.m. where a curtain blocked the view of the death chamber. At 6 p.m. the curtain was opened and Grossman was revealed lying strapped to a gurney with an IV inserted into both arms. The warden contacted the governor's office for any final instruction. There would be no last minute reprieve.

The execution began at 6:02 p.m. As the lethal chemicals flowed into his body, Grossman closed his eyes and looked like he was going to sleep. At 6:07 p.m. the warden called out Grossman's name, shook his body and brushed against his eyelashes to make sure he was unconscious, and then the final chemical was administered to stop his heart.[15]

At 6:16 p.m. the attending physician appeared from behind a wall within the execution chamber. The doctor used a stethoscope to check Grossman for a heartbeat. At 6:17 p.m. the doctor pronounced Grossman dead.

Mike Deeson, a reporter who witnessed Grossman's execution, wrote, "Having covered some of the Peggy Park murder, and now being a witness at the execution of her killer, it seems as if Park's death was more traumatizing. She was beaten over the head more than twenty times with her flashlight and then shot in the head with her service revolver. And while the execution brings some closure, it will never end for the Park family."[16]

It's not clear where Grossman's remains were laid to rest. Some 25 years before Grossman took his last breath, the family of Peggy Park had her body cremated and her ashes were scattered near the eagles' nests she worked to protect in Florida. A nature trail was named for her in Pinellas County Park and a memorial plaque was installed near the place where she was murdered.

It is unlikely that any effort was made to memorialize the sad and unfortunate life of Martin Grossman.

CHAPTER 8

Michael Adam Sigala, Texas.
Executed March 2

Plano, Texas, is an affluent suburb of Dallas. Voted one of the most livable cities in America, Plano is home to Oracle, Frito Lay, Dr. Pepper, Siemens and a number of other major corporations. In 2000, there were just five murders in Plano, the lowest homicide rate of any U.S. city with a population of 250,000 or more. Two of those murders rocked the Dallas-Fort Worth Metroplex.

During the summer of 2000, Michael Sigala was serving 10 years probation for a 1999 robbery conviction. After serving 30 days in the local jail, he was assigned to a drug treatment center in Wilmer, Texas, a town south of Dallas. Having previously violated his probation for illegal drug use, this was the second time he was sent to drug treatment.

Although he had never served a prison sentence, Sigala had a long and troubling history of violent criminal activity and had spent time in local lock-ups. As a juvenile, he was on probation for theft, and then received jail time for marijuana possession and another jail stint for theft. At age 13, he was arrested for burglary. Not long after the burglary, he was expelled from school for carrying a gun.

On August 22, 2000, he was out on a one-day pass from the Wilmer Treatment Center to look for work. While away from the center, he broke into the apartment of Kleber and Lilian Dos Santos.

Kleber's work as an engineer brought him to Texas from Brazil in January 2000. A month later he was married to Lilian. She remained in Brazil to continue her veterinary studies at the University of Sao Paulo and was visiting her husband during a summer break from school.[1]

"So often in criminal cases, people will sometimes put themselves in bad circumstances. But this one, these people seemed completely blameless," said Debbie Harrison, a Collin County assistant district attorney who prosecuted the case.[2]

* * *

What Sigala did to Kleber and Lilian Dos Santos shocked northern Texas.

According to court records,[3] once Sigala got inside Dos Santos' apartment, he executed Kleber with a single gunshot to the head. He then forced Lilian to remove her clothes and wash herself. In the bedroom, he bound Lilian's hands and neck with telephone cords, and then dripped hot wax from a nearby candle onto her vagina. He then whipped her buttocks with a belt or something rod shaped, and cut the inside of her thigh. While torturing Lilian, Sigala masturbated and ejaculated on the floor.

Evidence showed that, for several hours after her husband was killed, the 25-year-old woman was raped and fatally shot in the face and again in the side of the head.

After the murders, Sigala lingered at the apartment. He attempted to wipe his fingerprints off of everything he touched, and he cleaned the carpet where he had ejaculated. He also helped himself to a drink and watched television. He went through the apartment, collecting the couple's wedding rings and some other items including a camera. Finally, he left. The bodies were found by a neighbor after Kleber failed to report to work.

"It was pretty sad, especially when you think of your husband being killed in front of you, then you're dragged off, your clothes taken off, being tied up and who knows what," said Harrison.[4]

Sigala was arrested about two months after the murders when the camera he took was found at a pawn shop in Arlington, some 30 miles southwest of Plano. That led investigators to the couple's wedding rings, which had been pawned in Dallas.

In a videotaped statement to police following his arrest, Sigala initially denied any involvement but later said he shot the couple in self-defense because Dos Santos struck an accomplice of his with a baseball bat. He contended that he and the friend, who he knew only as Billy, went to the apartment to sell Dos Santos some heroin.

Most of what Sigala told police did not add up. Authorities found no evidence Dos Santos or his wife ever used drugs. A toxicology report found no illegal drugs in either victim. Testing of the semen discovered on the floor next to the bed revealed an "exact" DNA match to Sigala. A firearms expert testified that all of the bullets recovered from the scene were fired from the same weapon. Although Sigala attempted to blame Lilian's assault on another person, authorities found no evidence of a second attacker.

Eventually, he confessed to killing Kleber, ejaculating as Lilian lay on the bed, and stealing the couple's rings. "I freaked out," Sigala told detectives. "I didn't mean to hurt nobody."

"He was in the apartment a very long time," Harrison said. "He sat down and watched TV for a while. He cleaned the apartment immaculately. Everything was wiped down." The reason why Sigala selected the Dos Santos apartment for the attack remains a mystery.[5]

* * *

On October 8, 2001, Sigala was convicted of first degree murder. All capital murder trials come in two phases, the guilt phase and the penalty phase. After a determination of guilty, the jury must then decide death or life in prison. In order to make that decision, the jury hears additional evidence during the trial's penalty phase.

During the penalty phase of Sigala's trial, the prosecution presented evidence that he was a drug abuser, had washed out of drug rehab, had been expelled from school, and later dropped out. His long criminal record of thefts, drug possession, robbery, and burglary were also presented to the jury.

A mental-health expert testified that Sigala had an antisocial personality disorder and could be described as a "sadistic sexual predator." Sigala believed that women wanted sado-masochistic sex. He told his mother that he was a sociopath; he found it funny when others were in pain, and he had no remorse for killing Kleber.[6]

According to the testimony of an FBI agent presented during the trial's penalty phase, Sigala was "a member of a unique, particularly vicious subclass of offenders that are dangerous, but also represent a continuing threat to the community." The FBI agent observed that Sigala had rehearsed the crime, was comfortable at the crime scene, and enjoyed a sense of accomplishment afterwards. A psychiatrist also testified that Sigala suffered from antisocial personality disorder, which indicated that he would commit violent acts in the future.[7]

Defense attorneys argued for a life sentence. Sigala's attorneys told the jury that his drug use, upbringing, educational failure and mental health problems contributed to his criminal activity.

On October 15, 2001, Sigala was sentenced to death.

* * *

Sigala declined to speak with reporters as his execution date neared. A week before his scheduled execution the U.S. Supreme Court refused to review his case. He filed no new appeals; death was inevitable.

On the day before Sigala was to be executed, he was transferred to the Texas State Penitentiary at Huntsville on March 1, 2010. According to the department of corrections, Sigala ate a final meal of deep-fried burritos and chocolate pudding.

As he laid strapped to a gurney, Sigala made his final statement, "I would like to ask for forgiveness of the family. I have no reason for why I did it. I don't understand why I did it. I hope that you can live the rest of your lives without hate."[8]

As the lethal three-drug protocol was administered, he snored at least once and then gasped. Nine minutes later, at 6:20 p.m. he was dead.

Relatives of Kleber and Lilian Dos Santos did not speak with reporters afterward, but the parents of both victims issued statements saying they were grateful justice had been done. "For many people facing such tragedy, life would be worthless. For us, however, we have faith, and we find meaning in an eternal life that our merciful God will provide us. We really believe that we will meet our dear son and daughter-in-law one day in heaven."[9]

CHAPTER 9

Joshua Maxwell, Texas. Executed March 11

Rudolfo Lopes was a sergeant with the Bexar County Sheriff's Department in San Antonio, Texas. He was scheduled to work at the county jail from 10:00 a.m. to 9:00 p.m. on October 11, 2000. Lopes left for work that morning in his gold four-door Chevrolet pickup truck. As he did every day, Lopes carried a briefcase and his department issued Glock pistol. However, it turned out to be anything but a routine day. Lopes never returned home from work that night.

According to court records,[1] Lopes' body was discovered in a field behind a strip mall near San Antonio. He was blindfolded and lying face down with his arms inside his shirt with both wrists bound together by a clear telephone cord. There was also a white cotton cord tied around one of his wrists and his hands bound together. Police found a spent shell casing on the ground near his body.

A week later, two police officers on patrol in downtown San Francisco, California, observed a gold pickup truck speed through an intersection almost hitting a pedestrian. The officers stopped the truck, exited their vehicle, approached the truck from the rear, and asked the driver to turn off the engine. Instead, the driver, Joshua Maxwell, drove away and led the police on a chase through downtown San Francisco.

During the chase, Maxwell shot at the police. The bullet hit the officers' windshield and came within inches of striking one of the officers. Glass from the windshield sprayed the inside of the police car, injuring one of the officers.

Additional police officers joined the chase. Maxwell continued shooting, and the police returned fire. Pursuing police officers said that at one point during the high speed chase, the driver "reached out with his left arm and hand and raised his middle finger and flipped us off."[2]

The pursuit finally ended when the truck became stuck in traffic. The driver and a passenger were identified as Maxwell and Tess McFarland. Maxwell was wearing a gold chain necklace belonging to Lopes when he was arrested.

The police searched the truck and found Lopes' badge, a credit card belonging to Lopes, and a State of Indiana identification card for "Trina Dorris" bearing McFarland's picture. Police also found Lopes' Glock pistol, a Chinese 9-millimeter pistol, and a briefcase.

Maxwell agreed to speak with the officers and gave a taped interview. During the interview Maxwell admitted that a month before killing Lopes, he killed Robbie Bott in Indiana. Maxwell and McFarland kidnapped Bott and made him buy expensive items at department stores and withdraw cash from automatic teller machines. Maxwell admitted he killed Bott by shooting him in the face and strangling him. They put him in the trunk of his own car and set him and his car on fire.

Early in the morning of September 12, 2000, Bott's abandoned car was found aflame about fifteen minutes from his Mooresville home. His charred, hogtied body was found in the trunk.

* * *

Maxwell was arrested and extradited to Texas for the murder of Deputy Lopes. He was convicted of the murder of Bott and received a 91-year sentence.

Nearly a year after Lopes' murder, while he was being held in detention at the Bexar County Jail awaiting trial, an incident occurred which ultimately would incriminate Maxwell in Lopes' murder.

Two corrections officers reported that Maxwell was upset about not receiving his commissary account balance earlier in the day. Maxwell called one officer a "black, mother-fucking nigger" and said that he would "bust his face if he could get out of his cell."

He also said "if he could get out of that cell, he'd kill him, just like he had killed his home-boy, Lopes." The officer told Maxwell to calm down and went back into the office. Maxwell, using a "pleading-type of voice," then mimicked how Lopes had begged for his life, stating repeatedly, "Please don't kill me." Maxwell used a stronger, higher, and more authoritarian voice when he described his response: "Shut up, bitch ... I'm going to kill you anyway."[3]

* * *

At trial, Debra Guzman, who lived in a residential area behind the strip mall, testified that she and her husband were watching the presidential debate on the evening of October 11. She heard one loud gunshot between 9:00 and 10:00 p.m.

The medical examiner who performed Lopes' autopsy testified that his death was caused by a single gunshot wound to the top of his head. The 9-millimeter bullet entered the top of Lopes' head, exited his chin, re-entered his body through his chest, and lodged between his sternum and his heart. A firearms examiner testified that the Chinese 9-millimeter pistol found in Lopes' truck was the weapon that fired the bullet recovered from Lopes' chest and the shell casing found near his body.

The corrections officers testified about Maxwell's outburst in jail—admitting to executing Lopes. Tessie McFarland, a former stripper, also testified against her boyfriend at the trial. She pleaded guilty to capital murder and was sentenced to life in prison. She also pleaded guilty to confinement and arson in Bott's killing and received a 30-year sentence.[4]

On February 27, 2002, the jury found Maxwell guilty of first degree murder. Two weeks later, the jury reconvened to determine Maxwell's sentence—life or death.

Evidence regarding the murder of Botts was presented during the penalty phase of trial. Maxwell's history of criminal activity was also an issue. He had a juvenile and adult criminal record. From the age of 13 in 1991, Maxwell had juvenile court adjudications for resisting law enforcement, auto theft, theft, criminal mischief, escape, disorderly conduct and residential entry.

After Maxwell left the juvenile system in 1994, he established an adult criminal record for auto theft, firearm possession, criminal trespass and marijuana possession. In 1997, he pleaded guilty to a felony theft charge in Marion County, Indiana, and received a three-year sentence, which ran concurrently with a three-year sentence for attempted theft in Johnson

County, Indiana. In fact, when he killed Botts in September 2000, Maxwell had been out of prison about five months.[5]

Penalty phase evidence also showed that Maxwell was a member of, or connected with, street gangs. Additionally, he had broken into his sister's house in Marion County, Indiana, and had stolen jewelry, clothing and shoes and then tried to pawn the items. The mother of one of Maxwell's daughters acknowledged that she had taken out a restraining order against Maxwell and that he had never supported his daughter financially.

Maxwell's mother acknowledged that her son had stolen jewelry, guns and a car from his family. Additionally, before McFarland and Maxwell left Indiana in September 2000, they left McFarland's infant son with Maxwell's mother. They promised to retrieve the child in a few days but never returned. He also assaulted a jail guard after being denied television privileges.

On March 12, 2002, following a lengthy penalty hearing, the jury sentenced Maxwell to death.

* * *

Maxwell had three teenage children living in Indiana. "I love my kids, and I regret the fact that this guy's family is going through this," he said during a final interview as his execution neared. He also acknowledged he committed a number of robberies, still unsolved, during the trek from Indiana to Florida, Texas and California. However, he continued to protest his pending execution; "I need to be locked up, no doubt about it, but me dying isn't going to solve anything."[6]

Maxwell did not go down without a fight. After his conviction, he filed an appeal. His case took an interesting turn when he alleged that there was juror misconduct during the penalty phase of his trial.

According to court records,[7] during the penalty phase, a juror, Morgan Miles, called her brother, Robert Lee, an attorney in Dallas, to ask him "what a 403 was." Miles testified that Lee was appalled that she would ask him such a question and informed her that if she had any questions, she should present them in writing to the judge. They did not discuss the facts of the case, and their conversation lasted less than a minute. Lee called back "like five seconds later" and told Miles that she should not have called him and that she could have caused a mistrial.

Lee testified via telephonic conference call regarding the details of his conversation with Miles. He told the court, "Well, if I were to provide you any information or you were to get any information and impart that to your fellow jurors, you would have a nullification of the trial and it would be like a mistrial. And it would be completely improper for me to say anything."[8] The trial court denied Maxwell's motion for a mistrial.

Maxwell filed an application for state habeas corpus relief. In November of 2004 the Texas Court of Criminal Appeals affirmed the conviction and sentence. In the summer of 2008, the U.S. District Court denied federal habeas corpus relief. The United States Court of Appeals affirmed the U.S. District Court's denial of relief and only ten days prior to the execution date, the U.S. Supreme Court refused to hear Maxwell's appeal. No last minute court appeals were filed.

* * *

On March 11, 2010, Joshua Maxwell woke up for the last time. He was transferred to the death house at the Huntsville Prison. Like 450 condemned prisoners before him, Maxwell would not leave the Texas State Penitentiary at Huntsville alive.

In the hours leading up to his execution, he sat down for a final meal of six pieces of fried chicken with ketchup, three bacon cheeseburgers, six cans of Mountain Dew Red, a brownie and French fries. He walked the strangely choreographed 17 steps to the execution chamber. His chest, arms and legs were strapped to a gurney. Corrections staff inserted an IV into his arm through which lethal amounts of three drugs would be administered.[9]

With the family of his two victims behind a glass partition inside an observation room adjacent to the death chamber and his own family in a nearby room, Maxwell was asked if he had any last words.

As he fought back tears, his voice cracking with emotion, Maxwell apologized repeatedly for killing Bott and Lopes during the cross-country crime spree with his girlfriend.

At the time of the crime spree, Maxwell and McFarland were compared to the main characters in the 1994 film *Natural Born Killers*. The movie couple went on a murderous road trip. The couple was also compared to Bonnie Parker and Clyde Barrow, the 1930s bank robbers and killers whose notoriety gained resurgence with a movie in 1967.[10]

"The person that did that 10 years ago isn't the same person you see today," he said moments before the lethal drugs began flowing through his veins. "I hurt a lot of people with decisions I made. I can't be more sorry than I am right now."[11]

Maxwell told relatives of the victims that, "[I] put you through some things that I can't take back." Then, in defiance, he added that his execution was "creating more victims.... This is not going to change anything."[12]

After speaking to the victims' families, Maxwell turned his attention to his own. His mother, half-sister and son huddled together and cried as they listened to him. "I hurt the Lopes family. Let this be a lesson," he told his son. "Your decisions affect everybody. Look after your sister for me." Dylan Maxwell, wearing a shirt with his father's picture, touched the glass and told him, "I love you."[13]

* * *

As he faced death, Maxwell's contrition did little to win over those close to this gut-wrenching case that lasted nearly ten years. "Absolutely cold-blooded murders," said Jim Kopp, the Bexar County assistant district attorney who prosecuted Maxwell.[14]

"I'm still very angry," Lopes' sister said when asked about Maxwell as his execution approached. "Maxwell, when he was housed here in Bexar County, he mocked my brother. He mocked that he begged for his life, and I'll always remember that ... I don't think there's closure," she said. "I don't know what that is. But, it's a way of moving on."[15]

Maxwell was pronounced dead at 6:27 p.m. nine minutes after the lethal dose of drugs began flowing through his body. As she left the death chamber, Bott's mother grasped a heart-shaped locket hanging around her neck. "I have my son's ashes in here," she said. "I wanted him to be here."[16]

CHAPTER 10

Lawrence Raymond Reynolds, Jr., Ohio.
Executed March 16

Loretta Mae Foster was worried about her neighbor. Foster was a matronly 67-year-old woman who was popular in her neighborhood. She frequently babysat for neighbors and was known for lending a helping hand.

The neighbor she was worried about wasn't ill or elderly. He wasn't in need of sympathy or a hot meal. The neighbor Loretta Foster was worried about was an unemployed alcoholic who lived only a few doors down.

Apparently, a few weeks before her death, Foster wanted to help that neighbor who had been down on his luck. She hired the guy, Lawrence Reynolds, an Army veteran, to paint her basement.

Soon after, Foster told her son that Reynolds returned after the job and said he needed to put a paint can in her basement. Later, Foster complained to her son that Reynolds had been knocking on her door after dark. She told her son that she was afraid of Reynolds.

A few days later, Foster's sister-in-law, Norma Haubert, drove Foster to a doctor's appointment. Foster told Haubert that a neighbor had been acting "weird." He would knock on the door, hide and then jump out. Foster told her doctor about Reynolds in an effort to explain why her blood pressure was elevated.[1]

* * *

On a cold and snowy January night in 1994, Brian Baker and Jim Ferrando headed to the Northgate Lanes in Cuyahoga Falls, Ohio, to keep out of the cold and shoot some pool with friends. January had been an extremely cold month in eastern Ohio. In fact, just that week, Cuyahoga Falls recorded one of its coldest temperatures in history—minus 25 degrees Fahrenheit.

According to court records,[2] Ferrando and Baker met up with Lawrence Reynolds and his brother Jason. Reynolds told his buddies that this would be his last night to party with them because he had killed someone and was leaving town the next day.

Reynolds told them in graphic detail about the murder. He said he had knocked on a neighbor's door and told her that he had something to give her from his sister. He had rope and a tent stake with him. Loretta Mae Foster opened the door and a struggle began. Reynolds hit Foster, and she fell to the floor. He began to rummage through her purse. When he realized she was attempting to reach for the phone, he cut the phone line, "tied her up" and hit her once or twice with the tent stake. He tried to strangle her with his hands but was unsuccessful.

At some point during the struggle, Reynolds received a rope burn on his hand, which he showed Ferrando and Baker. Reynolds told them that he had left Foster lying naked in the living room, and that he had taken 40 dollars in cash and a blank check from her checkbook before leaving through the back door.

The group proceeded to another bar where Reynolds continued to talk about how he had killed Foster. Baker and Ferrando did not know whether to believe Reynolds, so they left the bar and went to Foster's house. They looked into the living room window and saw Foster's nude body lying on the floor.

Lawrence and Jason also went to Foster's house after leaving the bar. Jason was stunned to see Foster's body. Lawrence picked up a glove and the tent stake that he had left on the ground outside Foster's house. Then they returned to their parents' home.

Baker and Ferrando went to see a friend whose father was a police officer. They told Joe Orsine, a Cuyahoga Falls police officer, what Reynolds had told them and described what they had seen at Foster's house. They later went to the police station and made a statement. Police officers went to Foster's home. After finding the victim's body, the police obtained an arrest warrant for Lawrence Reynolds.

The police went to the Reynolds home and arrested Lawrence. While the officers were there, Lawrence's father consented to a search of his home. He specifically consented to a search of Reynolds's bedroom and basement. Police seized a camouflage outfit, gloves, a tent pole, white rope, a knife and a blank check belonging to Foster.

*   *   *

Reynolds was a drunk and had been for some time. During his high school years, he drank as many as 12 cans of beer a day. After high school, he enlisted in the Army for four years and then re-enlisted for two more. He served in Korea for 18 months and according to his family was often drunk when he telephoned home.[3]

When he got out of the Army, his girlfriend and their son did not move to Ohio with him. His depression fueled his drinking. He worked at a replacement window company but was fired because of alcohol-related tardiness and absenteeism.

In 1992, Reynolds had been arrested for driving under the influence and failing to comply with a police officer's order. He moved in with his parents and completed an alcohol treatment program; however, he continued to drink. He paid rent to his parents when he first moved home but had not given them any rent for about four months.

He was unemployed and drinking heavily. He sold personal items to support his drinking. When he had nothing left to sell, he decided it was time to steal money. Unfortunately, Loretta Mae Foster was the closest, easiest target.

Reynolds was not shy when it came to talking about his murderous exploits. Even after he landed in jail, he boasted about the murder. While sitting in the Summit County Jail, Reynolds told his cellmate the same story he had told his friends. Reynolds also stated that he had taken off Foster's blouse to enable him to see her hands at all times. When asked about a newspaper article that suggested that the victim was found with her pants off, Reynolds initially claimed that Foster's pants had come off in the struggle, but he later told his cellmate that "he tried to stick his meat in her."[4]

The autopsy showed that Foster had been strangled. Although she had also been subjected to blunt force trauma, there was no physical evidence of sexual assault.

At trial, the defense did not deny that Reynolds was responsible for Foster's death. Instead, the defense attacked various elements of the offenses charged and attempted to show that Reynolds had been drunk and had not gone to Foster's house intending to kill her.

The jury found Reynolds guilty of all charges and recommended the death penalty.

* * *

Reynolds filed an appeal and, among other things, argued that he was denied effective assistance of counsel because his lead attorney was appointed to represent him only two weeks prior to trial.

Attorneys George Keith and George Pappas were appointed to represent Reynolds. After pretrial hearings, but before the trial began, the trial court discovered that neither attorney was certified to act as lead counsel in a death penalty case. Keith moved to withdraw from the case and requested that an attorney certified as lead counsel be appointed. The trial court appointed Kerry O'Brien, a lead-counsel certified attorney. Jury selection began two and a half weeks later.

Reynolds contended that it was unreasonable to expect counsel to prepare for a capital trial in two weeks. O'Brien prepared for the trial by reviewing materials that had been prepared by Pappas and Keith. Pappas remained on the case and provided continuity of representation for Reynolds.

The Ohio Supreme Court found that Reynolds did not demonstrate that he was harmed by lead counsel's belated appointment. The Court found no evidence that O'Brien was hampered by his late appointment. The Court affirmed Reynolds' conviction.[5]

* * *

In Ohio, death row inmates approaching execution are placed under a 72-hour watch. Prison guards are instructed to keep inmates under regular observation, logging those observations for a minimum of every 30 minutes. Death row inmates are not completely isolated. They have access to recreational areas and may have limited interaction with other inmates.

That's the way it works in theory. That is not the way it worked for Reynolds as he waited on death row. Just hours before Reynolds was to be transferred from a state correctional facility in Youngstown to the state's death chamber at the Southern Ohio Correctional Facility at Lucasville, he managed to take an overdose of pills in his cell on death row and was found unconscious.[6]

Governor Ted Strickland issued a seven-day reprieve and rescheduled Reynolds' execution for March 16, 2010. This was the second time the state readied Reynolds for execution. He was scheduled to die in October of 2009, but Strickland delayed the execution so the state could review its lethal injection procedure. Since then, Ohio switched from a three-drug protocol to a single-drug protocol.

During his 24 hours at the Lucasville prison, Reynolds asked for and was given anti-anxiety medication on three occasions. Reynolds sat for his final meal virtually alone. He had few family visits while in prison, and his parents wanted nothing to do with his request for clemency the previous summer. Only his spiritual advisors and his attorney kept him company in his final hours. He ate a final meal of a porterhouse steak with A-1 Steak Sauce, pork chops with barbecue sauce, jumbo fried shrimp with cocktail sauce, fried mozzarella sticks, French fries, onion rings, fried mushrooms, chocolate fudge, black cherries, black walnuts and a Dr. Pepper.[7]

Reynolds appeared unstable and off-balance when he got to his feet in his holding cell. He needed assistance to make the 17-step walk to the death chamber. Reynolds' arms, legs and chest were strapped to a gurney in the death chamber. As prison medical technicians connected IV lines to his right and left arms, he lay motionless, staring at the ceiling.

"I came in like a lion and go out like a lamb," Reynolds said in a brief final statement from Ohio's death chamber. Addressing two women he didn't identify, he said, "Erin and Emma will forever and always hold the heart of the lion." Reynolds then addressed other inmates on death row and his unsuccessful legal challenge of Ohio's new execution method. "To my brothers, I hope they will never have to walk these 15 steps I walked today," he said. "I have tried to bring attention to the futility and flagrantly flawed system we have today. Stop the madness."[8]

In the witness room, Denise Turchiano, Foster's niece, replied, "It's going to stop right now."[9]

The single lethal dose of sodium thiopental drug began flowing at 10:19 a.m. Within two minutes, Reynolds' eyes closed, and shortly after that he laid motionless on the gurney in the death chamber.

*   *   *

Seated adjacent to the death chamber were three relatives of Loretta Foster: "The law has been upheld and justice has been served," said Patty Solomon, a granddaughter of Foster's who witnessed the execution of Reynolds. Patty was also a neighbor of Reynolds.[10]

She read a statement to reporters after the execution noting the "hurdles" her family has overcome and that even Reynolds' death could not change the fact that her grandmother was "senselessly taken from us. It is now our time to heal." Patty went on to say, "It is time to put this behind us and move on with our lives," she said. "Our hearts are as broken today as they were 16 years ago."[11]

Solomon sat with Turchiano and Foster's great-niece, Kelly Redfern, while witnessing the execution. The women held each other as they sat in the death house for nearly 30 minutes. Redfern held a butterfly ornament; Solomon clutched a crucifix. Solomon barely spoke throughout the process, but on occasion, Turchiano would whisper in Solomon's ear, wink and chuckle.[12]

The Reverend Ernie Sanders, who met with Reynolds prior to the execution and served as the inmate's spiritual advisor, said Reynolds intended to apologize to the Foster family.

Sanders said the suicide attempt March 7 was done to prevent the "sideshow" of an execution. Governor Ted Strickland delayed the execution for a week to allow Reynolds time to recover from the near fatal overdose. "He just kind of wanted to die all by himself," Sanders said.[13]

Reynolds was pronounced dead at 10:27 a.m. about ten minutes after prison personnel began the lethal injection procedure. Reynolds was the tenth man executed in the U.S. in 2010.

CHAPTER 11

Paul Warner Powell, Virginia.
Executed March 18

On a fair Virginia evening, March 18, 2010, Paul Warner Powell entered the death chamber at the Greensville Correctional Center. The facility is located in southern Virginia near the North Carolina border. Powell entered the death chamber through a door on the right side of a room used exclusively for carrying out executions. He was restrained in handcuffs and shackles and escorted by a team of corrections officers.

He wore a light blue shirt and dark blue pants, with the right pant leg cut off above the knee. His head and right leg were shaved to facilitate the method of execution that Powell has selected—electrocution.

A few days before the scheduled execution, Powell was moved from death row at nearby Sussex I Correctional Center, 32 miles away. He was placed in one of three holding cells that directly adjoined the death chamber at Greensville.

Powell spent the day of his execution preparing to die. Powell barely ate, and his last meal request was not released to the public. His last day was filled with the company of his mother, brother and lawyers.[1]

Josh White of the *Washington Post* witnessed the execution. He wrote that Powell looked gaunt and pale as he entered the death chamber. He had a stern look and held his chin high. He was placed in the chair while at least six guards affixed eight straps around his ankles, wrists, upper arms, waist and chest. A clamp was attached to his right leg below the knee. Sponge-lined contacts were also placed on the leg to complete an electrical circuit and a metal skullcap was placed on his head with a chin strap.

Powell swallowed hard and his eyes darted around the room.[2]

At 8:58 p.m. an official switched on a microphone in the room, and Powell was asked if he had anything to say. He just stared straight ahead and said nothing. A minute later, a face mask was put in place, covering him from forehead to chin with just his nose exposed. A guard wiped Powell's face and leg with a white towel.[3]

* * *

According to court records,[4] just before noon on January 29, 1999, Stacey Lynn Reed arrived home from school early, having completed an exam given that day. Stacey was a friendly, headstrong girl who decided as a freshman in high school she wanted to be the first female Navy SEAL and a week later shaved off all her hair.[5]

Paul Warner Powell, a neighbor, was waiting for her at her home in Manassas when she arrived. When Powell learned that Robert Culver, a friend of Stacey's mother, would be home shortly for lunch, he left. Powell returned at about 12:45 p.m. after Culver had left. Powell was armed with a couple of knives, a box cutter and a pistol.

Stacey was talking to her boyfriend, Sam Wilkerson, on the telephone when Powell returned. After Stacey ended the telephone conversation, Powell confronted her about her relationship with Wilkerson. Wilkerson was African-American and Powell was an avowed racist and white supremacist. He demanded that Stacey end her relationship with Wilkerson.

Powell and Stacey began to argue, and the argument grew into a struggle. Powell pulled a knife from his belt and as he described it Stacey "got stuck." Powell denied deliberately stabbing Stacey. The struggle continued briefly until Stacey collapsed on the floor in her sister's bedroom.

Although Powell did not know whether Stacey was still alive, he made no effort to assist her or call for medical assistance after the stabbing. Powell walked through the house, got some iced tea and had a cigarette.

Kristie Erin Reed, 14 years old at the time, arrived home from school shortly after 3 p.m. and was met at the door by Powell. He told her that Stacey was in her room, but moments later Kristie then discovered her sister's body in her bedroom. She dropped her schoolbooks and began to cry.

Powell told Kristie to go to the basement. Kristie, who knew that Powell was usually armed, complied because, as she said later, she "didn't want to die." In the basement, Powell ordered Kristie to remove her clothes and to lie on the floor. Powell then raped Kristie, as she "begg[ed] him not to kill her." Powell later admitted that he knew that Kristie was a virgin.

While Powell and Kristie were in the basement a friend of Kristie's came to the house and knocked on the door. When Powell heard the knock, he tied Kristie's legs together and tied her hands behind her back with shoelaces he cut from her athletic shoes. Powell then dressed and went upstairs.

While Powell was upstairs, Kristie managed to loosen the rope on her hands and attempted to "scoot across the floor to hide" under the basement steps. Hearing Powell coming down the steps to the basement, she returned to the floor where he had left her. Powell then strangled Kristie with a shoelace and she lost consciousness. While she was unconscious, Powell stabbed Kristie in the abdomen and slit her wrists and throat.

He returned upstairs and searched for items to steal. He got another glass of iced tea, and left Stacey and Kristie both for dead. He went to a friend's house and then drove to the District of Columbia to buy crack cocaine. Stacey was in fact dead, but Kristie survived the brutal attack.

*   *   *

In 2000, Powell was convicted of the murder of Stacey and sentenced to death. In addition, Powell was convicted of the abduction, rape, and attempted capital murder of Kristie.

At trial the medical examiner testified that the autopsy on Stacey's body revealed that she died from a knife wound to the heart. He further testified that there was a single entrance wound and two exit wounds indicating that the knife had been withdrawn, at least partially, and then reinserted into the heart.

The trial also revealed that the DNA profile obtained from the blood found on Powell's survival knife was consistent with the DNA profile of Stacey's blood. The DNA profile obtained from sperm fractions swabbed from Kristie's vagina and perianal area was the same profile as that obtained from Powell's blood.

The prosecution used Powell's own words against him. While in jail, he wrote letters to friends wherein he admitted having committed the murder, rape and attempted murder because of Stacey's relationship with a black man. He further claimed that he had planned to kill Stacey's family and steal the family's truck. He also wrote to a female friend and asked her to "get one of [her] guy friends ... to go to a pay phone and call Kristie and tell her [that] she better tell the cops she lied to them and tell her [that] she better not testify against me or she's gonna die."[6]

Powell told another inmate that he had become angry with Stacey when she refused to have sex with him after talking to Wilkerson. He told the inmate that he stabbed Stacey twice. He went on to say and that when he attempted to cut Kristie's throat, his knife was too dull, "[s]o he started stepping on her throat trying to stomp her throat." To another inmate, Powell described Stacey's killing as a "human sacrifice" and expressed satisfaction in raping Kristie because she was a virgin.

In June 2001, the Supreme Court of Virginia reversed Powell's murder conviction. The Court found that the trial judge erred by allowing a pretrial amendment of the indictment to include two new aggravating circumstances that were not considered by the grand jury. Virginia's capital murder statute includes fifteen aggravating circumstances, which when accompanied with the "willful, deliberate, and premeditated killing" of a person, make the defendant eligible for the death penalty.

What Powell did next cost him his life. When Powell learned that he was getting a new trial he was under the mistaken belief that he could not again face the death penalty. While awaiting retrial Powell wrote a letter to the Commonwealth's Attorney. In the letter Powell intended to taunt the prosecutor. However, he also disclosed new evidence about Stacey's death.

Powell's obscenity-laced letter included the following passages, "I figured I would tell you the rest of what happened on Jan. 29, 1999, to show you how stupid all y'all ... are." Admitting that he "planned to kill the whole family" on that day. Powell further stated that "I had other plans for [Stacey] before she died." Powell described how he had attempted to initiate consensual sexual intercourse with Stacey, which he had previously admitted. Powell then revealed that when Stacey resisted his advances, he pushed her on her bed and, while sitting on top of her, told Stacey "that we could do it the easy way or the hard way."[7]

Powell described how Stacey had "started fighting with me and clawed me [sic] face." He stated that he "slammed her to the floor ... sat on top of her and pinned her hands down again." Powell claimed that Stacey relented "and I told her if she tried fighting with me again I would kill her."

Powell wrote that Stacey began to disrobe but stopped when the telephone rang. Stacey put her clothes back on so that she could answer the telephone. Powell refused to allow Stacey to answer the telephone and ordered her to resume disrobing. When she refused, Powell "pushed her back and pulled out [his] knife." When Stacey attempted to leave the bedroom, Powell stabbed her. Stacey fell back and Powell removed the knife. Stacey then stumbled to another bedroom and collapsed. Powell "saw that she was still breathing" and "started stomping on her throat" until he "didn't see her breathing anymore."[8]

"It was heart-wrenching to read that letter. To know a lot of the details that we couldn't prove or didn't know in the first trial," said Lorraine Reed Whoberry, Stacey and Kristie's mother. "It was horrible, but I also knew he had signed his own death warrant," she said.[9]

* * *

Armed with this new evidence, the Commonwealth decided to withdraw the indictment in the original case, under which it was limited to trying Powell for first degree murder and sought a new indictment against Powell for capital murder. On December 3, 2001, the grand jury returned an indictment charging Powell with the capital murder of "Stacey Lynn Reed during the commission of or subsequent to the attempted rape of Stacey Lynn Reed."

In January 2003, Powell was convicted of the capital murder of Stacey during the commission of rape or attempted rape of Stacey and sentenced to death.

Lorraine Reed Whoberry has forgiven Powell. During a conference call the night before the scheduled execution Powell and Whoberry spoke. The call lasted, with some interruptions, for an hour to an hour and a half. "As the conversation went on, he was able to open up a little bit more. He wasn't belligerent, he didn't raise his voice. It was very civil," Whoberry said. "It was just a simplistic, 'I'm sorry,' and I accept that."[10]

"The questions that we asked, he answered to the best of his ability," said Whoberry. "I did ask him at some point if he had forgiven himself, and he got emotional and he said, 'No.' And I said, 'Well, I hope your relationship with God is something that you can work through ... before tomorrow night,' and we let him know that we are praying for him and his mom, his family," Whoberry added.[11]

"I need to know that he's gone, that we don't have to deal with this anymore," said Kristie Reed, now 25 and an advocate for rape victims. "I was totally against the death penalty before this happened, and I didn't know why people would want to do it. But those people haven't been through what we've been through. Now I'm totally for it. He definitely deserves to die. He needs to die for what he did to Stacey."[12]

* * *

In January of 2010, the U.S. Supreme Court decided it would not intervene to stop Powell's execution. Soon after, Virginia Governor Bob McDonnell also said he would not stay the execution. It was the first capital case to come before the new governor, who had taken office on January 16, 2010.[13]

Powell chose to die in the electric chair instead of by injection. Virginia death row inmates were given the choice starting in 1995. If an inmate refuses to choose, injection becomes the default method. The electric chair uses two cycles of electricity, each lasting 90 seconds with a slight pause between them.[14]

At exactly 9 p.m. the time scheduled to carry out the execution, the electricity began to surge into Powell's body. There was a thump as Powell's body jerked back into the chair. His hands clenched into tight fists and veins swelled as his arms turned red. Smoke rose from his leg.[15]

There was a second major jolt, smoke and sparks emitted from Powell's right leg. His knee appeared to swell and turn purple. His knuckles went white.

At 9:03 p.m. the electricity stopped. Everyone waited in silence for five minutes as Powell's lifeless body slumped as much as a body strapped to a chair could slump. At 9:08 p.m. a guard walked up to Powell and opened his shirt. A doctor emerged from a door on the left side of the room and placed a stethoscope on Powell's chest in search of a heartbeat. There was none. He was pronounced dead at 9:09 p.m. The curtain was drawn.[16]

Lorraine Whoberry and Kristie Reed watched the execution from behind a glass partition separating the death chamber and the observation room. Also in the room was Commonwealth's Attorney Paul B. Ebert. As a prosecutor, Ebert was responsible for sending ten killers to their death by execution in Virginia. That number represents nearly ten percent of all the people executed in Virginia since the death penalty was reinstated in 1982.

Ebert witnessed his first execution in November 2009, when sniper John Allen Muhammad was executed by lethal injection. Three more people Ebert has prosecuted are on Virginia's death row, and another committed suicide before he was executed. Ebert felt lethal injection was an anticlimax, as it appeared Muhammad simply went to sleep. Electrocution, Ebert said, appeared to have more finality to it. "It was a little more vivid," Ebert said afterward. "It felt more meaningful and impressive. But it was still a much more gentle death than Stacey's."[17]

Powell was the first and only person executed in Virginia in 2010. Virginia courts sentenced 121 killers to death prior to Powell receiving his death sentence. Virginia has executed 108 offenders, second only to Texas. After Powell's execution only 15 people remained on Virginia's death row.

Virginia's death penalty appears to be anything but arbitrary. The state executed more than 90 percent of all offenders on death row.

CHAPTER 12

Franklin DeWayne Alix, Texas. Executed March 30

One of the last things Franklin DeWayne Alix said before he died was, "I'm not the monster they painted me to be."[1]

Alix was part of a six-month crime spree in which he committed four murders, attempted to kill two others and pulled off nine robberies, four kidnappings and two aggravated sexual assaults.[2]

Alix wrote on a Canadian anti–death penalty website that he "has five children which I love very much." The remainder of what he wrote is replete with errors. His efforts to entice a pen pal to correspond with him consisted of the following:

> I am not a religious person anymore, but I do believe and practice to be a respectable of others and myself kind of person for the rest of my living life I can live ... I love reading Black history books (when fortunate), Auto & Biographies, and NF books of enlightenment that will help me deal with everydays' mind challenges as I dwell in an oppressive place.[3]

In his youth, court records revealed, Alix had been active in his church, singing in the choir and teaching Sunday school. One witness described him as having been a "typical fun-loving teenager."[4]

*   *   *

One of the four murders Alix committed cost him his life. According to court records,[5] in the early morning of January 3, 1998, Alix abducted 19-year-old Karyl Bridgeford at gunpoint after she parked her car in front of her family's townhouse located outside of Houston.

Alix forced Karyl into the trunk of her car and then drove off with her inside. He threatened to kill her unless she could give him some money. Karyl told Alix her credit card cash limits were maxed out and that she could not remember her PINs. She suggested Alix take items from her home and pawn them to get money.

He drove Karyl back to her house, pointed his gun in her face, and told her, "Do you see this? Anything goes wrong in here, and I'll kill you and anyone else in the house."

Alix pushed Karyl through the townhouse while he looked for items with value. Ultimately, several items, including two televisions, a videocassette recorder and a Nintendo game, were taken from the home. Karyl and Alix were still in the house when her brother, Eric, returned home with a friend. Eric's return probably saved Karyl's life, but cost him his own. The two young men ran from Alix, who then shot Eric in the back and fled the area on foot. Eric died as a result of the gunshot wound.

On January 6, 1998, Houston police arrested Alix and obtained his videotaped confession, wherein he admitted to Eric's murder. Alix led officers to the murder weapon, an examination of which confirmed that the bullet recovered from Eric's body was fired from Alix's gun.[6]

*   *   *

In less than five months, Alix had been responsible for the death of four innocent, law-abiding Houston area residents, including Bridgeford. On August 8, 1997, he fatally shot Gregorio Ramirez during a robbery attempt in the parking lot of an apartment complex. On October 5, 1997, he shot and killed Selemawi Tewolde in an apartment complex parking lot. He killed Bridgeford on January 3, 1998; and on January 4, 1998, he shot Christopher Thomas in the head, killing him.

Less than a year after Alix's reign of terror, a Harris County jury convicted Alix of capital murder with regard to Bridgeford's death. During closing arguments in the punishment phase of his trial, Alix became belligerent and had to be removed from the courtroom. He was sentenced to death.[7]

The Texas Court of Criminal Appeals affirmed Alix's conviction and sentence. However, in 2006 the Houston Police Department's crime lab became embroiled in controversy after lawyers representing convicted offenders questioned analysis practices and mishandled evidence.

In Alix's case, lawyers argued that the crime lab failed to report during his punishment hearing that his DNA was not found on evidence from Gregorio Ramirez's murder. The appeals courts, however, ruled that Alix's "long history of violence" constituted a "larger body of proof" and that one set of disputed DNA results did not undermine the jury's decision to sentence him to death.[8]

Alix's attorneys challenged DNA testing arguing that it had been performed by the Houston Police Department's "scandal-rocked" crime lab. Subsequent testing of evidence in the case yielded ambiguous results, the Texas Court of Criminal Appeals reported, and the trial judge held that a crime lab chemist's testimony was unreliable. Still, appeals court judges found no reasonable probability that the jury would have changed its decision based on the question of the chemist's credibility. Furthermore, the court found "without a reasonable doubt" that the chemist's testimony did not contribute to punishment.[9]

During his federal appeal, Alix also contested the testimony of the medical examiner, arguing the deputy examiner who conducted the autopsy wasn't licensed and that the district attorney's office knew and suppressed the information. The Texas Court of Criminal Appeals said a medical examiner may delegate duties to a deputy who is not licensed. Additionally, the Fifth Circuit said that even if the state court was wrong, there was no constitutional violation for evidence improperly admitted under state law.[10]

The appeals court also found that Alix's lawyers were diligent in their defense, that they were aware the Harris County Medical Examiner's Office was under investigation for its practices and that they had questioned the coroner about the investigation in their cross-examination at trial.[11]

In early 2009, the U.S. Court of Appeals for the Fifth Circuit affirmed the lower court's denial of habeas corpus relief. Habeas corpus is a legal procedure in state and federal court that requires the review of a prisoner's detention. Habeas corpus is Latin for "you are to have the body." Thereafter, Alix filed a second federal habeas petition. The district court denied this petition, declined to issue a certificate of appealability and granted summary judgment in favor of the state of Texas.[12]

In October 2009, the U.S. Supreme Court refused to hear Alix's appeal.

* * *

"I just got myself caught up in a web," Alix told a reporter in an interview from death row. He said he owed a friend "a couple of thousand dollars" and was forced to turn to robbery to get money. "I wanted to do the right things in life, but I got caught up with the wrong folks."[13]

"I killed the dude," he said, referring to Eric Bridgeford. "I wasn't trying to, but I did. When the dude charged at me, the gun went off ... I don't want to die. I'm remorseful. But I won't apologize," he said. He denied raping Karyl Bridgeford and said that she "volunteered to give me her TV" if he wouldn't kill her.[14]

Of his other crimes, Alix said, "I'm not saying nothing happened to those people." He admitted committing "some of the robberies," but "no other murders" and no rapes. Karyl and her mother, Janey, attended Alix's execution, as did members of Christopher Thomas' family.[15]

"Our lives are forever changed, but we need to go on," Janey Bridgeford said after watching her son's killer die. "It was hard. I didn't take pleasure in that. I have forgiven him. I didn't think I'd get a verbal apology from him. I understood he may not come clean with everything."[16]

That message of forgiveness was echoed by Thomas' sister, Fernellifa Jolivette. "I have to accept it and I have to forgive in order for me to find peace within myself and a place in Heaven," Jolivette said afterward. "If you don't, it will consume you. It will eat you alive.... In the end, he has God to answer to."[17]

* * *

Like the 451 condemned killers who preceded Alix to the death chamber of Texas Corrections Facility at Huntsville, he was provided an opportunity to make a final statement. He took advantage of the opportunity. While strapped to a gurney in the death chamber, only minutes before the injection of the lethal three-drug mixture, Alix admitted he had made mistakes leading up to the Bridgeford murder.

Considering his horrific record of death and violence, Alix seemed to take some solace in first denying that he had been an alcoholic or a drug user. "I made lots of mistakes that took your son. I messed up, made poor choices. I'll take it to the grave, I will be at peace." He added, "It is what it is. I got peace in my heart."[18]

Alix offered an apology to the Thomas family as well. "I've been wanting to apologize to y'all for your son," he said. "They told me not to do it in court. I wrote him a letter, but they told me that they tore it up in court." Alix again admitted that he "made lots of mistakes." He finished by expressing love to his family.[19]

Alix was declared dead at 6:20 p.m.—seven minutes after the lethal injection was administered. He was the 1,200th person executed in the U.S. since the death penalty was reinstated in 1976.

CHAPTER 13

Darryl M. Durr, Ohio. Executed April 20

A few days after Super Bowl Sunday, during the winter of 1988, Billie Jean O'Nan was desperately searching for her daughter, 16-year-old Angel Vincent. Angel disappeared from her Elyria, Ohio, home while her parents attended a Super Bowl party to watch the Denver Broncos play the Washington Redskins at San Diego's Jack Murphy Stadium.

O'Nan confronted her daughter's friend, Deborah Mullins, one of the last people to see Angel before she disappeared. Mullins' boyfriend, Darryl Durr, told O'Nan, "You know how kids are, she probably ran away."[1]

* * *

According to court records,[2] on the evening Angel disappeared, Deborah Mullins had asked Darryl Durr to drive her to the house of one of Angel's friends to retrieve a package of cigarettes for Angel. Durr and Mullins had a child, a newborn daughter named Angel. Mullins lived down the street from Angel Vincent and Durr was obsessed with Angel, hence naming their child Angel.

Durr agreed to drop the cigarettes off at Angel's house. Durr's obsession would now turn deadly.

It wasn't long before Durr returned to Mullins' house. He didn't come in the house; instead he threw stones at her upstairs bedroom window and blew his car horn to get Mullins' attention. Mullins and their baby left the house and got in the car. Durr had a knife and brandished it toward both of them.

As Durr was driving, Mullins heard noises from the back seat. She turned and discovered her friend Angel gagged with her hands tied behind her back on the rear floorboard. Although she was in obvious distress, Mullins did nothing to help Angel, to stop Durr, to alert Angel's family or to call the police.

Mullins asked Durr, "What's going on?" He said that he intended to "waste" her because "she would tell." Mullins made no further inquiry. After threatening the life of both Mullins and their baby, Durr dropped Mullins and the baby off at home and left Angel in his car. Again, Mullins did nothing to help Angel.

Several hours later, Durr returned to Mullins' house. He told Mullins that he had "wasted" Angel and that she should pack her things because they were leaving.

Durr and Mullins had a tumultuous relationship. In the fall of 1998, about nine months after Angel disappeared, Mullins had it with Durr. He had been arrested for two rapes. Apparently the murder of her friend was not enough in itself to break off the relationship. Rape, on the other hand, was something she would not tolerate. Mullins went to the Cleveland Police and began talking about Angel's disappearance.

Mullins told police that on the evening of Angel's disappearance Durr drove Mullins and their baby to his wife, Janice Durr's, Cleveland apartment. After dropping his girlfriend and the baby off at his wife's apartment, he left with a duffle bag containing two shovels.

When Durr returned, he was wet and covered with snow. He placed a ring and bracelet that belonged to Angel on a coffee table. As he was falling asleep, he told Mullins that he had strangled Angel with a dog chain until she "pissed, pooped and shit and made a few gurgling sounds." He then took her body to a park, wrapped it in a blanket, placed it between two orange traffic barrels placed end-to-end near some railroad tracks.[3]

The following day, Durr burned a bag of clothing in the basement of his wife's apartment building and asked Mullins to model the black acid-washed jeans that Angel had worn on the evening of her abduction.

He then drove Mullins, Janice Durr and their children to the west side of Cleveland where he burned another bag of items, and while driving out of Cleveland, he threw Angel's jean jacket out the car window.

When Mullins got home her mother told her that Angel's mother, Mrs. O'Nan, had come over and asked if Mullins knew anything about Angel's disappearance. Mullins was warned by Durr to tell Mrs. O'Nan that Angel had been talking about running away; otherwise he would kill Mullins and the baby.

Mullins also testified that Durr took her and their baby to Edgewater Park where he threw Angel's glasses over a cliff into the lake. A month or so later, while driving past the Cleveland Zoo, Durr pointed to a location near a bridge and said, "Over there." When Mullins asked what he meant, he replied, "You know what I am talking about."

Durr was convicted of first degree murder and sentenced to death largely on the testimony of Mullins. Prosecutors said Mullins knew facts about the case that she could not have known without Durr telling her, including where the body was found.

* * *

In early spring, three boys noticed a foul odor coming from two orange traffic barrels while playing in Brookside Park. The barrels had been placed open end to open end, and were underneath a railroad tie. Upon separating the barrels, the boys discovered a severely decomposed female body that had been wrapped in a dirty old blanket. A portion of a leg was visible through a large hole in the blanket.

As a result of the information provided by Mullins, an ankle X-ray obtained from Elyria Memorial Hospital, and dental records, the body discovered in Brookside Park was determined to be that of Angel Vincent.

Mullins, who had spent part of Angel's last day with her, did nothing to stop her murder and lied to Angel's anguished mother, yet her testimony would be the key to putting Durr on death row.

* * *

There were television screens inside the side-by-side witness rooms that abutted the death house at the Southern Ohio Correctional Facility in Lucasville, Ohio. The monitors showed medical personnel preparing Durr for execution in a holding cell. It was April 20, 2010, and Durr was preparing to die.

He lay motionless as an IV site was established in each arm, a process that took about 13 minutes. Durr was then escorted into the execution chamber. The prison warden stood over Durr as the execution team strapped him at the ankles, knees, chest and wrists.

Witnessing Durr's execution that calm and cool April morning were Durr's attorney, Kathleen McGarry; his spiritual advisor, Rev. Georgina Thornton; and Matthew Princehorn, a friend of Durr's.

Angel's family was also there to witness the execution. Norma Godsey (formerly O'Nan); Angel Vincent's mother; Wesley Brewer, her uncle; and Corennia Hatfield, her aunt, all were seated in the execution chamber behind a glass partition.

Godsey was using a portable oxygen tank. She wheezed and sniffled as she walked into the death chamber. She sat down and asked for a bucket in case she became nauseous. She never had to use it.[4]

As he prepared to die, Durr was still defiant. Only minutes from his execution, he refused to admit the killing, apologize for the terror he inflicted on Angel Vincent or ask for forgiveness for the suffering he caused her family.[5]

At 10:22 a.m., the warden reached for the microphone and offered Durr a chance to speak his last words: "To the Vincent family who I believe are here and who believe I have caused so much pain and believe I have murdered their daughter, I am truly sorry you believe that way, having been through that pain myself. I had hoped DNA testing would allow me to prove my innocence, but unfortunately, that's not going to happen."[6]

* * *

As his execution approached, Durr would not go to his death without a fight. In what many legal observers called an unusual legal maneuver, Durr's lawyers revealed a week before the execution that they discovered that their client was allergic to anesthesia.

At the time, Ohio used a single lethal dose of anesthesia, sodium thiopental, to execute condemned inmates. Ohio was the only state using a single drug protocol in early 2010. In fact, Durr was going to be the fifth offender executed using the single drug method since its introduction in Ohio during the fall of 2009. Ohio has since moved to a single lethal dose of pentobarbital.

Durr argued that no one knew how his body would react to the drug. The state countered that there was no proof that an allergic reaction would occur before Durr was already deeply unconscious and that the worst reaction would be death from low blood pressure and impaired breathing, effects that would be irrelevant in the context of an execution.[7]

Attorney Kathleen McGarry informed Ohio District Court Judge Gregory Frost that she found evidence that Durr was allergic to anesthesia after reviewing his medical history report.

McGarry said in court documents that she wasn't aware of the exact allergy Durr had but wanted to make sure it did not include sodium thiopental. "One of the things the Ohio Constitution guarantees is that he has a quick and painless execution," McGarry told the Associated Press. "If he's going to react to the anesthetic drugs in such a manner that he's going to have a violent reaction, either vomiting or seizures or whatever the spectrum is that could happen, then obviously the execution has problems."[8]

A Columbia University Medical Center anesthesiologist filed an email as part of Durr's appeal saying if he did have an allergy to sodium thiopental, it may pose a problem. "An allergic or other adverse reaction to some component of a general anesthetic might present a serious problem for an execution by lethal injection," the email from Mark Heath said.[9]

McGarry cited other cases involving adverse reactions to execution methods in her appeal. In 1989, Texas death row inmate Stephen McCoy began choking and seizing after receiving lethal injection chemicals causing a witness to faint, according to reports. In 1992 death row prisoner Robyn Lee Parks' muscles in his jaw, neck, and abdomen began to spasm about two minutes after the drugs started to flow during his execution in Oklahoma. However, according to reports, the exact cause for those reactions was undetermined in each case.[10]

Judge Frost allowed the records to be reviewed, but only days before the scheduled execution, he ruled there was not enough evidence to support that the allergy could, in fact, impact the execution. Judge Frost also said in his ruling that Durr's legal team waited too long to file this appeal and relied too heavily on speculation for the appeal. "Durr presents this court with an unproven allergy that might have an unknown effect on his execution and asks for time to fill in details that may or may not rise to the level of demonstrating a likelihood of success," wrote Judge Frost. "Speculation is not evidence, however."[11]

The U.S. Supreme Court declined to intervene, upholding Judge Frost's ruling that Durr waited too long to raise the allergy issue and then relied mainly on speculation to ask for time to investigate. Dennis Sipe, one of two attorneys who witnessed the execution on behalf of Durr, said Durr's reaction more likely stemmed from physical pain rather than his feelings about being executed. "I think he had come to terms with the fact that the state was going to end his life," Sipe said.[12]

* * *

Durr did not request a special last meal and had spent his last day alive not eating or drinking, observing what he called a religious fast. "He didn't request a special meal at all," said prison personnel at the Southern Ohio Correction Facility at Lucasville. "The staff said he was very quiet, very easy to work with."[13]

He finished his contrition-less final words with, "To my momma minister, we are born in this life in struggle and I planned to go out in a struggle, but I want to make you proud. I'll go out in peace. To my cousin, please take care of my children. Tell my children and my wife I love them. To my wife, I love her. It's been 20 years in this life and I will see her in the next life."[14] The wife he refers to, Janice Durr, is the woman he abandoned to have a child with Deborah Mullins.

At the conclusion of his final statement, a five-gram dose of sodium thiopental was injected into Durr's body. Within minutes, Durr raised his head and shoulders off the table and appeared to look in the direction of the witnesses—even though he was strapped down—and grimaced for a few seconds.

His head then fell back and his mouth opened wide to exhale as the drug took affect. Durr's eyes closed, but his chest heaved several times, and his throat convulsed spasmodically as if he was swallowing or gasping for air. His mouth kept moving, as if he was mumbling. His left fist remained clenched. Durr lay motionless for a few minutes before a member of the execution team checked his breathing.[15]

One witness began to wail, another witness cried, "Oh, God! Oh, Jesus!" according to Durr's spiritual adviser, the Rev. Georgina Thornton. A curtain was closed blocking the witnesses' view of the execution chamber. A coroner examined Durr and declared him dead about 11 minutes after the drug was administered.[16]

*   *   *

"That son of a bitch is dead," said Wesley Brewer, Angel's uncle and one of the three witnesses from the victim's family. Godsey, Angel's mother, tried to quiet Brewer, but he continued. "It was too humane. I'd rather have seen him in an electric chair."[17]

Godsey said she began to drink and smoke heavily after her daughter's death. Once a big sports fan, she was attending a Super Bowl party the night that Angel was murdered, she told reporters she had not watched a baseball or football game since her daughter's death. She said she even tried to take her own life so that she could be with her daughter.

Godsey told reporters that she was unhappy that Durr had neither acknowledged that he killed her daughter nor apologized for it. "I just wanted him to ask me for forgiveness," Godsey said. "I just wanted him to tell me he was sorry ... he was a monster," she added. "He took everything from me."[18]

CHAPTER 14

William Josef Berkley, Texas.
Executed April 22

William Berkley called himself "Little Capper." On the street that means "Little Killer." Little Capper, who had no criminal record, planned a robbery to help a friend pay his court costs.

A self-described marijuana-smoking, baggy-jeans-wearing, "sarcastic smart ass," Berkley was born in Germany, where his father was posted with the U.S. Army. His family moved to El Paso when he was about 10 years old. He dropped out of high school by the tenth grade.[1]

Michael Angelo Jaques was Berkley's friend who owed the court costs. The two of them went to a bank ATM drive-thru in El Paso, Texas, looking for someone to rob. Jaques sat in a car while Berkley hid in the bushes. Within minutes, Sophia Martinez, an 18-year-old on her way to meet a blind date, pulled up. It was March 10, 2000.

According to court records,[2] bank security cameras recorded what happened next. The video showed that at 10:22:35 p.m. Sophia drove up to the ATM and withdrew $20. Exactly 90 seconds later, Berkley approached the passenger side of Sophia's car with his arms extended. He pointed a pistol at Sophia at 10:24:09 p.m. and the passenger side window shattered. Berkley then moved around to the driver's side and got into the backseat. Sixty-six seconds later, a bleeding Sophia withdrew $200 from her account. Sophia and Berkley then pulled away.

Jaques left the bank parking lot and drove to a nearby hospital to visit his wife who was a patient. Jaques arrived at the hospital at about 10:45 p.m. and told his wife that Berkley had just robbed someone at an ATM.

*　　*　　*

Around 2:30 a.m. a nurse came into the hospital room and told Jaques that a friend was waiting downstairs. Jaques went downstairs and met Berkley. Sophia's car was in the parking lot with its right front passenger side window shattered.

Berkley told Jaques that he had tried to open the passenger door but it was locked. He tried to break the window with the butt of the gun but it would not break. He fired a shot, but the window only shattered. When he went around to the driver's side, he noticed Sophia had been shot in the face. Berkley told her to open the automatic locks, and he got in the backseat. As Sophia tried to drive off, Berkley put the gun to her head and told her to withdraw $200.

He then forced her to drive to "the spot," a secluded area, in the desert outside El Paso.

Berkley told Sophia to get out of the car. He then shot her in the face twice. Once she fell to the ground, Berkley continued to shoot Sophia until his gun was empty.[3]

Sophia's murder generated a great deal of community outrage and was featured on Crime Stoppers and *America's Most Wanted*. A reward was offered for information about the case. On September 30, 2000, Heather Jaques, Michael Jaques' wife, contacted the FBI with information about Sophia's death.

Heather reported finding a set of unfamiliar car keys and Sophia Martinez's driver's license on the kitchen counter of the apartment where she and her husband lived. Berkley burned the driver's license on a grill. When the woman later saw a newspaper report of Martinez's murder, she recognized Martinez from the driver's license. Heather received $51,000 in reward monies for coming forward with information.[4]

* * *

The morning after the murder, Sophia's abandoned vehicle was located by New Mexico State Police in the desert not far from El Paso. There were numerous blood stains inside the vehicle. Later that day, El Paso police found Sophia's lifeless body by a dirt road in an isolated area near a well. An autopsy revealed Sophia had been shot five times in the face and head and that Berkley's semen was found in Martinez's body.[5]

On October 1, 2000, Berkley was living with his parents when Heather Jaques went to the FBI. A police search of his parent's home produced a black "beanie" hat that was identical to the one seen on the man in the ATM surveillance video. The police also recovered a .22 caliber revolver from the nightstand in Berkley's father's bedroom, latex gloves in Berkley's bedroom at his parents' house, and Martinez's car keys from the roof of the apartment complex where Heather lived. Berkley was arrested, and confessed in writing.[6]

Two days after Berkley gave his first written statement, Berkley's father notified police that Berkley wished to make another statement. In his second, far more detailed, written statement, Berkley added that the murder weapon was a .22 caliber handgun he had secretly taken from his father and that he later burned "the girl's" driver's license in a barbeque grill.[7]

* * *

At his trial in April of 2002, Berkley pleaded not guilty and did not acknowledge any involvement in the crime.

Regarding the DNA findings, his father testified that William had dated Martinez and once introduced her to him. However, neither of Berkley's confessions included any indication Berkley knew his victim. Finally, Sophia's mother testified she was very close to Sophia, that she had never heard of Berkley before Sophia's murder, and that she was not aware of Sophia ever having dated Berkley.[8]

Berkley had no prior criminal record, but several people testified about his violent nature. A former girlfriend testified that he once choked her to unconsciousness and threatened to kill her. Others testified that he bragged about occasions where he beat, stabbed, cut, or pushed people. Two of Berkley's friends testified, however, that many of his boasts were lies.

Berkley gave a written confession at the time of his arrest. The confession was so ridiculous that it would have been funny had a young woman not been brutally murdered. He told investigators that he approached Martinez's vehicle at the ATM with a gun. As he approached the car, the gun "went off." He then directed Martinez to withdraw $200 and drive away. Once they arrived at the secluded location, she initiated sexual intercourse with him. While they were having sex, his gun "went off" again. He passed out. When he awoke, the woman was lying on the ground. He then panicked and drove her car away, then abandoned it and walked home.[9]

As an alibi, Berkley said he and Jaques were going to break into a home to steal some cocaine the night Martinez was killed. Then the plan got sidetracked, and Berkley "got picked up by four girls." Though he didn't know the women's last names, Berkley said he went off with them.[10]

An El Paso County jury convicted Berkley of capital murder and sentenced him to death. Jaques was sentenced to life in prison for planning the robbery and hiding evidence.

*   *   *

At approximately 4 p.m. on April 22, 2010, the U.S. Supreme Court turned down Berkley's final appeal. He would be dead in little more than an hour.

While on death row, Berkley maintained his innocence. "I'm not exactly sure what happened," he told a reporter shortly before his execution. "I wasn't there." He said he and Jaques had planned to commit a robbery the night Martinez was killed, but their plans got sidetracked when he was hitchhiking, "got picked up by four girls" and went off with them. "I screwed up and signed two confessions," he said in another interview. "But I could not read what I was signing because I did not have my glasses. I was told that the stuff I was signing was to get the attorney I requested present."[11]

Again, even facing imminent death Berkley concocted an outlandish story to support his invented claims of innocence.

He said he had consensual sex with Martinez, having dated her for several months. "She was a cool chick," he said.

The victim's sister, MaryAnn Martinez, called Berkley's declaration "absolutely ridiculous." She commented, "We knew who she would date. There was no reason she would hide it."[12]

After speaking to the media the day before his scheduled execution, Berkley spent his final hours sorting through property, writing a letter and cleaning his cell at the Texas State Penitentiary at Huntsville. Prison officials logged his last day alive, recording him pacing in his cell at 11:45 p.m. on the eve of execution, sleeping at 3:45 a.m. and showering at 6:35 a.m.

He ate his final meal at 3 p.m. It consisted of two BLT cheeseburgers, two jalapeño cheeseburgers, fried okra, French fries with ketchup and mustard, brownies, chocolate and vanilla ice cream, and three root beers. After finishing his last meal, Berkley took the short escorted walk from his holding cell to the death chamber.[13]

His final words were not directed at the family of Sophia. He went to his death without admitting his crime or apologizing for the pain and sorrow he caused Sophia and her family. Berkley addressed his last words to his girlfriend, Samantha Ann Gray; his lawyer, Cori Harbour; and his spiritual advisor, Irene Wilcox. The three were Berkley's personal witnesses at the execution. "Samantha, I love you with all my heart and soul. Cori, thanks for everything.

Make sure my princess is all right. Death before dishonor. Cori, I think you should continue with criminal law. It's your decision. They need lawyers out there that will fight. Death before dishonor. Warden, let her rip. Thank you for coming, Irene."[14]

* * *

Sophia's mother, Lourdes Licerio, and Sophia's two sisters, Dulce Enriquez and MaryAnn Martinez watched the execution.

After the execution, MaryAnn Martinez read a statement. The family did not take questions. "Sophia was our flesh and blood, our beloved," Martinez said. "The night she was murdered, she had no fanfare, no witnesses, no chaplain, and no last meal.... Today is not about anyone else other than my sister."[15]

Martinez said she and her family attended the execution so that their loved one wasn't forgotten. "Today is not about revenge. That's not in our hands.... Making peace with her death and absence only comes from God."[16]

Jaime Esparza, the El Paso district attorney who prosecuted Berkley, said there was plenty of evidence the condemned inmate killed Martinez, including a signed confession where he admitted shooting the teenager. "His guilt really was overwhelming," said Esparza, who also attended the execution.[17]

* * *

"Warden, let her rip" were nearly the last words out of Berkley mouth just before the lethal injection was administered, staying true to his "smart ass" reputation.[18]

The drugs were administered to Berkley at 6:09 p.m. ending at 6:13 p.m. After the first injection, Berkley gave a loud swallow. He had his eyes closed. At one point, he opened them, made a loud snoring sound and then closed his eyes again. He gasped at least twice. Gray began to cry as Wilcox attempted to comfort her.[19]

At 6:18 p.m. a priest was standing at Berkley's feet, praying. A prison official checked his vital signs, and then moved the white sheet over his face. He was dead.

CHAPTER 15

Samuel Bustamante, Texas.
Executed April 27

On January 18, 1998, the police discovered the body of Rafael Alvarado in a ditch along a road outside of Rosenberg, Texas. He was wearing a watch, a gold necklace and a ring. His wallet contained $100. Alvarado had been stabbed multiple times. By all indications, he was not the victim of a robbery, but why was he murdered?

Alvarado had left a bar in Rosenberg at about 2 a.m. He offered some guys in a pick-up truck money to give him a ride across town. There were four men in the truck: Samuel Bustamante, Walter Escamilla, Arthur Escamilla and Derrick Depriest.

Earlier in the evening, Escamilla suggested that the four men go "shopping." According to Bustamante, "shopping" consisted of picking up "wetbacks" (illegal immigrants) when they leave bars at closing time, under the pretense of giving them a ride. Once in the vehicle, "you beat the heck out of them" and take their money and jewelry.[1]

Bustamante spent the day eating and drinking in El Campo, about 70 miles southwest of Houston. After midnight, he and his buddies took off on their "shopping" spree.

As the four men pulled up in Rosenberg, it was just about closing time for the local bars. The group spotted Alvarado. Bustamante would say later that Alvarado was "dressed real decent," his watch appeared to be "real" and looked expensive, "like a yellow gold."[2]

* * *

Alvarado had no idea that the four men were as interested in him as he was interested in getting a ride. His fate was sealed when he jumped in the truck. In fact, only Bustamante really knew what was going to happen. According to court records,[3] about 15 minutes into the ride, Bustamante leaned forward and asked Escamilla a question, and Escamilla told Bustamante to wait. Bustamante stood up and stabbed Alvarado ten times with a knife. Alvarado managed to break free and fall out of the truck to the ground.

Escamilla shouted at the driver to stop, but by the time the truck stopped, they were unable to find Alvarado after searching for several minutes in the darkness.

The four men stopped at a truck stop after looking for Alvarado. Walter Escamilla, Arthur Escamilla, and Depriest went inside, and when they came out, they found Bustamante trying to get into a car. The car windows were down a bit, because someone was asleep in the car. The three men with Bustamante intervened and told him to stop. As they drove away, the other men expressed their concern that Bustamante was "crazy."

Later in the day, Bustamante's brother, Bill Bustamante, drove them back to the scene to search for the body. Their search was unsuccessful.

* * *

Bustamante was listed in prison records as 5-foot–7 and 264 pounds. Known as "Fat Boy," he was a cold-blooded killer.[4] He confessed to a second murder about a month after killing Alvarado. He said that he and his brother killed Lloyd Harold Turner, a homeless man, to "work out some aggravation." He stabbed Turner ten to twenty times while his brother beat him with a baseball bat. They left Turner's body under an overpass of highway U.S. 59 in Fort Bend County, Texas.[5]

Bustamante already served three different prison sentences prior to the murders. In December 1988, he began serving a five-year sentence for burglary. He was paroled a year later. While on parole, he received a new conviction for possessing a weapon. He served six months of a four-year sentence before receiving parole again in February 1991.

After receiving parole a second time, Bustamante moved to North Carolina. He was quickly back in prison again, serving a one-year sentence for forgery that began in April 1991. He was paroled after serving five months. After that, he racked up convictions for shooting a gun within city limits, carrying a concealed weapon, making threatening communications, resisting arrest and possessing marijuana. After his last conviction in December 1992, he returned to Texas.[6]

When Bustamante was arrested, he told detectives, "I don't need a judge and I don't need a jury to tell me I'm guilty."[7]

At his trial, Bustamante admitted that he stabbed Alvarado to death. He also admitted that he conspired with the others to travel to Rosenberg to rob an unsuspecting illegal immigrant who needed a ride. However, inexplicably, he claimed that he did not intend to rob Alvarado. The sole reason for denying his intention to rob the victim appears to be an effort to avoid the death penalty. Committing a murder in the course of a robbery is an aggravating circumstance that could result in a sentence of death.

In addition to Bustamante's own incriminating testimony, Derrick Depriest testified that after Alvarado was stabbed, he jumped from the truck. The four men searched for him in the darkness. During the search, Bustamante told the others he wanted Alvarado's boots. This testimony was important to substantiate the intent to commit a robbery and to secure a sentence of death.

The trial was not without its problems. During the guilt phase of the trial, Bustamante's brother, Bill, was called to the stand and refused to testify. Thus, Bill's written statement was not admitted into evidence. The statement contained information about the murder as related by Bustamante to Bill. In addition to the facts regarding Alvarado's murder, it was also disclosed that on at least one other occasion, Bill had gone "shopping" with Bustamante.

At the conclusion of the guilt phase of the trial, Bill's written statement was inadvertently submitted to the jury with the properly admitted exhibits. The statement was labeled "Exhibit 107" and another properly admitted exhibit was given the same number. Realizing that the exhibit might have been erroneously provided to them, the jurors notified the trial judge, who questioned the jurors.

The questioning revealed that three jurors had read the statement or portions of it either silently or aloud. Nine jurors had not read it themselves but had heard some or all of it read aloud. Five jurors said that "they learned nothing new from the statement, three said that they learned that [Bustamante] had 'gone shopping' before, and four said they learned about an incident at a truck stop, after the murder, in which [Bustamante] apparently started to break into another vehicle occupied by a sleeping person." Additionally, "[o]ne juror said she also learned that [Bustamante] had told his brother before leaving for Rosenberg that he intended to rob someone."[8]

The jury convicted Bustamante of capital murder in March 2001 and sentenced him to death. The Texas Court of Criminal Appeals affirmed the conviction and sentence in June 2003. All of his subsequent appeals in state and federal court were denied. He was also sentenced to 40 years in prison for Turner's killing.

Derrick Depriest, Walter Escamilla, and Arthur Escamilla pleaded guilty to aggravated robbery and received eight-year sentences. Bill Bustamante is still serving a 40-year sentence for Turner's murder.[9]

*   *   *

Bustamante's Houston lawyers, Philip Hilder and James Ryttner, argued that their client was mildly mentally disabled and therefore covered by the Supreme Court's 2002 ruling that banned the execution of the mentally disabled.[10]

In the summer of 2002, in the case of *Atkins v. Virginia*,[11] the court ended capital punishment for the mentally disabled and overruled its prior holding in *Penry v. Lynaugh*.[12] The court cited evolving standards of decency.

The court cited the action of a significant number of state legislatures abolishing the death penalty for the mentally disabled. Although six years later, the court would rely less on legislative action when banning the death penalty for child rape.

Historically, the Supreme Court has utilized a four-pronged analysis in determining evolving standards of decency. The court considers recent state legislative enactments, the position of nationwide organizations, sentencing data and, of course, the court's own analysis.

In *Atkins v. Virginia*, the high court found that the action of 30 states in outlawing the execution of the mentally disabled indicated a national consensus opposing the practice. The court cited the nation's evolving standards of decency. Just 13 years earlier in *Penry v. Lynaugh*, the court had decided that executing the mentally disabled was not cruel and unusual punishment. As a result, the court found that "today our society views mentally disabled offenders as categorically less culpable than the average criminal."

Darryl Atkins gained national notoriety when his appeal to the U.S. Supreme Court outlawed the execution of the mentally disabled. It all began with the tragic murder of Eric Nesbitt. In August of 1996 Atkins, along with an accomplice, forced their way into Nesbitt's car. They took his money and shot him eight times.

In Virginia, where the murder occurred, only the shooter can be sentenced to death. At trial, Atkins' accomplice implicated him as the shooter. The defense failed to present evidence that Atkins was mentally disabled. Prior to trial, an expert determined that Atkins had an IQ of 59 with the cognitive ability of a child between nine and 12 years of age. He was convicted and sentenced to death.

The decision in *Atkins* had some shortcomings: Most notably, the court did not define mental disability. Identifying mental disability is exceedingly difficult for a variety of reasons. The court left the job of defining mental disability up to individual states. Left to their own devices, the states implemented a potpourri of procedures with regard to the mentally disabled. The problem was no more evident than in Virginia.

Atkins' case was sent back to Virginia for further review. It was here that his case took its first bizarre turn. Virginia now had a law that defined mental disability as having an IQ below 70. In August of 2005, a third jury found that Atkins was not mentally disabled and sent him back to death row. Although the *Atkins* decision resulted in the commutation of hundreds of death sentences, Atkins himself would not benefit by the decision.

In 2006, the Virginia Supreme Court overturned Atkins' death sentence for a third time. The Virginia high court declared that the third jury should not have been told that a prior jury sentenced Atkins to death.

As Atkins' lawyers prepared for a fourth sentence hearing, the case took a second bizarre turn. A lawyer who represented Atkins' accomplice came forward after ten years and informed the court that his client's testimony at Atkins' trial was manipulated by the prosecution. Attorney Leslie P. Smith contended he was barred by an ethical responsibility to his client not to divulge the misconduct.

Smith originally sought the advice of the Virginia Bar Association in 1998. He was advised that his first responsibility was to his client and any disclosure could jeopardize his client and his own license to practice law. Smith recently asked the bar association to reconsider the matter, and he was advised to inform the court of the alleged misconduct.

As a result, Atkins' death sentence was commuted to life in prison. Ironically, it was not because of the landmark Supreme Court decision that bears his name but because of the prosecutorial misconduct that landed him on death row in the first place.

The Texas Court of Criminal Appeals, the state's highest criminal court, refused Bustamante's appeal relating to the issue of mental disability. The Texas Board of Pardons and Parole also declined a clemency request.[13]

*   *   *

Bustamante granted a reporter's request for an interview prior to his execution, but he failed to keep the appointment. On an anti–death penalty web site, Bustamante stated, "I did do wrong, yet there is a lot more good in me than bad. We are all human and make mistakes. Yet, do we not deserve the benefit of the doubt?"[14]

In Texas, executions are scheduled for 6 p.m. No visitors are permitted after 12:30 p.m. on the day of execution. In the morning of Bustamante's execution, he met with friends, the warden and a prison chaplain. "He answered questions with, 'Yes' and 'No'" said a prison spokesman. "He was very quiet."[15]

At the time in Texas, condemned prisoners are allowed a last meal of their choosing, up to a cost of $52. About one prisoner in five declines the last meal. In 2011, Texas changed the last meal policy. Under the new policy, a condemned inmate's final meal is the same as every other meal served in the institution that day.

For his last meal, Bustamante ordered four fried chicken legs and thigh quarters, macaroni and cheese, fried okra, jalapeno peppers, 10 flour tortillas and a six pack of cola.[16] The meal is served between 3:30 p.m. and 4 p.m. Following the last meal, an inmate is then allowed to have a shower and put on fresh clothes.

Shortly before 6 p.m. approved witnesses to the execution are ushered into rooms adjacent the death chamber.

There are two separate rooms, allowing the victim's and condemned's families to be isolated from each other. Bustamante's death was witnessed by four friends. No friends or relatives of the victim were present. Fred Felcman, the prosecutor in Bustamante's case, said the victim's family members could not be located in Mexico.[17]

Bustamante was escorted by guards into the death chamber and onto a gurney where he was secured by thick, leather straps with his arms outstretched in the shape of a cross.

Two IVs were inserted in veins in his arms and legs by corrections staff and medical personnel. Once the lines were attached, a saline solution began to flow. Lines containing the three chemicals led from the gurney through a hole in the wall.

Bustamante's execution began about 90 minutes after the U.S. Supreme Court declined to review an earlier state court decision that rejected his mental disability claim.

After Bustamante was readied for the lethal injection, the curtains in the observation rooms were opened, allowing the witnesses to view the final procedure.

A ceiling-mounted microphone was lowered down to Bustamante and the warden invited him to make a final statement. Bustamante said nothing, shaking his head, no admission, no prayer, and no plea for forgiveness.

A technician seated behind a one-way window began the lethal injection process after being directed by the warden. The chemicals are introduced one at a time: sodium thiopental to sedate him, pancuronium bromide to collapse the lungs and diaphragm, and potassium chloride to stop the heart.

Bustamante took several nearly inaudible breaths as the lethal drugs took effect and then slipped into unconsciousness as his four female witnesses looked on. The entire procedure took about 20 minutes. The drugs took about eight minutes to kill Bustamante after they were administered. He was pronounced dead at 6:22 p.m. He was the seventh Texas prisoner executed in 2010.[18]

After Bustamante was pronounced dead, the witnesses were escorted from the observation rooms and his body was immediately taken to a waiting vehicle and delivered to a funeral home. Felcman, the prosecutor, witnessed the execution and told reporters, "Bustamante liked killing." He added that Bustamante "[E]njoyed it. He bragged about it.... He meets all the qualifications of a classic serial killer."[19]

CHAPTER 16

Kevin Scott Varga and Billy John Galloway, Texas. Executed May 12 and 13

Kevin Scott Varga and Billy John Galloway were on their way to Mexico when they left Sioux Falls, South Dakota, on the first day of September 1998. The two met in prison in South Dakota. Varga was paroled in May 1998 after serving about half of a ten-year prison term for grand theft. Galloway, originally from Onondaga, New York, was paroled a month later. He served time for theft, a parole violation, and attempted robbery.[1]

Galloway credited his charisma and what he called his "Manson complex" for being able to persuade his girlfriend, Deanne Bayless, Varga and Varga's 17-year-old girlfriend, Venus Joy Anderson, to make the road trip.[2] It would be the last trip without handcuffs and shackles that Varga and Galloway would ever make. In fact, 12 years later, only hours apart, Varga and Galloway would make their final trip, the death chamber at the Texas State Penitentiary at Huntsville.

* * *

According to court records,[3] as Varga, Galloway and their companions headed south, Varga asked Anderson if she knew what it meant to "roll" someone. Varga explained rolling someone like this: Anderson would go to a bar, meet a man and take him back to their hotel room where Varga would be hiding. When she had the man with his pants down, Varga would come out and blackmail the man for his money. Anderson agreed to the plan. Varga provided specific instructions to Anderson. Choose a "mark" that is older, somewhat weak and not too heavy.

They decided to carry out the plan in Wichita, Kansas. Before leaving their hotel room for a bar, Anderson saw Varga swing a metal pole around the room and heard him complain that it was too long.

The four went to a bar where Anderson and Bayless, pretending to be sisters, met David McCoy. The girls picked up Galloway and McCoy, and the four rode in McCoy's car to the hotel where Varga was hiding in the room with the metal pole. Varga jumped out from his bathroom hiding place and began beating McCoy with the pole.

Anderson ran out of the room during the beating. She stepped back into the room to hear Galloway yell out "that's enough." McCoy was lying on the floor. Varga, Galloway, and Bayless began to celebrate the success of their macabre plan. They jumped around and hugged and kissed each other. One of the three shouted, "[T]he first murder was always that way,

75

you know." Unbeknownst to Anderson the plan switched from blackmail to murder. The three hugged and kissed Anderson as well.

When Bayless discovered just 80 dollars in McCoy's wallet, Galloway started kicking and spitting on McCoy's body and calling him names. Before leaving the room, they cut out the portion of the carpet soaked with blood and attempted to wipe blood from the walls. They wrapped McCoy's body in blankets and loaded it into the back of Galloway's Bronco. They left the Bronco in a parking lot when it broke down a few blocks from the hotel.

McCoy's body was found several days later in a state of advanced decomposition. The medical examiner found that the skull fractures in the back of McCoy's head were severe: "The bone was broken into so many small pieces they simply fell to the autopsy table." In addition, there was a fracture at the base of the skull that most commonly occurs in car accidents. Both cheekbones, the jaw area and the left eye socket were fractured. There were numerous lacerations about the head, including some that split the left ear in half.

After dumping McCoy's body and the Bronco, the four continued south in McCoy's car. In Texas, the four began to discuss "rolling" another victim. They went to a Holiday Inn in Greenville, where Anderson and Bayless went into the lounge and met David Logie. They eventually left with him in his car with Bayless driving. Galloway and Varga followed in McCoy's car. Bayless drove to a deserted area of town behind a building. Bayless and Logie got out of the car. Logie thought that he and Bayless were going to have sex on the hood of the car.

Immediately Logie was attacked by Galloway who began punching him. Logie pleaded for his life. He screamed, "Please don't kill me, please. You can have my money ... my car, anything, but please, please, don't kill me," but Galloway kept hitting him.

After several minutes, Varga handed Galloway a ball-peen hammer. Logie was still lying on the ground screaming. Galloway began striking Logie with the hammer for several more minutes.

After taking Logie's wallet, the four dragged his body into the woods. They drove McCoy's car into the woods and set Logie and the car on fire.

The medical examiner found extensive injuries to Logie's head. There were multiple fractures of the bones above the left eyebrow, fractures to the orbital ridge, the cheeks, the nose, the upper and lower jaws, mandible, teeth, also multiple lacerations about the head and upper body which were consistent with having been struck with a hammer or a tree limb. Police later found a ball-peen hammer and part of a tree limb with blood on it near Logie's body.

The foursome continued south in Logie's car, arriving in San Antonio where Anderson and Bayless went shopping at a mall with Logie's credit cards while Varga and Galloway went to a strip club. When Anderson and Bayless left the mall, they were pulled over by the police. Anderson confessed to the two murders and surrounding events when placed in the patrol car. Varga and Galloway were arrested at the strip club.

*   *   *

Varga and Galloway both took similar routes through the criminal justice system. They were both convicted of first degree murder in Hunt County, Texas, and sentenced to death by a Hunt County jury. The Texas Court of Criminal Appeals affirmed Varga's and Galloway's conviction and sentence on direct appeal.

During Galloway's direct appeal, he made an interesting argument with regard to Equal Protection of the Law and gender discrimination. Galloway argued that his prosecution for capital murder and exposure to a potential death sentence was based solely upon his gender, thus denying him Equal Protection under the Fourteenth Amendment to the United States Constitution.

Galloway suggested that, while the state tried, convicted and sentenced him to death for his involvement in the instant offense, the prosecution gave both of the women involved plea bargains for a lesser charge and lesser punishment. Varga, the other male involved, was sentenced to death. Anderson served a reduced seven-year prison term in exchange for her testimony. Bayless is serving 40 years for murder. She will not be eligible for parole until 2018.[4]

The law is clear with regard to the issue of gender discrimination. The party who raises the issue of equal protection has the burden of proving the existence of purposeful discrimination by providing "exceptionally clear evidence" that the state decided to prosecute for an improper reason.

The Texas Criminal Court of Appeals found that Galloway did not provide exceptionally clear evidence for his claim. The evidence presented throughout the case showed that the four persons involved in the charged offense acted with varying degrees of involvement. The differences in charging and punishment indicate that the prosecutor weighed each individual's culpability, as well as the state's ability to prove each case when making the decision about whom to prosecute and for what.[5]

*   *   *

"People are trying to make me a monster," Galloway said in an interview from death row. "I'm not a monster. I made some bad decisions in my life." On the other hand, Galloway said he persuaded the others to make the fateful road trip to Mexico. Galloway did not make any last-day legal moves to attempt to prevent his execution. "I guess I've come to the realization that this is it," he said.[6]

Keith Willeford, a former Hunt County district attorney, said Galloway was "a pretty violent son of a gun, a nasty dude. These were brutal, horrible murders, just absolutely disgusting."[7]

Varga took a little different approach in his final interview from death row. Varga stated that he has never claimed to be completely innocent in regard to his part in the murders but does maintain that he did not actively participate in their deaths. "I am not saying I am innocent, but I did not take an active part in the deaths," he said. "I don't believe I am a total innocent as that would indicate no culpability at all. It was my idea to rob the men, but I maintain that I never intended for anyone to die," he said. "I am guilty in that I did not do anything to stop it."[8]

Criminally negligent homicide, Varga's lawyers contended, would have been a more appropriate charge for his part in the robbery-murder—a charge that, if convicted, carries a maximum prison sentence of two years in Texas. "I have served my time four times over now," he said. "This is not even close to being a just punishment for me. It is ironic because Texas considers South Dakota to be a backwater place, yet I find the opposite to be true," he continued. "The moral standings and ideologies of people here are foreign to me." Varga went on to say, "The fact that Texas still maintains (the death penalty) with such fervor indicates to me a backwards way of thinking."[9]

Attorney Toby Wilkinson tried convincing a jury during Varga's trial that he was not a participant because there was little blood on him. "There's no doubt he was there," Wilkinson said. "If Kevin helped in the beating, there would have been blood everywhere. But when he participated in the Wichita murder, and he stays with these people, then I think your average person says he deserves what he got because he knew what they were going to do and didn't leave.... That's kind of what we were facing. Had we not had that first murder, the jury might have been more acceptable."[10]

Although he felt he was unjustly punished for his role in the murder of McCoy and Logie, Varga was contrite when he faced the victims' family. He was upbeat and smiling as the lethal drugs were delivered into his arms. "I know I took someone very precious to you," he told the parents and friends of Logie as they watched through a window. "I wish what was torn from you was not ... I would pay it back a thousand times to bring back your loved ones. I would pay it gladly." He said he loved them, asked them for forgiveness but said he didn't require it "because God has forgiven me ... I hope you find peace."[11]

Twenty-four hours later Galloway expressed his own apology. "If I can go back and change the past, I would," Galloway said, looking at Logie's father and widow, who were watching through a window adjacent to the death chamber. "There's nothing I can do. I'm sorry."[12]

*　　*　　*

Galloway's execution provided Logie's family some closure, but little consolation for the fact that Logie was no longer with them. "The fate of these individuals was determined by them," Diane Logie said about Galloway and Varga during a press conference after the execution. "They are solely responsible for the reason we are all gathered here."[13]

Dianne Logie went on to say that their experience in dealing with her husband's death changed their perspective on how they view the death penalty. "[Galloway and Varga experienced] a much more humane death than they inflicted on their victims," she said. "They [were] able to say good-bye to their families and express their love, which is more than what was granted for us. If our beloved David had to die, we are glad it was in Texas where justice is their main goal."[14]

When asked for their feelings on Galloway's apology and Varga's request for forgiveness, Jack Logie, the victim's father, did not hesitate to respond with, "His death left a void in our lives and hearts that can never be filled. Our lives will never be the same for as long as we live." Logie's father dismissed Galloway's apology and Varga's more extensive but similar comments from the death house. "I cannot forgive," he said. Logie's mother, Norma Logie, felt differently, silently mouthing the words, "I can."[15]

*　　*　　*

Varga and Galloway ate their final meals 24 hours apart. Varga ate five white meat pieces of deep fried chicken, ranch dressing, tater tots, deep fried mushrooms, two double cheeseburgers and French fries, six Mountain Dews, a pint of chocolate overload ice cream and pepper jack cheese. Galloway had two BLT sandwiches, a bacon cheeseburger, French fries, a piece of chocolate cake, two glasses of milk and two cans of Mountain Dew.[16]

In their final comments, they also addressed their families. Varga directed comments to the witnesses there on his behalf, which included his mother, Beth Varga, and his spiritual advisor Kathryn Cox. "Mom, you are my strength ... you didn't do anything wrong," he said. "This is nothing. I am going to go to sleep and wake up with Jesus. This is the only way God could save me." After thanking the warden, a chaplain and God, he declared his readiness to the warden; the lethal injection was administered through the IVs into Varga's body at 6:12 p.m. His mother said, "I love you so much, Kevin."[17]

After his brief statement to Logie's family, Galloway turned his attention to his family, father William Galloway, stepmother Mary Galloway, friend Adonya Buzinis and Kathryn Cox the same spiritual advisor who ministered to Varga the day before. "I love you, Adonya," he said. Galloway kept eye contact with his family as the lethal injection began to flow through his system, beginning at 6:09 p.m. and concluding five minutes later, at 6:14 p.m.[18]

Varga's last few words, "Oooh! Thank you, Jesus. I am going, Mom," were uttered just before succumbing to the injection.

"That's it," Galloway said. He gasped slightly and then began snoring quietly. Ten minutes later, as his pale skin turned purple, Galloway too, was dead.[19]

Varga and Galloway both died at 6:19 p.m.—exactly 24 hours apart.

CHAPTER 17

Michael Francis Beuke, Ohio.
Executed May 13

Michael Beuke wanted to be a serial killer. A serial killer is defined as a person who murders three or more people over a period of time, with an opportunity to "cool off" between each murder, and whose motivation for killing is largely based on psychological gratification.

The only thing that kept Beuke from reaching his goal was the resilience of his victims. Beuke committed one murder. He had every intention of killing at least two more. In every other manner, Beuke fit the definition of a serial killer. He even bragged to a co-worker that he was the "homicidal hitchhiker" shooting good Samaritans who would stop to pick him up in suburban Cincinnati.[1]

Over a three-week period in the spring of 1983, Beuke terrorized an entire region. According to court records,[2] it began on the morning of May 14. Gregory M. Wahoff picked up Beuke hitchhiking along an Ohio road. Beuke pulled out a .38 caliber revolver and demanded that Wahoff drive east on I-275. Beuke told Wahoff that he just wanted to take his car. After exiting the freeway to get gas at a Sohio gas station, Wahoff re-entered the freeway and was told to drive to Trustee Road, a small dirt road in Hamilton County, Ohio.

At the end of the road, Beuke told Wahoff to stop the car and get out. After getting out, Wahoff offered his wallet to Beuke. Leaving the wallet where it fell, as Beuke was not interested in money, he ordered Wahoff to walk to a wooded area. Wahoff refused, Beuke asked, "Do you want to die here?"

Wahoff ran at Beuke and tried to get the gun from him. He was unable to get the gun but kept on running. He didn't get far. Beuke shot Wahoff in the back—the bullet lodging against his spine—and Wahoff fell to the ground, paralyzed. When he caught up with Wahoff, Beuke placed the gun against Wahoff's face and fired a second shot. Fully conscious, Wahoff played dead. Beuke was confident he killed Wahoff. He then got into Wahoff's car and drove away.

On June 1, 1983, a woman named Kim Wilson was walking down a road in Claremont County, Ohio, when she saw a red hat on the side of the road. As she drew near, she saw a body in the bushes down in the ditch. The local police and an investigator with the Clermont County Prosecutor's office responded. The body was identified as being that of Robert S. Craig, a resident of Hamilton County.

Two hundred and sixty dollars were found in Craig's shirt pocket. He had been shot twice in the head and once in the chest. One gunshot wound was between his eyes. Craig's car was later found in the parking lot of the Tri-County Mall in Hamilton County. In the car's trunk, police found fresh fish in storage containers.

Craig was employed by Inland Reef, a fresh fish supplier located in Hamilton County. He had a history of picking up hitchhikers and engaging them in conversation about religion. On June 1, 1983, at approximately 11:00 a.m., Craig left Inland Reef to make a delivery of fish to a restaurant in Hamilton County via I-275 and I-71, which he often traveled. The June 1 delivery, however, was never completed.

On June 3, 1983, Bruce B. Graham saw Beuke carrying a red gas can while Graham was driving down I-74 toward Cincinnati. Graham assumed that the man had run out of gas somewhere on the expressway. He picked up Beuke and offered him a ride to the next exit to buy some gas.

While Graham drove, Beuke pulled a short-barreled revolver out of his jacket and instructed Graham to drive a certain route, telling him that he "needed" his car and that he was just going to tie him up loosely so that Graham could later escape.

He ordered Graham to exit the freeway in Indiana and drive to a secluded rural area. When Graham stopped the car, Beuke shot him. The bullet grazed Graham's head, inflicting a minor but bloody wound. Beuke and Graham began to struggle for the gun. Graham eventually jumped out of the car and took off, but, as he fled, Beuke fired several shots, striking Graham in the shoulder. Graham made his way to a farmhouse and Beuke drove off in Graham's car. Graham had approximately $160 in cash. Beuke never asked Graham for money.

Graham was taken to a hospital where the bullet was removed from his shoulder and given to Indiana police. A description of Graham's car was disseminated and a few hours later the car was discovered at I-74 and North Bend Road, not far from the Hamilton County site where Graham first picked up Beuke. There was a bullet hole in the windshield and blood splattered in the car.

*   *   *

Beuke planned each encounter with his victims. He had no intention of robbing the victims, often leaving readily accessible money behind. He would try to calm his victims by telling them that he only wanted their car and would let them go. He even used the gas can as a ruse to lure a good-natured person to render aid. He fit the profile of a serial killer in every way but miraculously two of his victims survived multiple gunshot wounds including shots to the head.

The thrill that Burke got out of killing, and trying to kill, was too much to hold inside. Following Craig's killing, Beuke told a friend and co-worker, Michael J. Cahill, that he was the "mad hitchhiker" sought by the police in connection with shootings in the area. He told Cahill that he had been picked up by Craig on I-275 and that, before he actually killed Craig, Craig had forgiven him. Beuke also mentioned that, since that day, he always smelled fish even though no fish were around. Craig was delivering fresh fish on the day he was killed. Beuke also admitted to Cahill that he had shot another person.[3]

After the third incident, Cahill informed the police about the criminal activities Beuke had described to him. Beuke's home and car were searched. A green cup which had been taken from Wahoff's automobile, the gas can used in the Graham assault and a blood-stained blue and white football jersey were all found in the trunk.[4]

*   *   *

Beuke was indicted for aggravated murder. The aggravated specifications for seeking the death penalty included the attempt to kill two or more persons, including Craig, and causing the death of Craig in the course of a robbery. He was also charged with the attempted murder of Wahoff and Graham. The charges also included robbery for each of the automobiles belonging to Wahoff, Craig and Graham.

The vehicles were taken so that Beuke could return to his vehicle which he would park in the vicinity of where he would hitchhike. He did not attempt to rob his victims in the sense of demanding money or other valuables. Each time he stuck his finger out for a ride, Beuke's intent was to murder the unsuspecting driver who picked him up.

Beuke's jury trial began September 19, 1983. Evidence presented by the prosecution included the testimony of Wahoff, who was paralyzed for life and died in 2006.[5] Bruce Graham testified as well. Fingerprints belonging to Beuke found on the Wahoff and Craig automobiles and bullets removed from Craig and Wahoff were identified as having been fired from Beuke's gun. Beuke's statement to Cahill admitting that he was the hunted mad hitchhiker was also admitted at trial. Each piece of evidence helped create a disturbing picture of Beuke.

The prosecution demonstrated Beuke's familiarity with the areas where Craig, Wahoff, and Graham were taken and shot, as well as the locations where their cars were found. The trial concluded on October 5, 1983, after the prosecution presented a total of 39 witnesses. The defense failed to present any direct evidence and Beuke did not testify in his own defense.

The jury returned a guilty verdict on all counts as well as the two aggravated specifications making Beuke eligible for the death penalty.

The penalty hearing was held on October 7, 1983, although defense counsel sought more time to prepare for the hearing. In mitigation, the defense offered into evidence a presentence report, an investigation of the crime before sentencing, and presented only Beuke's parents as witnesses at the hearing. The parents' testimony focused upon the family's religious orientation, Beuke's active involvement in related activities, the Boy Scouts through age eighteen, and the family's personal and economic hardships.

The jury found that the aggravating factors for purposes of applying the death penalty outweighed the mitigating factors and recommended that Beuke be sentenced to death.[6]

*   *   *

Prison officials said Beuke was very emotional when he arrived at the Southern Ohio Correctional Facility at Lucasville, home of Ohio's death house, the day before his scheduled execution. He continued crying as he talked to his attorneys throughout the day. He did not ask for a special last meal; instead, he opted for the standard prison fare that he had grown accustomed to over the last 27 years, a dinner of chicken a la king, mashed potatoes, lima beans and peaches.[7]

Prison officials allowed him to have his piano keyboard for his final day, and he was heard crying and playing music throughout the day.[8]

Beuke's attorney, Dale Baich, a federal public defender from Arizona, filed numerous unsuccessful appeals in the final week of Beuke's life. Baich had originally represented Beuke when Baich was with the Ohio public defender's office. One appeal alleged that Beuke had brain damage; another argued that a prescription medication he took might interfere with the drugs used in the backup, intramuscular lethal injection method. The Ohio Supreme Court and the Sixth U.S. Circuit Court of Appeals rejected Beuke's last minute pleas.[9]

Beuke lost appeals before the U.S. Supreme Court, failing to convince a majority of justices that he had been on death row so long that the execution would violate the Eighth Amendment's ban against cruel and unusual punishment.

Beuke didn't give up. The Ohio Supreme Court denied a last-minute stay on the morning of the execution, turning aside an appeal related to a previously unsuccessful claim that brain damage contributed to Beuke's violent behavior. His lawyers said recent brain scans and expert opinions showed Beuke suffered from moderate to severe brain damage. Ohio Governor Ted Strickland also denied Beuke's clemency request.[10]

Among those who witnessed Beuke's execution were Susan Craig, the widow of murder victim Robert Craig, and Dawn and Paul Wahoff, the children of Greg Wahoff.

He apologized to the widows of his victims. Beuke said, "Mrs. Wahoff, I am sorry. Mrs. Craig, I am sorry. Mr. Graham, I am sorry." Wahoff's daughter, Dawn, clasped hands with her brother, Paul, and Susan Craig, who sat side-by-side in the adjoining witness room. Beuke then launched into a 17-minute recitation of the Roman Catholic rosary, the Lord's Prayer and other prayers.[11]

The 6-foot 4-inch Beuke occasionally whimpered while repeating the Hail Mary dozens of times and clasping rosary beads in his right hand. Beuke's eyes remained closed throughout the prayers. He then became still, looking upwards. Once the drugs started flowing, Beuke became completely still within three minutes.[12]

*   *   *

"The execution was carried out in accordance of the law for the state of Ohio. The execution went through without any complications," said a spokesperson for the Southern Ohio Correctional Facility. Michael Beuke was pronounced dead at 10:53 a.m.[13]

"The man who was executed today was not the same person who committed those crimes 27 years ago. His time in prison was a story of remorse and redemption," Dale Baich, Beuke's attorney, said.[14]

"I didn't take it lightly that a person died today," Susan Craig said during a news conference following the execution. "This is his debt to my family and JoAnn (Wahoff's) family, and today he paid it." Mrs. Craig called Beuke's apology unsatisfying: "Don't you think it's time you man up and be honest? Don't you dare tell me you're sorry."[15]

Robert Craig, Jr., named after his slain father, accompanied his mother to Lucasville but did not witness the execution. A grown man now, he never knew his father, who had been killed before he was born. "It's pretty much surreal," said Bobby Craig. "It's like we went full circle, we closed the circle today," said Susan Craig.[16]

Witnesses were shaking their heads before his repetitive statement was over; clearly impatient, it went on so long.[17] Dawn later reflected: "I was thinking, 'You're stalling the inevitable.' But it's his last minutes of his life.... There's nothing that is going to bring my dad back."[18]

Bruce Graham, now of Rising Sun, Indiana, had previously met with Beuke and had forgiven him. He asked the Ohio Parole Board to spare Beuke's life, writing that he believed Beuke "has reformed his life and his ways."[19]

Susan Craig said afterward, "June 1, Bob will be dead as long as he was alive; how sad is that? It's been a really long time. I was pregnant at the time he was murdered. Now we can talk about Bob and have happy memories and not talk about Michael Beuke."

Gregory Wahoff's wife, JoAnn, of Bright, Indiana, gave up her witness chair to her children. "I was content with watching the body brought out," she said afterward. "I'm just outraged," Mrs. Wahoff said of the decades of legal appeals. "It should not have gone on this long."[20]

CHAPTER 18

Rogelio Reyes Cannady, Texas.
Executed May 19

Rogelio Reyes Cannady represents one of the major flaws in the idea that life in prison without parole is an appropriate alternative to the death penalty. Cannady, already in prison for two murders, murdered his cellmate.

Even if Cannady had been sentenced to death rather than life in prison, he probably would not yet have been executed when he committed his third murder. Only two years had passed since his original murders. However, he would have had limited access to other inmates, especially those *not* on death row. Another human being would probably be alive today if Cannady had been sentenced to death for the original murders.

Cannady was a ruthless, cold-blooded killer. At 17, he was sentenced to 20 years in prison for assaulting another teenager while attempting to steal a bicycle. The day he was released on bond for the robbery charge, June 29, 1990, Cannady killed two runaway teenagers.[1]

Cannady and his friends were celebrating his release from the Cameron County, Texas, jail. That night he and four other teenagers murdered 16-year-old Ricardo Garcia and 13-year-old Ana Robles. The two victims had run away from a juvenile group home. Cannady stabbed Garcia 13 times, raped Robles and held her down while one of his friends strangled her to death.[2]

Cannady pleaded guilty to the killings and was sentenced to serve two consecutive life terms in prison.

*   *   *

In May of 1991, Cannady was transferred from the Cameron County Jail to the McConnell Unit of the Texas Department of Criminal Justice in Beeville. In addition to the two consecutive life sentences he was also serving a concurrent 20-year sentence for the earlier robbery and assault.

A little more than two years later, October 10, 1993, Cannady beat his cellmate, Leovigildo Bombale Bonal, to death with a weapon he assembled from prison issued items, a padlock attached to the end of his belt.

According to court records,[3] prison guards found Bonal lying on the cell floor with his hands tied behind his back with a belt. Cannady did not appear to be injured, but his boots and clothing were covered with blood. Blood was splattered on the cell walls, the bunk beds and the furniture in the cell. Concealed in a pair of boots, the officers found a belt and the face of a combination lock. The body of the lock had been dumped in the cell's commode.

Bonal, who was serving a 15-year sentence for murder from Tarrant County, died two days later. Cannady said he beat Bonal because Cannady thought Bonal caused the two of them to miss breakfast.

The murder was brutal. A technician from the Texas Department of Public Safety Crime Lab analyzed the blood spatters. Blood patterns were created on the ceiling by blood flying off a weapon, possibly a combination lock. She also discerned that the victim was stomped on while lying in the blood or that the victim's head bounced up and down in the blood.

Bonal's autopsy revealed numerous lacerations and abrasions on the scalp and face as well as lacerations, abrasions, and swelling on the arms, hands, and one leg. A circular imprint that matched the combination lock was found on his torso. He suffered two skull fractures and extensive hemorrhaging over the scalp and in the brain. One of the skull fractures was slightly circular in nature. The medical examiner matched the injuries to the lock retrieved from the cell.

The evidence was gruesome, yet Cannady contended that he killed Bonal in self-defense. He said he was in fear of being raped. On the night of the killing, Cannady said that he woke up when he thought he heard someone call "chow time." He allegedly got up to look out of the cell, but when he turned around, he saw Bonal was masturbating.

At that point, he confronted Bonal and hit him in the face. Cannady said he thought Bonal was trying to reach for something so, incredibly, with the threat of being assaulted, Cannady grabbed his lock and attached it to his belt. He then hit Bonal and kept hitting Bonal because Bonal kept coming toward him. Cannady admitted that he hit and kicked Bonal repeatedly. He also said he dismantled the weapon and tied Bonal's hands after Bonal became unconscious in order to prevent Bonal from striking back.[4]

*　　*　　*

Cannady had a lengthy criminal record. His troubles with the law began at the age of ten when he committed a string of thefts and burglaries. When Cannady was twelve, the State admitted him to a home for boys. However, due to his discipline problems and fighting, the home expelled Cannady three months later and returned him to his mother. Having regained his freedom, Cannady expanded his criminal resume to include a variety of offenses including drug dealing, assault, theft, violation of probation, felony criminal mischief, burglary, truancy, public intoxication and resisting arrest.[5]

Cannady was equally defiant while in prison. He was a considerable discipline problem. On two occasions, he refused to obey orders. On five occasions, he refused to work. His behavior only worsened after he killed Bonal in October 1993. Between November 1993 and May 1994, prison officials reprimanded him for possessing contraband, using state property in an unauthorized manner, damaging state property, creating a disturbance, spitting on an officer, possessing a weapon, possessing drugs and threatening medical personnel.[6]

*　　*　　*

In Texas, for a murder to qualify for the death penalty, one or more aggravating factors must be present. In most capital murder cases, the aggravating factor is that the murder was committed in conjunction with another felony, such as burglary, robbery or rape. In 1993, the Texas Legislature revised the capital murder statute. The new law made being a prisoner serving a life sentence an aggravating factor. This revised statute went into effect on September 1, 1993, 40 days before Cannady killed Bonal.[7]

Before his trial began, Cannady almost escaped the death penalty for a second time. His lawyers argued that the revised statute did not apply in his case because the offenses for which he received life sentences were committed prior to September 1, 1993. Cannady was the first Texas prison inmate being prosecuted under Texas Penal Code § 19.03(a)(6).[8]

The trial judge agreed with Cannady's position and reduced the charge against him from capital murder to murder.

The state appealed the trial court's ruling. The Texas Criminal Court of Appeals reversed the trial judge, holding that the effective date of the revised capital murder statute applied to the date that the instant offense was committed, not to the prior offenses that elevated the charge to capital murder. The "ex post facto" clause of the U.S. Constitution was not violated because Cannady's crime was defined as capital murder before he committed it. The U.S. Supreme Court declined to review the case, thereby allowing the appeals court's interpretation of the statute to hold.[9]

After his conviction and death sentence, Cannady raised on direct appeal the issue of the new statute in a different context. Cannady argued that he should have been allowed to have the jury decide guilty or not guilty on the pending murder before the jury received evidence about his prior convictions. Cannady asserted that the Texas statute is prejudicial on its face, meaning that the law allows evidence of his prior murder convictions to be admitted during the trial for the current murder. Without the new statute, the two murders would not be admissible in the current murder trial. He contends that the jury will look at him simply as a repeat killer and ignore the facts of the case before them.

Normally, the fact that an accused had committed a prior murder would not be admissible during a homicide trial. The theory is, as argued by Cannady, a juror is likely to conclude merely from the prior murder conviction that the accused is guilty.

Cannady argued that Texas law only permits prior offenses to be raised during the penalty phase of trial after the jury has convicted the accused of first degree murder. The statute reads, "[prior] convictions shall not be read until the hearing on punishment is held."

The Texas Court of Criminal Appeals found that the Texas Statute authorizing the death penalty for killing while serving a life sentence is an element of the crime of capital murder, and therefore must be proven at trial. The Court went on to write, "Although the details of the prior conviction may be more prejudicial than is warranted for admission at guilt/innocence ... the State is entitled to prove the fact of the commission of a crime listed and the sentence imposed as part of its burden to prove the crime of capital murder."[10]

*   *   *

In his later appeals, Cannady's case took a bizarre twist. He claimed that he did not commit the two murders in 1990 although he confessed and pleaded guilty. He was now contending the he was coerced into signing a confession. There are at least two different stories of what happened the night of the murders. There were original confessions signed by Cannady and an accomplice in 1990. Then there was the historically revised version concocted a decade later. One story was violent and ruthless, while the other was filled with deception and accusations against investigators.[11]

The confession of Cannady's accomplice, Francisco Solis, detailed how Cannady, known to his friends as Roy, stabbed Ricardo Garcia. The confession suggested that Cannady and Solis eventually threw Garcia in an irrigation canal behind Adams Gardens, a small community between La Feria and Harlingen in Texas. "When Roy was stabbing Rick with the knife, Roy was smiling..." the confession stated. "He was enjoying the killing."[12]

After Garcia was dead, Danny Kuhlke, Johnny Ray Lopez Garza, and Luis Acosta met Cannady and Solis, all teenagers, at the canal, according to Cannady's confession. Then, the five teenagers returned to Garza's mobile home. There, prosecutors said, Cannady took Robles, who had run away with Garcia, into a bedroom and shower where he raped her. Eventually, Solis and Cannady choked Robles to death with a red bandana and threw her into another canal behind Adams Gardens, according to the confession.

Autopsies proved that Robles had been raped and strangled while Garcia had 13 stab wounds. It was January 21, 1991, when Cannady and Solis pleaded guilty to murder in order to avoid the death penalty.

Affidavits filed with Cannady's last appeal to the U.S. Court of Appeals for the Fifth Circuit contended that the confessions of Cannady, and the others, were coerced. One accomplice, Francisco Solis, wrote a letter, dated April 28, 2010, to one of Cannady's lawyers denouncing the 1990 confession. That letter stated that he and Cannady were not present at the time of the murders.[13]

* * *

Cannady walked to the death chamber within the Texas State Penitentiary at Huntsville about 30 minutes after the U.S. Supreme Court rejected his appeal suggesting that there was no merit to his claim that his confession to the 1990 murders was coerced. He finished his last meal, seven beef-and-cheese enchiladas, pico de gallo, two cheeseburgers, fries and two pieces of fried chicken.[14]

In the death chamber, he smiled and nodded to his brother, Victor Villapando; niece, Adela Martinez; and three friends, Norma Baeza, Juana Bello and Gary Ojeda. He selected the three to witness his death and told them repeatedly that he loved them. "I was in there right now thinking how we grew up. You know how we grew up in the same house," Cannady said. "We need to take care of each other like we used to ... I'm going to be OK," he said as they watched through a window. "Y'all take care of yourself.... May God have mercy on my soul: I am going to be OK. I know where I'll be."[15]

Two of Garcia's brothers witnessed the inmate's execution. Cannady did not address them, and the brothers declined to speak with reporters afterward.[16]

As he waited for the drugs to take effect, he laughed and lifted his head from the gurney. "I thought it was going to be harder than this," he said, grinning. "I'm going to sleep now. I can feel it. It's affecting me." Then he began snoring. Cannady was dead at 6:19 p.m.[17]

* * *

Tina Church, an investigator for Cannady's lawyers since 1998, said that Cannady's execution was a bigger mistake than the 2004 execution of Cameron Todd Willingham, a convicted arson killer whom she also represented.[18]

Willingham was convicted of murder and executed for the deaths of his three young children during an arson in Corsicana, Texas. His case gained international attention in 2009 when an investigative report in *The New Yorker*, drawing upon arson investigation experts and advances in fire science, purported to demonstrate that, contrary to the claims of the prosecution, there was no evidence that the house fire was intentionally set, and that the State of Texas executed an innocent man.[19]

It is puzzling how Church could conclude that the execution of a confessed killer of two, who also murdered his cellmate, could be a mistake. At times people are so ardently opposed to the death penalty that the facts of a given case are of little consequence.

CHAPTER 19

Paul E. Woodward, Mississippi.
Executed May 19

Mid-summer brings warm temperatures and high humidity to southern Mississippi. July 23, 1986, was no different than most summer days in Perry County—hazy, hot and humid. It was around noon on that day when a woman who lived on a bluff along Highway 29, south of New Augusta the Perry County seat, noticed a logging truck with a white cab stopped in front of her driveway. A guy jumped out of the truck and walked toward the truck's rear. He returned with a blonde haired woman wearing yellow clothing.

According to court records,[1] as the man held the woman in yellow by her arm, he yelled, "Get in, get in!" He forced the woman into the truck through the driver's side door and drove off. Hearing a sound like a running motor, the homeowner walked to the end of her drive to investigate. On the highway in front of her house was an abandoned car with the motor running and the driver's side door open. She called the Sheriff's office.

At about the same time, the driver of a vehicle on the same highway saw a white colored logging truck without a load moving away from a vehicle. The automobile was blocking the lane of travel with the engine running. The driver's door was open and a woman's purse was sitting on the front seat. The motorist notified the police.

The car belonged to 24-year-old Rhonda Crane, a Jackson County Youth Court volunteer. She was on her way to join her parents on a camping trip.

Within a couple hours of Rhonda's disappearance, a deputy sheriff on routine patrol observed a white Mack logging truck that fit the description provided to law enforcement with regard to Crane's abandoned vehicle.

The operator of the truck was Paul E. Woodward. The police asked him specifically about Crane's disappearance. He told the deputy he knew nothing about it and had not noticed anything out of the ordinary. He was released and drove away.

However, the police had quickly figured out that Woodward unloaded logs at Leaf River Forest Products, a pulp mill, and departed the yard at 11:36 a.m. Woodward arrived at Walley Timber Company, a wood yard, at approximately 1:00 p.m. The yard manager noted that he was late arriving at the yard and was wet from sweating. A drive from the mill to the wood yard takes approximately 30 minutes.[2]

Woodward had an extra 54 minutes between the pulp mill and the wood yard. That short span of time cost Rhonda Crane her life, and 24 years later it cost Woodward his life as well.

* * *

"I thought this day would never come," said Rhonda's sister, Renee Lander, who witnessed Woodward's execution. "We waited a long time to see him put to death. I'm very glad to have seen him take his last breath. I wish it could have been brutal like Rhonda's death."[3]

Rhonda's death was indeed brutal. According to court records,[4] Woodward had a pistol in his hand when he forced Rhonda to get into his truck. He then drove the victim to an isolated area, forced her out of his truck and into the woods where she was raped at gunpoint. After raping her, Woodward shot Rhonda in the back of the head and left her in the woods to die.

Crane's family members joined law enforcement in her search. Her father and a friend found her body just off the road about 18 hours later. After the police pieced together a timeline for Woodward's whereabouts, he was apprehended a few hours before Rhonda's body was found. The key pieces of evidence were the witnesses who reported seeing Crane being kidnapped and hearing Woodward's truck tires screeching to a stop.

During the trial, Woodward's attorneys argued to the jury that Woodward had a "dark influence" over him and claimed to have conversations with the devil. It was also disclosed that Woodward previously had been committed to the state mental hospital and had been arrested at least twice before. "One reason for admitting these prior bad acts was our defense theory that Paul had been 'troubled' all his life and had wrestled with good versus evil," his attorney, Terryl Rushing, wrote in an affidavit contained in his appeal to the Mississippi Supreme Court. "He had always striven to do the right thing but was overwhelmed at the time he killed Rhonda Crane."[5]

Woodward's attorneys argued that executing a mentally ill inmate would be the same as executing a mentally disabled inmate or a juvenile, both of which have been banned by the U.S Supreme Court as cruel and unusual punishment.[6]

Some experts see mental illness as the next frontier of the death penalty.[7] However, unlike mental disability and age, mental illness is difficult to determine and not easily categorized.

Severe mental illness in itself should not categorically disqualify an offender from capital punishment. In cases in which mental illness produces functional impairments at the time of the offense that significantly reduce culpability, the Eighth Amendment should preclude the application of the death penalty.[8]

There are situations were severe mental illness may negate a defendant's criminal responsibility altogether. Most states recognize the defense of insanity in those situations.

Although most of the leading mental health organizations and professional associations have recommended that legislatures exempt those with severe mental illness at the time of the offense from capital punishment, most state legislatures have been reluctant to move in that direction.[9]

In fact, the absence of legislative action has separated mental illness from conditions like mental disability and age. When the U.S. Supreme Court considered mental disability and later juveniles, more than thirty state legislatures had already banned the death penalty for both. Should a mental illness exemption be recognized as a constitutional matter?

Some scholars suggest that imposing capital punishment on those severely mentally ill would not serve the goals of retribution and deterrence that underlie the death penalty. Execution under those circumstances would constitute an affront to human dignity. It should be banned as cruel and unusual punishment.[10]

When Woodward faced a jury in Perry County, the issue of mental illness and the death penalty had not been resolved by the Mississippi Supreme Court or the United States Supreme Court.

Woodward was sentenced to death on April 29, 1987. In 1993, the Mississippi Supreme Court granted him a new sentencing hearing because the prosecution had used words like "heinous," "atrocious," and "cruel" when arguing to the jury during the penalty phase of Woodward's trial.

A second jury was empanelled and listened to the penalty phase evidence. Again, Woodward was sentenced to death.

*   *   *

In the days leading up to his execution, Woodward visited with his attorneys, C. Jackson Williams and Nina Rifkind. He also visited with his spiritual advisor, William "Buck" Buchannan. Though he was believed to have had at least five children and 11 grandchildren, Woodward had no family visits in his final days and made no calls to relatives. "I think a reasonable person would assume he doesn't have close family ties," Corrections Commissioner Christopher Epps said. Woodward did not make any phone calls in his final days.[11]

Woodward was a big man and his appetite did not seem to be impacted by his impending death. The morning of his execution he ordered oatmeal, a roll, ham, milk, two eggs, and syrup. Woodward's lunch order consisted of a roll, pork, pinto beans, a piece of cake, four steamed cabbages and a carton of milk. According to prison records, he ate half a portion of cabbage, half a portion of pork, and drank the entire carton of milk.[12]

Described as active and talkative in his final hours, Woodward visited with his spiritual adviser and finished his last meal. He had a grilled hamburger—well done and seasoned with salt and pepper—dressed with mustard, mayonnaise, lettuce, tomato, onion and pickles; French fries with salt; fried onion rings; a bowl of chili without beans; a pint of vanilla ice cream and two 20-ounce root beers. He was joined at his final meal by a Mississippi State Penitentiary chaplain.[13]

Commissioner Epps said the 307-pound Woodward ate everything "except a few of his French fries." The inmate had been eating lighter earlier in the day. "He told me he was saving room for his last meal," Epps said. Woodward did not fight his execution beyond an appeal to Governor Haley Barbour for clemency, which the governor denied the day before the execution.[14]

*   *   *

Though he did not publicly express remorse or discuss Crane's death in the hours leading up to his death, Epps said he asked Woodward about it privately. "His voice started shivering and he said 'Yes sir, I do. I wish I could take it all back,'" Epps recounted. Woodward's final words were: "Thank you warden—I'm sorry, I mean commissioner."[15]

"The scary part to me is that the victim could have been any young lady—any female," said Commissioner Epps.[16]

Woodward declined a sedative before the execution. He was lucid and alert in the death chamber. "I would like to say the Lord's Prayer," Woodward said as he laid strapped to a gurney in the death chamber located within the state penitentiary at Parchman. He invited others in the execution room to join in prayer. After the prayer, Woodward took a couple of heavy breaths, turned his head toward the witnesses and closed his eyes.[17]

Three protesters wearing shirts with anti–death penalty slogans stood at the Parchman entrance as a mix of sodium thiopental, saline, pavulon and potassium chloride was pumped into Woodward's veins. He died at 6:39 p.m. His body was released to the University of Mississippi Medical Center at his request.[18]

Renee Lander said her family had been disappointed by repeated delays in Woodward's execution. She said she thought it should have happened years ago. "He had many, many appeals, and he gave Rhonda none," she said. Epps agreed 23 years is a long time for a prisoner to sit on death row. "We talk about finance and expense ... I think it's also important that we think about the victims' family and what they have to go through," he said. Lander said the delay of the execution created "anger" in her family. "It made my father ... more bitter knowing he was still alive," she said.[19]

"It is our agency's role to see that the order of the court is carried out professionally with dignity and decency. That has been done and justice was championed today," said Commissioner Epps who seemed to relish the prominent role he played in the government action carried out in Parchman. "In this final chapter tonight, it is our heartfelt hope that the family of Rhonda Crane may now begin the process of healing. Our prayers go out to you as you continue life's journey," said Epps.[20]

Former Sheriff Jimmy "Shorty" Smith investigated Crane's murder. He did not attend Woodward's execution, but he had strong feelings about it. "If any man ever committed a crime and deserves to die, he deserves to die. I'm not a bloodthirsty man," said Smith. "If the law would allow me to, I would go up there and have not any remorse to sit in there and watch him die for what he did to this young girl."[21]

Woodward was the first person executed in Mississippi in 2010. Mississippi courts sentenced 55 killers to death prior to Woodward receiving his death sentence. Although the state has executed 13 offenders since 1976, 61 inmates remain on death row.

CHAPTER 20

Gerald J. Holland, Mississippi.
Executed May 20

In Mississippi, the average length of time between a murder and an execution is about 15 years. Gerald James Holland was 72 years old when he was executed on May 20, 2010. He raped and murdered 15-year-old Krystal King in 1986. He was not the oldest person executed in Mississippi: that distinction belongs to John Nixon who succumbed to lethal injection at age 77. Holland's 24 years on death row was not the longest time spent there: that belongs to Richard Jordan who is pushing 35 years, and counting, on Mississippi's death row.[1]

Nonetheless, Holland deserved to die.

According to court records,[2] around 8:00 p.m. on a warm Thursday evening, September 11, 1986, a young guy named Willie Boyer ran into his friend, Krystal King, at the Biloxi Beach Arcade. They hung out at the arcade for a while and headed down to the beach and drank a six-pack of beer. At about midnight the beer ran out and Willie gave Krystal a ride to a house on Burton Avenue in Gulfport. Gerald "Jerry" Holland owned the house.

Holland had been drinking. Boyer and Holland had a drink together. Holland had a beer and Boyer had a beer and a little bit of tequila. Krystal did not have a drink. Boyer would later recall that Holland may have been drinking, but he did not appear drunk.

Boyer and Krystal's visit would continue for a couple of hours. They watched David Letterman on television and listened to Holland small-talk about his divorce and the "divorce papers" which he had just received in the mail. Around 2:30 a.m. Boyer decided to leave while Krystal remained behind. That was the last time Boyer saw Krystal alive.

*   *   *

Jerry Holland was not a native of Gulfport; he grew up in the city of his birth, Los Angeles, with his mom, dad, two younger brothers, and a younger sister. His dad worked various jobs as an electrician, truck mechanic and other positions involving general maintenance. His mom was a homemaker.

During the latter half of his teenaged years, Holland moved with his family to Memphis where he completed high school. He left home at the age of 21 and survived by working odd jobs. "As I got older, I worked selling shoes, became a dental technician, got into the electrical trade and stayed in it most of the time," explained Holland. He lived and worked in different places, married and divorced twice and fathered five children.[3]

He also ran into trouble with the law. His criminal record included convictions for burglary, auto theft and rape of a child. He received a four-year prison term in Texas for the rape; however, he served only one year before being paroled in 1976. He moved to Gulfport in 1981. In June or July 1986, Holland's second wife had left him and taken their only child with her. Holland was 49 years old and was working sporadically. He just found a roommate, 21-year-old Jerry Douglas. Douglas was a friend of Krystal's who introduced her to Holland.

* * *

Sometime after Boyer left, Douglas, who was sleeping in a bedroom adjacent to the living room, woke up when he heard some noise in the living room. He got up to go to the bathroom, get a drink of water and check on the noise. He opened the bedroom door, the lights in the house were on and the front door was wide open. He heard noise outside and saw Holland bent over a black object on the ground. Douglas asked, "Jerry, what is going on?" Holland answered, "Go back to bed. You don't want to know."[4]

Douglas then returned to the kitchen and watched Holland through the window. Douglas watched as Holland rolled the object, which made a loud thud when it hit, into the back of his pick-up truck.

Holland returned to the house with a wild look on his face, his eyes were very big and glassy looking, and he was shaking. Holland said, "My God, I killed her: I killed her."[5]

Holland told Douglas that he and Krystal had sex on the couch. He said that she picked up a hunting knife and started playing with it. Holland went on to say that he and Krystal went back to the bedroom with the knife. Holland told Douglas that he took the knife from her and stabbed her in the chest.

Holland changed his story a few minutes later. He told Douglas that he and Krystal were "wrestling around on the bed and [she] rolled off the bed and she fell onto the knife." Holland also told him that "he mutilated the body to cover up the stab wounds" and to "make it look like a sex fiend had done it." Holland told Douglas that he had placed the body in his truck "to ... bury it and try and cover everything up."[6]

Douglas, apparently under duress, accompanied Holland to bury Krystal's body. Douglas later contacted the Gulfport Police Department and informed homicide detectives about the murder.

* * *

On September 12, 1986, the Gulfport Police S.W.A.T. Unit entered Holland's home, arrested him and read him his Miranda rights. Detectives read Holland his rights three more times at the police station. Fully apprised of his rights Holland decided to waive those rights and confess to Krystal's murder.

Holland's confession consisted of the following:

> We had ... I think we had sex. I was pretty much drunk ... I don't even know if we did it or not and she was sitting in my lap and ... she saw my goddamned hunting knife. She started playing with it and she said let's go to bed, I'm sleepy. I said are you going to sleep on the couch or do you want to sleep with me? She says, "I'll sleep with you," so we went to the bedroom and she ... still had that goddamned knife in her hand. She was messing around with it like Zorro and all that bullshit. Typical kid at that point, I mean ... I was dodging [the knife] ... and I grabbed her wrist and I was going to take it away from her before one of us got hurt with it and then I bumped into her chest and she says "I'm dead." Then things got kind of black there for a minute.[7]

After confessing, Holland accompanied detectives to the spot where he dumped Krystal's body. Her body was found in a shallow grave in a rural area of northern Harrison County. Krystal's nude body was recovered beneath about one and one-half feet of sand. A bed sheet, plastic garbage bags, chunks of cement and a cement bag were on top of the body.[8]

An autopsy revealed that Krystal had been brutally battered. The pathologist described her injuries and their sequence. The first injuries were of the face, the lips, over the nose and eyes. They were more swollen, and they were the most advanced. About the same time frame, next in line, the injuries of the arms, forearms, wrists, knees and shins. In that same time pattern, the injuries to the genital region, the stretching, scraping and tearing of the vagina and rectal tissues occurred.

The stab wound to the chest went through the heart and the aorta. There was a ligature around her neck, the result of tying a shirt tightly around her neck and catching her hair in it. The last injury consisted of a pair of underpants which were stuffed down her throat—down as far as her voice box.[9]

The pathologist opined that Krystal probably remained conscious during the entire ordeal until finally, "she died of asphyxiation because of the ligature placed around her neck which closed off her airway, and the stuffing of clothing down her throat that obstructed her windpipe." She probably did not die from the stab wound. Indeed, she could have lived "as long as several hours" after being stabbed had she not been strangled. The stab wound did, however, contribute to her death. The mutilation of her genital area occurred post-mortem.[10]

On November 17, 1986, a grand jury returned an indictment against Holland for killing Krystal with "malice aforethought" while "engaged in the commission of the crime and felony of rape." On November 30, 1987—after numerous hearings on pre-trial motions—the trial began.

At trial, Holland's attorney Steven Orlansky argued Holland suffered from a brain injury caused when he was a teenager. Orlansky suggested that Holland was remorseful. "Gerald's actions on September 12, 1986, were the horrific results of anger and frustration related to his divorce, which had just been finalized, fueled by extreme alcohol abuse throughout the preceding day and night. He was immediately consumed with remorse as evidenced by his crying throughout the next day and asking one of the arresting officers to shoot him."[11]

Twelve days later, the jury found Holland guilty of murder and sentenced him to death.

*　*　*

Holland apologized to Krystal's sister, Marcie Walker, who was 11 when Krystal was killed. "I want you to know I'm sorry.... It was because of alcohol, despair and temper," Holland said as he lay strapped to a gurney moments before he was administered the lethal injection.[12]

Until the end, Holland was talkative and took responsibility for killing Krystal. Governor Haley Barbour refused Holland's request for clemency. The U.S. Supreme Court also rejected his last minute appeals. Holland's attorney gave him the news late in the afternoon on the day scheduled for his execution.

Afterward, Holland told Mississippi Corrections Commissioner Chris Epps, "I got the news, but it wasn't good news." Epps, who has witnessed 13 executions, said Holland knew his chances of avoiding death were slim. But Epps said he did not get the sense Holland was remorseful. "He admitted killing Krystal, but he didn't give a reason why," Epps said. Holland also denied raping the teenager, but tests revealed she was raped by Holland at least twice.[13]

Family members of Holland visited with him in the weeks leading up to the execution. However, no family members were present on his final day. Holland had been married twice, but Epps said he did not appear to have close family ties. His sister, brother, sister-in-law and nephew were on his visitation list, but Holland requested that they not witness his execution. He didn't even want his attorney present.[14]

Mississippi State Penitentiary Chaplain James Whisnant was the only person Holland wanted with him during the execution. For his last meal, Holland consumed a 14-ounce T-bone steak, baked potato, brussels sprouts, salad and apple pie. He drank a liter of Pepsi.[15]

Holland was put to death by lethal injection on May 20, 2010, at the Mississippi State Penitentiary at Parchman. He was declared dead at 6:14 p.m. He was the second Mississippi death row inmate to be executed in less than 24 hours. In the very room that Holland died, deep within the facility at Parchman, Paul E. Woodward died a day earlier at 6:39 p.m. the result of lethal injection.

"He has consistently expressed that remorse to me throughout the years that I have known him and would have done anything if he could turn back the clock to give back the young life he took," said Orlansky.[16]

Krystal's sisters, Marcie and her twin, Malissa King Adams, were 11 years old when Krystal was killed. As they spoke to the media after Holland's execution, they held a picture of the smiling teenager with flowing, shoulder-length blond hair. "We had 11 years with our sister," Walker said. "I'm not having nightmares anymore." The pair called Holland a monster for what he did to their sister.[17]

The victim's mother, Kathy King, said she did not want to see the execution but sent a handwritten letter. In that letter, she said, "24 years ago, my daughter Krystal was stabbed, beaten, raped and finally suffocated to death by Mr. Holland. She was just a child. Tonight, Mr. Holland finally received what he should have gotten 20 years ago." Although it ended the family's lengthy nightmare, she said the execution was not justice because it could not bring her child back.[18]

Holland requested his body be released to Mississippi Department of Corrections. He was buried on prison grounds in a casket constructed by inmates. Holland was the oldest person executed in 2010. He was 49 years old when he killed Krystal. At the time he committed the murder, he was older than any other offender executed in 2010.

CHAPTER 21

Darick D. Walker, Virginia.
Executed May 20

Darick Demorris Walker was on this earth for 37 years. Moments before his death, the only thing he had to say was, "Last words being: I don't think y'all done this right, took y'all too long to hook it up. You can print that. That's it." Those were the final words to stream across Walker's lips as he slipped into a lethal slumber strapped to a gurney in the death chamber of Greensville Correctional Center in Virginia.[1]

Walker's attorneys argued that he should not be executed because he suffered from mental disability. His final statement may have lent some credence to that argument. A man facing imminent death who can only conjure up a statement that complains about the process which he had immediately completed in preparation of his death is facile at best.

A social history prepared on Walker's behalf in 2003 when he was 30, said he functioned at the level of an 11-year-old, that he may have suffered from fetal alcohol syndrome, and that he had a family history of mental illness and mental disability. Walker's history also included two unprovoked, brutal murders.[2]

*   *   *

Walker was a vicious killer. He forced himself into two different homes in less than seven months and killed two men in front of their families in separate shootings. Under Virginia law, the death penalty may apply to anyone who commits two premeditated murders within three years. The two murders are themselves an aggravating circumstance with regard to the death penalty.

Catherine Taylor and her children, Monique, Bianca, and Sidney, lived in Richmond's University Terrace Apartments with Stanley Beale, the children's father. According to court records,[3] on the evening of November 22, 1996, Taylor heard a loud banging noise coming from the living room. Taylor left the bedroom where she had been with Sidney, an infant, and as she entered the living room, she saw a man kick in the locked front door and enter her home. Taylor knew the man standing in her living room as "Todd."

The man was actually Darick Walker. He was holding a gun yelling, "Where is he?" Walker continued yelling and asked Beale, "What you keep coming up to my door? What you looking for me for?" Beale, who was standing in the doorway to the kitchen, told Walker that he did not know him and did not know where he lived. Bianca, who was 13 years old at the time, screamed that her father did not know the intruder. Walker began shooting at Beale as Taylor ushered Bianca and Monique into the bathroom to hide in the bathtub. Walker shot Beale three times, killing him.

Bianca told the police that she also knew Walker as "Todd" and subsequently identified Walker in a photo line-up as the person who killed her father.

Tameria Patterson, a 14-year-old girl who was visiting a friend in the University Terrace Apartments, testified that on the night of the murder, she saw "Todd" enter her friend's apartment and say, "I shot him." When shown a photo spread, Tameria identified Walker as the person who had entered the apartment.

About six months later, on the night of June 18, 1997, Andrea Noble and Clarence Threat were sleeping in their bedroom when they were awakened by a "pop" coming from the screen door, followed by a knock at the door. Noble went to the door and looked outside through a small window in the door. She did not see anyone.

Later, she again heard a knock and went to the door, but again did not see anyone. Sometime after the third knock, the door was knocked down. Noble went to the living room and saw a person she knew as "Paul" standing with a gun. The man was actually Darick Walker. Walker pointed the gun at Noble as she backed into the bedroom. When they reached the bedroom, Walker struck Noble with the back of the gun and then shot Threat in the leg. In the bedroom, Walker and Threat exchanged words and Walker continued to shoot. Threat sustained a total of seven gunshot wounds. He died as a result of a gunshot wound to the chest. Walker told Noble that if she told anyone, he would come back and kill her and her kids.

At trial, Andrea Noble identified "Paul." During the punishment phase of the trial, prosecutors introduced Walker's prior convictions for a sex offense, forgery, assault and auto theft. The evidence also showed that Walker regularly stole from friends and acquaintances and, in a rage, had punched a pregnant woman in the stomach. In addition, as the trial court noted in imposing sentence in accordance with the jury's recommendation, the commission of two brutal, unprovoked murders within a six month period is a "strong indication ... that he is prone towards violence."[4]

* * *

Darryl Atkins, whose name is synonymous with the issue of mental disability and the death penalty, is also from the Commonwealth of Virginia. Atkins successfully challenged his execution based on mental disability.

In *Atkins v. Virginia*,[5] the Supreme Court held that the Eighth Amendment prohibits the execution of mentally disabled offenders. Relying on *Atkins*, Walker filed a petition for federal habeas corpus relief, a Latin term meaning "you have the body." The writ of habeas corpus is used to test the constitutionality of a state criminal conviction. Theoretically, the writ pierces through the formalities of a state conviction to determine whether the conviction is consistent with due process of law.

While Walker's first habeas petition was pending in the district court, the U.S. Supreme Court decided *Atkins*. The High Court concluded that a national consensus had developed against the execution of the mentally disabled. The Court held that the Eighth Amendment's ban against cruel and unusual punishment bars the execution of the mentally disabled.

Although the court banned execution for the mentally disabled, the Court also noted in a rather cryptic manner that it may not be so easy to determine who is mentally disabled and who is not. The Court wrote in *Atkins*, "to the extent there is serious disagreement about the execution of mentally retarded offenders, it is in determining which offenders are in fact retarded.... Not all people who claim to be mentally retarded will be so impaired as to fall within the range of mentally retarded offenders about whom there is a national consensus."[6] That means there is no bright-line standard to determine mental disability. The Court did not specifically say, for instance, that a killer with an IQ below 70 is mentally disabled.

In addition, the Court "did not provide definitive procedural or substantive guides for determining when a person who claims mental disability will be so impaired as to fall" within the class of defendants ineligible for capital punishment.[7]

Instead, the Court expressly left to the states the "task of developing appropriate ways to enforce the constitutional restriction upon [their] execution of sentences."[8] Furthermore, "states ... have responded to that challenge by adopting their own measures for adjudicating claims of mental retardation."[9]

The Virginia General Assembly responded to *Atkins* by enacting a statutory scheme to determine capital defendants' claims of mental disability. The General Assembly mandated that a capital defendant has the burden of proving mental disability by a preponderance of the evidence, and it defined the term "mentally retarded" as:

> [A] disability, originating before the age of 18 years, characterized concurrently by (i) significantly subaverage intellectual functioning as demonstrated by performance on a standardized measure of intellectual functioning administered in conformity with accepted professional practice, that is at least two standard deviations below the mean and (ii) significant limitations in adaptive behavior as expressed in conceptual, social and practical adaptive skills.[10]

For Walker, who had completed his direct appeal and state habeas proceeding as of the effective date of the legislation, the General Assembly specified that "he shall not be entitled to file any further habeas petitions in state and his sole remedy shall lie in federal court."[11]

The federal district court held a multi-day evidentiary hearing without a jury, during which the parties introduced a substantial amount of evidence on the issue of Walker's mental disability. This evidence included Walker's scores on various standardized tests; documentary evidence from school, prison, and medical records; and declarations from his family, acquaintances, and fellow inmates. The court also heard testimony from several witnesses, including designated experts who testified on the issue of Walker's mental disability. Eventually, the federal district court denied Walker's petition. A split panel of the 4th U.S. Circuit Court of Appeals agreed and ruled that Walker did not prove that he fit the legal definition for mental disability.[12]

*   *   *

Governor Bob McDonnell denied Walker's clemency request about a week before the scheduled execution. The night before Walker's execution the U.S. Supreme Court turned down his appeal and request for a stay of execution. A U.S. Supreme Court spokeswoman noted that three justices—John Paul Stevens, Ruth Bader Ginsburg and Sonia Sotomayor—would have agreed to a stay of execution. A spokesperson for Governor McDonnell said he found no compelling reason to commute Walker's sentence to life in prison.[13]

Walker, a tall man wearing sandals and blue prison clothing, was escorted into the death chamber by several corrections officers. He was cooperative and appeared calm as he looked around the room and toward the observation rooms. In one of those rooms was his attorney, Danielle Spinelli. Walker was strapped to a gurney, and a curtain was pulled to block the view of witnesses while the intravenous lines were attached to his arms.[14]

A corrections spokesperson acknowledged that prison officials had difficulty getting one of the IVs started, but said there were no other problems. There were no visible problems with the injection.[15] Perhaps the difficulty with the IV was the reason for Walker's bizarre, detached final statement.

The first of three chemicals used in the execution began flowing. Walker took several deep breaths, his breathing grew shallow, and then it stopped.[16]

Reached by telephone before the execution, Alice Threat-Skipper, Threat's mother, said she has never gotten over the crime. "It's been a long, hard 12 years," she said. She said she learned her son had died by an early-morning telephone call from a relative of Threat's girlfriend.

Threat-Skipper said her late son was raised in Richmond and was one of six children. As a child, he enjoyed playing baseball and bowling. Threat-Skipper continued, stating as an adult, he had a good job and helped care for his two children.[17]

Though she did not wish to stop the execution, Threat-Skipper said she does not believe in capital punishment and would have been satisfied had Walker been sentenced to prison without the possibility of parole so he could not harm anyone else.[18]

Walker died at 9:24 p.m. Outside the Greensville Correctional Center four death-penalty protesters stood in silence, holding candles.

CHAPTER 22

John Avalos Alba, Texas. Executed May 25

On August 5, 1991, the day after John Avalos Alba was released from jail, he went to a pawn shop in Plano, Texas, and purchased a .22 caliber semiautomatic pistol and a box of ammunition.

Alba had been in jail only a couple of months following his June 1991 arrest for fondling a 12-year-old girl during a slumber party at the apartment he shared with his wife Wendy.

According to court records, Alba and Wendy had a rocky marriage marked by alcohol abuse, infidelity and domestic violence. Only a few months earlier, the police responded to a domestic violence call at the Alba residence. Wendy had two black eyes, red marks on her neck and body and a shoe imprint on her back.[1]

Alba told one of the officers who arrested him for beating Wendy that he knew where the officer lived and was going to kill his wife and children. Other officers testified that they had responded to similar domestic violence calls from Wendy. Neighbors and friends told police that they frequently heard yelling and screaming, saw Wendy with bruises and black eyes, and saw Alba abuse and threaten her. Alba's ex-wife also testified that he was violent towards her during their marriage.[2]

Although Alba had no prior felony convictions, in June of 1991, he was arrested for fondling the 12-year-old girl at his apartment. When the police arrested Alba in June, he was allowed to speak with Wendy before he was transported to Allen City Jail. When Wendy told Alba that she would not help him get out of jail, he said, "Wendy, you better come get me out of jail or I'll kill you."[3]

While Alba was in jail, he wrote numerous threatening letters to his wife. Meanwhile, she moved in with friends Robert Donoho and Gail Webb in their apartment in Allen, north of Dallas. She was also trying to establish residence in a women's shelter.[4]

*   *   *

According to court records,[5] on August 5, 1991, at about 10 p.m. Alba tracked down Wendy at Donoho and Webb's apartment in Allen, Texas. Alba tried to force his way into the apartment while Wendy and Webb attempted to hold the door closed. Alba fired his pistol into the door and forced his way into the apartment. He angrily told Wendy and Webb that "you bitches deserve this." Alba grabbed Wendy by the hair and pulled her halfway out of the apartment where he beat her with his pistol and shot her in the back of her head, her buttocks, and the middle of her back severing her spinal cord.

Alba next went after Webb who had run into the kitchen and was attempting to hide by crouching on the floor. He stood over her and said with a snicker, "You deserve to die, bitch." He then shot her six times. Webb survived the attack. At the same time, Donoho had gone to the back bedroom to call the police. When he came out to check on Wendy and Webb, Alba challenged, "You want some of this?" and fired a shot at Donoho's head, missing him by about a foot.

The final wound he inflicted on Wendy was an afterthought. Before leaving the apartment, Alba shot Wendy one last time as she lay prostrate on the floor. Wendy died after being transported to the hospital.

As Alba left the apartment, he was confronted by the apartment manager, Misty Magers, her boyfriend, and a neighbor. When the manager ran to call for help, Alba fired a shot in her direction and yelled, "I'm going to get you too, Misty." He then turned the gun on the other two and continued his challenge, "Do you want any of this?" They let Alba pass. As he was attempting to finally leave the complex, he ran into a police officer responding to the call of shots fired. Alba excitedly told the officer, "I'm getting the hell out of here. There's a crazy son of a bitch over there shooting people." Alba then ran off. The officer did not detain him because he was unaware that Alba was actually the shooter.

Alba jumped in his car and took off at a high rate of speed. He later abandoned his vehicle in Plano and fled on foot to a bowling alley. There he came upon Ryan Clay, a teenager, working on a car in the parking lot. Alba asked for a ride, and when Clay stated that it was not his car, Alba pointed his gun at him and again asked for a ride. Clay complied. However, before they could leave the parking lot, sixteen-year-old Michael Carr, the owner of the car, stopped them. Carr, realizing something was not right, drove Alba to a nearby neighborhood.

The next morning, Alba returned to the apartment complex where he had killed his wife. Seeing a police officer, he ran to a shopping mall and set off a two-hour standoff with police, during which he held a gun to his head and threatened to kill himself. A S.W.A.T. team used a stun grenade and tear gas to subdue him.[6]

A website operated by a supporter of Alba described the circumstances of the murder quite differently than the trial record. According to the site, Wendy Alba also physically abused John and had sexual affairs with several other men. The site also stated the friends she moved in with were drug dealers. John went to visit his children and got into an argument with Wendy over the environment where his children were living. "He asked Wendy if she had been unfaithful again, and tragically, the gun was in his possession at the same time of the chilling details of Wendy's latest liaisons were revealed."[7]

* * *

A jury convicted Alba of capital murder in May 1992 and sentenced him to death. The Texas Court of Criminal Appeals affirmed the conviction and sentence in June 1995.

However, a case unrelated to Alba's resulted in his death sentence being overturned.

In 2000, Texas Attorney General John Cornyn revealed that Dr. Walter Quijano, acting as an expert witness for the prosecution, offered racially biased testimony during Victor Saldano's capital punishment hearing. Specifically, Quijano stated, "because [Saldano] is Hispanic, this was a factor weighing in favor of future dangerousness." Following this disclosure, Cornyn reviewed all the capital cases in which Quijano testified and resulted in a death sentence. In June 2000, he announced that six other cases, including John Alba's, were tainted by racially biased testimony from Dr. Quijano, and recommended that all of their death sentences be vacated. The U.S. Fifth Circuit Court of Appeals vacated Alba's death sentence in August 2000.[8]

The state of Texas held a new sentencing hearing for Alba. At this hearing, he testified that he did not deliberately kill his wife; it was a "bad reaction." He stated that he bought the gun on the day of the shooting as protection from a cousin. The second jury sentenced Alba to death a second time in March 2001. The Texas Court of Criminal Appeals affirmed the sentence in April 2003. All of his subsequent appeals in state and federal court were denied.[9] It was the end of the line for John Alba.

*   *   *

According to Alba's oldest brother Rudy who still lives in Elgin, John grew up in Elgin and resided in Bastrop County for a time before moving to the Dallas area in the 1980s. When asked about his younger brother and the many years he spent on death row, Rudy said the murder conviction was never a topic discussed during prison visits.[10]

Rudy indicated that the family has now come to terms with the inevitable execution of his brother. "It's [the execution] going to happen is all I know," Rudy said as the execution approached. "He [John] has told our brother George that 'even though I lost everything, I'm ready to go anyway.'" Rudy said he planned on visiting his brother before the execution but would not be present for the execution.[11]

Alba declined to speak with reporters as his execution date neared. He visited with some family and his legal counsel in the days preceding his execution.

Alba headed to the death chamber after eating a hearty last meal that consisted of 4 pieces of crispy fried chicken (two thighs and two breasts), four fried pork chops (well done), six cheese enchiladas (two beef, two cheese, two pork), one bowl of pico de gallo, onion rings, salad, one onion, six slices of white bread, a bottle of ketchup, and six cold Cokes.[12]

Alba was strapped to a gurney, when the warden asked whether he had a final statement, he responded, "I wish I could go back and change it, but I know I can't." He also addressed his son and daughter, who watched through a window. "Just tell everyone I love them," he said. "Y'all will be OK. I will, too. OK, warden," he said. "Do it."[13]

The Texas Court of Criminal Appeals rejected a request for a reprieve the day before the scheduled execution. The motion requesting a stay of execution argued that Alba's sentence was improper because he wasn't eligible for life without parole under a law passed just a few years ago: his Hispanic race illegally figured into his sentencing, he should not have been charged with capital murder, and his sentencing was unconstitutional. The U.S. Supreme Court declined to grant the stay about 30 minutes before he was taken to the death chamber. The Texas Board of Pardons and Paroles also denied a clemency request.[14]

Alba's execution was attended by members of the victim's family, the parents of the girl he was accused of molesting and his own son and daughter. "I am sorry for taking someone so precious to you and to my kids," he said in his last statement. Turning to his loved ones, he said, "Thanks for being beside me. I appreciate you always standing by me and everything y'all have done." Alba said he could taste the chemicals as the lethal injection process began. He said, "I am starting to go," and then lost consciousness. He was pronounced dead at 6:19 p.m.[15]

Alba was not new to death. On a website, he wrote about his time on death row and his regular encounters with the idea of impending death. Alba posted the following on Death Penalty News[16]:

I have been thinking back on these past 14-years and I am trying to remember how many men have been executed, but it's been so many that I have lost count. I know, at least, 250 men, some who were my friends, or most who I had met over the years. It was a somber experience to be speaking to these men, knowing that in only a few days, sometimes the next day, they would be dead. Some accepted it, some didn't. One man, whose image stays in my mind, I will never forget. As they were taking him out of our wing to be executed, he stopped at my cell to tell me "good-bye." It was his eyes, his eyes were wide open with fear. I felt his fear (if that is possible to explain) it was so overwhelming. That took place in 1997, and more than 5-years later, I still see his eyes.

Alba's eyes are now forever closed.

CHAPTER 23

Thomas W. Whisenhant, Alabama.
Executed May 27

The night he brutally murdered his third victim, Thomas W. Whisenhant hosted a birthday party for his daughter and even drove his mother home to the same Irvington, Texas, home where he grew up. Within hours of dropping off his mother, he had kidnapped, raped and shot a 23-year-old convenience store clerk.[1]

Whisenhant was married with a one-year-old daughter and a baby on the way. He was also a serial killer. Between November 21, 1975, and October 16, 1976, Whisenhant killed Patricia Hitt, Venora Hyatt and Cheryl Payton. First, he shot and killed Hitt, a clerk at a regional convenience store known as Compact. Six months later, he raped, mutilated and murdered Hyatt after kidnapping her from a 7-Eleven in a rural part of Alabama. Five months later, Whisenhant raped and killed Payton, another Compact Store clerk.[2]

Whisenhant had a dark past that haunted him throughout his adult life. As one psychiatrist suggested, his past may have led him to the diabolical rape, murder and mutilation of three women.

*   *   *

Claude Brown, a psychiatrist, became involved in Whisenhant's case when Whisenhant was ordered to Searcy Hospital in Mt. Vernon, Alabama, for a psychiatric examination and evaluation. According to court records,[3] Brown and two other psychiatrists were appointed by the superintendent of Searcy Hospital to form a commission to thoroughly evaluate him.

On three occasions, Brown interviewed Whisenhant at the hospital. Additionally, Brown reviewed available records and psychology reports. In total, Brown spent approximately 30 hours evaluating Whisenhant. Four of those hours were spent in actual interviews with Whisenhant.

Brown's opinion painted a guy with a troubled past but not enough psychological trauma to meet the legal definition of insanity. At the time, this diagnosis would have meant that Whisenhant would have been not guilty by reason of insanity.

In the aftermath of John Hinckley's attempt to assassinate President Ronald Reagan, the insanity defense came under scrutiny across the country when a jury found Hinckley not guilty by reason of insanity. Five states abolished the insanity defense altogether, and 10 other states, including Alabama, restored the antiquated M'Naghten rule with regard to the insanity defense.[4]

The rule had been abandoned in Alabama as far back as 1871 but was reinstated in the early 1980s. In order to prove insanity, the M'Naghten rule requires that, at the time of committing the offense, the accused party was laboring under such a defect of reason, from disease of the mind, as not to know the nature and quality of the act the offender was doing or the offender did not appreciate that the act was wrong.

Brown testified that Whisenhant was aware of the murders that he had committed and that when they occurred he was not under the influence of any drugs or in an impaired state of consciousness. However, Whisenhant had no idea why he was killing and mutilating his victims.

Brown suggested that Whisenhant was reared in a home that was a "markedly abnormal one." His home was one in which women, particularly his mother who was the dominant figure in the Whisenhant family, "ran the show." His father, a "non-entity," was denigrated, "cast down and cast out, literally as well as figuratively." Whisenhant viewed himself as receiving the same treatment as did his father. As he grew up, he was by all accounts a shy, relatively reserved person who had few friends and no girlfriends. Whisenhant "remained extensively dominated by Mother," and was "early in trouble."[5]

Whisenhant was involved in purse snatchings and an unprovoked assault upon a female soldier when he was in the Air Force. Whisenhant spent seven years in a military prison for the latter. While in prison he threatened a female teacher in one of the prison's scholastic programs.

Following the birth of his daughter, Whisenhant became preoccupied, complaining of "very vague physical pains" and saying that his "head didn't feel like it was there at times." He also had little interest in sexual relations with his wife, and their relationship "became more aloof." His wife became fearful of him.

Brown considered the timing of the murders of the three women to be in specific reference to his wife's giving birth to the first child. The first murder occurred approximately six weeks after the birth of his daughter; the second, in the same month that his wife told him she was pregnant again; and the third, on the night of his first child's first birthday.

Brown further explained the purpose for the mutilation of the bodies of the last two victims. The amputation of the breasts, the cutting of the vagina, and slitting of the stomach all amounted to removal of gender identification; that is, he made his victims "not female anymore."

As to a diagnosis of Whisenhant's "disease," Brown classified him as a "severe schizoid personality with marked paranoid traits, with the traits of necrosadism, that is, the sadistic destructive act with bodies that are dead."

In Brown's opinion, Whisenhant was afflicted with a mental disease. Whisenhant "knew right from wrong" (and that was the key to him being convicted); however, when he killed Cheryl Lynn Payton, he had so lost the power to select right from wrong, because of duress of that mental disease, that his ability to prevent himself from killing her was destroyed.

*   *   *

According to court records,[6] Tris Lowe lived in Irvington, Alabama, in Mobile County. On October 16, 1976, Lowe and his fiancé stopped at the Compact Store at approximately 10:00 p.m. No one was in the store and no vehicles were in the parking lot. Lowe saw a Coke machine open with the keys in the lock, a broken "six-pack" of Coca-Colas on the floor and a mop in a bucket nearby. He attempted to use the pay phone outside; however, the receiver had been torn from the phone booth. Lowe also noticed a Miller High Life pony bottle inside the phone booth. Lowe then went to the store's phone and called the police and remained at the scene until sheriff's deputies arrived. Cheryl Lynn Payton was the clerk who was to be working at the Compact Store.

Two days later, Charles Edwin Trippe, Sr., was notified by a neighbor that a strange man was walking along his property in Irvington, where he farmed about 5,000 acres of land. Trippe drove down to his property. When Trippe walked out into the field, he discovered the body of a woman clad only in "knee-high" stockings and a blue denim shirt. Trippe returned to his house and called police.

When Trippe returned to the field about 15 minutes later, the body was gone; however, there were marks where it appeared the body had been dragged. Trippe and the officers followed the marks, discovering Payton's body in a thicket and covered with boards. At this time Trippe observed cuts on the body that he did not see when he first discovered the body. A carton of Miller beer pony bottles was near the victim's head.

Mobile County Sheriff's Detective Sergeant Larry Tillman was assisting in the organization of a search party to find Payton, who was at that time considered missing. Tillman, along with Trippe, and other law enforcement personnel were present when Payton's body was discovered.

Tillman noticed the front end of a pickup truck stopped at the top of a hill a quarter of a mile down the road. Tillman then took off after the truck. The chase continued at speeds from 80 to 100 miles per hour until the truck crashed through an electrical fence and into the woods.

Whisenhant surrendered to the police without resistance. He was taken to the sheriff's office where he was questioned by the detectives. Whisenhant was given Miranda warnings, he acknowledged that he understood and agreed to talk with police.

*　　*　　*

Miranda warnings derive from a U.S. Supreme Court case of the same name. *Miranda v. Arizona*[7] is the landmark Supreme Court decision that has become a part of American culture. Miranda's conversion from legal holding to cultural icon is due mainly to the nation's insatiable appetite for television crime dramas. Everyone with a TV has heard Miranda warnings: "You have the right to remain silent. Anything you say can and will be used against you. You have the right to an attorney. If you can't afford one, one will be appointed for you."

What did Miranda do to earn his place in the American consciousness? In 1963, Ernesto Miranda was arrested for robbery. While in the midst of a custodial interrogation by police, he confessed to raping an 18-year-old woman. At trial, prosecutors offered his confession into evidence. Miranda was convicted of rape and sentenced to 20 to 30 years in prison. Miranda appealed and his case made its way to the U.S. Supreme Court.

The Supreme Court ruled in favor of Miranda and suppressed his confession. The court imposed the following procedures to safeguard a suspect's Fifth Amendment privilege against self-incrimination: the person in custody must, prior to interrogation, be clearly informed that he has the right to remain silent, and that anything he says will be used against him in court; he must be clearly informed that he has the right to consult with a lawyer and to have the lawyer with him during interrogation, and that, if he is indigent, a lawyer will be appointed to represent him.

* * *

The police began an interview of Whisenhant that covered more than 40 typewritten pages. Sometime later, there was another interview. Prior to the interview, he was again Mirandized. The second session was also lengthy.

The interview turned into an interrogation, and the interrogation turned into a confession. Whisenhant not only confessed to killing Payton, but Hyatt and Hitt as well. Whisenhant told the police that on October 16, 1976, he abducted Payton from the Compact Store. He drove her to a secluded wooded area in rural Mobile County, raped her on the front seat of his pickup truck and then shot her in the head one time with the .32 caliber pistol. The murder took place in a field near the truck. He then dragged her body into a wooded area and left the scene.

The next day, he returned to her body, cut off a large section of her breast and slit her abdomen. He was ultimately observed near the crime scene.

With evidence obtained from Whisenhant, law enforcement authorities verified his confession. All three murders involved extensive sadistic mutilation of dead bodies. All three victims were unknown to Whisenhant.

* * *

Whisenhant was a condemned man for 32 years, eight months and 20 days. He spent more time than any prisoner has ever spent on death row in Alabama. However, that time was drawing to a close. Whisenhant spent his last day reading the Bible and visiting with friends. His final visits included Bill Hodel, a death penalty opponent who began corresponding with Whisenhant and visited him for nine years before moving from Mobile to St. Louis.[8]

One of the other visitors was Mara Tillman, whose uncle, Larry Tillman, arrested Whisenhant in 1976. Richard Cohen of the Southern Poverty Law Center, one of Whisenhant's attorneys, said Tillman wrote to Whisenhant trying to understand his actions and gradually transformed from someone who hated him to someone who regularly visited. A corrections spokesman said Whisenhant designated Tillman in his will as the recipient of all his belongings including a 13-inch black and white television, a Bible, a radio, a Timex watch, two packs of cigarettes and a check for $96.94 from his inmate account.[9]

Cohen said Whisenhant recently was baptized. He expressed concern for his two children and sister. According to Cohen, in the visitation room before the execution, the group sang "Amazing Grace."

Whisenhant declined breakfast on the morning of his scheduled execution. Later, he ate his last meal at Holman prison, home of Alabama's death chamber. He ate a meal of chicken leg quarters, French fries, American cheese, orange drink, coffee and chocolate pudding.[10]

* * *

Whisenhant was dressed completely in white when prison officials pulled back the curtains on a pair of adjacent observation rooms for witnesses. It was about 6 p.m. and the witnesses could now see Whisenhant as he lay strapped to a gurney. The warden read aloud the execution order and asked Whisenhant if he had any last words. He chose not to speak. He would end his life without an explanation or an apology. Whisenhant's friends waved to him moments before the lethal injection process began. He tried to raise his left hand which was impeded by a strap and he smiled.

The three lethal drugs were introduced into his body through intravenous tubes that protruded from a rectangular slot in the death chamber wall. A chaplain knelt by Whisenhant in the death chamber of the Holman Correctional Facility. An observation room containing three reporters, three of Whisenhant's friends, and his attorney's, was utterly quiet except for a few muted sobs. Family members of Whisenhant's victims watched from an adjacent room.[11]

Whisenhant fidgeted uncomfortably before closing his eyes and half opening his mouth. After several tense minutes, his chest stopped moving. Corrections officers drew the curtains, and a doctor checked him for a heartbeat. The time was 6:20 p.m. Whisenhant was dead.[12]

* * *

Relatives of Cheryl Lynn Payton interpreted Whisenhant's failure to apologize or acknowledge the victims' families as hostility. "He had no remorse—none," said her widower, Douglas Payton. "He died a much easier death than my wife." Payton's brother, Edward Gazzier said, "There really wasn't justice served today. We watched him die an easy death."[13]

"Through many trials, retrials, appeals and excuses, our family has endured an enormous heartache and severe suffering," said Susanna Payton, a family member of the victim, in a prepared statement read to reporters after the execution. Family members said watching the quiet, antiseptic execution did not make them feel better. "He showed no remorse. He wouldn't even look at us," said Vivian Gazzier, Cheryl Payton's mother, who held a picture of Cheryl during the news conference.[14]

"There comes a time when everybody says it's over, but it's never over," said Ken Curry, son of Venora Hyatt.[15]

Attorney Cohen spent 23 years on Whisenhant's case, arguing that his client should not be executed because he was insane. "I know there are a lot of people in Mobile who are jubilant and are saying this is a long time coming," said Cohen. "But upon reflection, this is a sad day for the state of Alabama because the state is executing a man who is clearly mentally ill, and it's very, very sad."[16]

Whisenhant was the first person executed in Alabama in 2010. Alabama courts sentenced 130 killers to death prior to Whisenhant receiving his death sentence. Although the state has executed 50 offenders since 1976, 201 inmates remain on death row.

CHAPTER 24

George A. Jones, Texas. Executed June 2

George Alarick Jones told a friend that he killed Forrest J. Hall "so he wouldn't get to see his son."[1] Jones had no beef with Hall. In fact, he didn't even know him before Jones abducted Hall as part of a carjacking at a Dallas, Texas, mall.

Five months later, Jones and a friend, Darrick Rodgers, kidnapped and killed Kindra Buckner. Jones and Rodgers drove the 20-year-old victim to a secluded spot, forced her to strip naked, searched the contents of her purse, and then shot her twice in the head. Fearing that Buckner might have survived, Jones and Rodgers returned to Buckner's body and shot her in the face with a shotgun. They burned her car to cover their tracks.[2]

"I wasn't there when the dude got shot," Jones said in an interview from death row about a month before his execution. "I never had a fair trial. I've never been one fearful of death, but I don't want to surrender to it, either. If I had a fair trial, I could deal with it."[3]

For Jones it was all about a fair trial. Jones did not claim he was innocent—only that he did not get a fair trial. He did claim his innocence and point the finger at his accomplice. But, the statement, "If I had a fair trial, I could deal with it," merits closer examination. Does that mean if he were wrongfully convicted, but got a fair trial, it would be all right to face the death penalty? Or, does it mean "I killed two people," but my trial caused me to get a death sentence?

This is the logic of a man with the word "killer" tattooed on his right arm.[4]

*   *   *

According to court records,[5] on April 13, 1993, Hall's lifeless body was found along a road in Lancaster, Texas. Hall had been shot twice in the back of the head at point blank range. Police recovered two spent .380 automatic shell casings near Hall's body. The following day, Dallas police officers recovered Hall's vehicle abandoned on a street near the Fair Park neighborhood of Dallas. Hall's car had been stripped—the tires and rims were missing, as were the car's stereo and speakers.

Within a week, the Lancaster police were involved in a pursuit of a suspected stolen vehicle. The driver of the vehicle fled on foot and the police recovered a .380 automatic pistol that was later found to be the weapon used to kill Hall. The driver that day was presumably either Hall or Rodgers.

Sometime soon after Buckner's murder, Derrick Rogers was questioned by the Dallas police and confessed. He implicated Jones in Hall's murder. At trial, Rogers testified that he had known Jones for over two years and that, on an April afternoon in 1993, Rogers and Jones, along with two others, went to a shopping mall in Dallas to look for someone to rob.

The group drove to the mall and waited. Rogers and Jones, armed with a .380 automatic pistol, saw Hall leave the mall. They forced Hall into his car and drove to a secluded area in south Dallas. The others followed them in a separate car. Jones ordered Hall out of the car and down to the ground. Jones shot him twice in the head as he lay in the grass. Afterwards, Rogers and Jones took Hall's car and rejoined the others at a nearby restaurant.

Once Jones had been implicated in the murder, the detectives got a warrant and arrested him at his home in South Dallas. Within hours, Jones also gave a three-page voluntary written confession admitting his involvement in the murder. Jones also admitted that a car stereo and speakers found in his house belonged to the victim and the tires and rims were pawned at a nearby pawn shop.

At trial the jury heard from Derrick Rogers' girlfriend, who confirmed much of Rogers' testimony. She testified that she saw Jones, armed with a pistol, force Hall into his car and drive away from the shopping mall. She then followed Jones, Hall, and Rogers to south Dallas. There she saw Hall step out of the car with his hands raised as Jones held a gun on him. As she drove away, she heard two gunshots.[6]

* * *

Jones' written confession blamed Rogers for Hall's slaying but said he "accidentally" shot Hall once in self-defense. His lawyers later challenged the confession, which Jones said was written by police, but it was admitted into evidence during his 1995 trial.[7]

In addition to the murders, Jones had actively participated in at least five other armed robberies. The facts of the various robberies are very similar. In each, Jones, along with one or more other individuals, confronted a victim in a public place, and armed with a handgun, a rifle, a shotgun, or some other weapon, forcibly took the victim's car. The victim of at least one of these aggravated robberies was shot at several times, and another was maced as he used a public pay phone. The cars that were eventually recovered had been destroyed or stripped of all their specialty equipment such as the tires, rims, and stereos.[8]

* * *

On March 22, 1995, a Dallas County jury found Jones guilty of murder and sentenced him to death. His conviction and sentence were automatically appealed to the Texas Court of Criminal Appeals.

Jones did not go down without a fight. He had an aggressive advocate in Dallas Attorney Richard Anderson. At Jones' trial, Anderson alleged that the judge wrongly allowed prosecutors to exclude a prospective juror perceived as friendly to the defense, thus effectively giving the state a numbers advantage in jury selection. The Court of Criminal Appeals ruled 6–3 in September 1998 that the trial judge had made an error, but it found that the mistake had not prevented Jones from having an impartial jury and a fair trial. Anderson was livid. He felt that the exclusion of the juror went to the heart of a fair trial. He suggested that one holdout juror can be the difference between life and death for Jones.[9]

In his motion for the court to reconsider, Anderson wrote that it comes as a "great surprise to both the casual observer and the seasoned legal veteran" that the court can "sit back and piously declare that the fundamental right guaranteed in the Constitution to a fair and impartial jury is not affected."[10]

In its opinion, the Texas Court of Criminal Appeals held that Jones is guaranteed the right to an impartial jury, but that the exclusion of a potentially defense-friendly juror does not mean he did not receive one. "A defendant has no right that any particular individual serve on the jury. The defendant's only substantial right is that the jurors who do serve be qualified."[11]

Since Jones did not show that the jury he received was biased, he cannot argue he had an unfair jury. The court affirmed Jones' conviction and his death sentence.[12]

Jones filed various state and federal appeals. Each time, the court rejected Jones' claims. The U.S. Supreme Court refused to consider Jones' appeal on January 10, 2005.

Jones was originally scheduled for execution on January 27, 2005. On January 12, 2005, Jones filed a second state application for a writ of habeas corpus, alleging that he is mentally disabled and thus constitutionally ineligible for execution pursuant to *Atkins v. Virginia*.[13]

After determining that Jones' second application satisfied all statutory requirements, the Texas Court of Criminal Appeals issued a stay of execution and remanded Jones' application to the trial court for consideration.

On February 24, 2010, agreeing with the trial court's conclusion that Jones is not mentally disabled, the appeals court denied relief on the merits of Jones' second claim. Jones did not seek review by the U.S. Supreme Court.

*   *   *

On June 2, 2010, Jones awoke to his last day on earth. He was being housed adjacent to the death chamber at Texas State Penitentiary at Huntsville. He ate a final meal of pizza, oatmeal cookies, French fries and sweet tea.[14]

He was strapped to a gurney, and IV lines were placed in his arms by prison personnel. When asked by the prison warden if he had a final statement, Jones thanked his parents "who have been my pillar of strength in this situation" and his brothers and sisters "who have loved me despite my faults and imperfections."[15]

Jones' relatives did not witness the execution. Jones did have his spiritual advisor at the execution. The victim's relatives watched through a window. Jones told them that he hoped the punishment "brings you closure or some type of peace. I hope it helps his family, son and loved ones. This has been a long journey, one of enlightenment," he added. "It's not the end, it's only the beginning."[16]

Jones did not accept responsibility for the murders nor did he apologize for his conduct.

"They were putting cases on me in places I never was," Jones said as he met with reporters from a visiting cage outside death row. "If I do something, I own up to it. How can I feel sorry for nothing I had to do with?"[17]

After a gasp and loud snores, Jones stopped breathing. He was pronounced dead at 6:18 p.m. eight minutes after the lethal drugs began flowing. His arms were partially covered by his white shirt and the tape around the intravenous tubes carrying the drugs. One needle in his right arm was opposite his "killer" tattoo.[18]

"It was a bitter, bitter situation," Hall's uncle, Theron Nash, said after watching the execution. "We thank God for this day and we ask God's mercy upon George Jones' mother."

Another uncle, Kelvin Hall, believed the punishment brought justice but seemed too easy. "It was like laying down and going to sleep," he said after watching Jones' death. "My nephew suffered." Even after 17 years, his nephew's slaying for him "is as fresh as the day it happened," Nash added.[19]

Doug Parks, Jones' lead defense counsel at his trial, said Jones had come from a good family and "never wanted for anything." Parks said Jones was acting out to fit in with the wrong crowd. "My take on George always was he was a 'schoolboy' and was trying to make inroads with his peers to be more like some of the folks who didn't come from such good families," Parks said.[20]

Greg Davis, one of the prosecutors who handled Jones' trial, said there was "absolutely no doubt" authorities had the right man. Davis said of Jones' claim of innocence, "That's just a lie."[21]

CHAPTER 25

Melbert Ray Ford, Jr., Georgia.
Executed June 9

Melbert Ray Ford had a plan for exacting vengeance from his ex-girlfriend. Ford wanted to kill Martha Chapman Matich, and he was not shy about telling people.

According to court records,[1] Ford talked to several people about robbing the store where Matich worked. He told one guy that he intended to kidnap Martha, take her into the woods, make her beg, and then shoot her in the forehead. Ford told a friend that he "was going to blow her ... brains out." There was one problem; Ford did not have a car, and he needed one to get to Matich.

Authorities say anger drove Ford to plot his ex-girlfriend's death and that he was so infuriated that he sought the help of several friends to drive him to the Newton County, Georgia, convenience store where Matich worked. When no one offered to help, an exasperated Ford exclaimed, "Isn't there anybody crazy around here anymore?" As he became more frustrated with the lack of help, he looked to anyone, even people he was not that well acquainted with.

Ford finally found an ally in his scheme to kill: Roger Turner, a 19-year-old who was out of a job and nearly out of money. Ford got Turner drunk, promising him that they could make a big score. Ford talked Turner into helping him, and they drove in Turner's car to Chapman's Grocery Store, arriving just after closing time.

It was March 6, 1986, and Martha and another woman were working at the store. Martha's co-worker went home sick before closing time. Martha's 11-year-old niece, Lisa Chapman, was at the store playing with the minnows and crickets sold as bait and didn't want to leave her aunt alone at the store.

As the two prepared the store for closing, Ford shot his way through the locked front door. Turner, waiting in the car, heard screams and gunshots. Then Ford ran from the store to the car, carrying a bag of money.

At 10:20 p.m. the store's burglar alarm sounded. A Newton County sheriff's deputy arrived within minutes. Martha was lying dead behind the counter, shot three times. Lisa was discovered in the bathroom, shot in the head but still alive, sitting on a bucket, bleeding from the head and having convulsions. She would not survive.

Ford and Turner were arrested the next day. Turner confessed first and was brought into Ford's interrogation room to tell Ford that he had told the truth. Ford told him not to worry, that Turner was not involved in the murders. Afterwards, Ford told the police that the shooting began after Matich pushed the alarm button. He told police that if he had worn a mask, the killings would not have happened. Ford lied to Turner and to the police.

Prosecutors dropped murder charges against Turner, a key witness at Ford's trial, and he was sentenced to 20 years in prison on robbery charges. He was paroled in 1991.

Ford was abusive toward Matich throughout the year-and-a-half-long relationship. At one point, he tied her up in the trailer the two shared and burned and tortured her. Eventually, Martha had to have a police escort home every night after working at the store.

At trial, Ford claimed he was too drunk to know what was happening and that Turner was the one who entered the store and killed Matich and her niece.[2]

In October of 1986, following a trial, a Newton County, Georgia, jury convicted Ford and sentenced him to death. The jury deliberated only an hour and a half before finding Ford guilty and only one hour before imposing two death sentences.[3]

Ford's attorney, Brian Mendelsohn, had argued that his client should not be executed. Carrying out his sentence would violate the Eighth Amendment ban against cruel and unusual punishment because Ford sat on death row for about 24 years.[4]

Ford contended that prosecutors suppressed evidence about Turner's drug use the night of the killings and claimed that his trial lawyer was ineffective.

The seminal case in the area of ineffective assistance of counsel is *Strickland v. Washington*.[5] The U.S. Supreme Court set forth a two-prong test. First, trial counsel's performance must be deficient. In order to find a deficient performance, the defendant must demonstrate that counsel's representation fell below an "objective standard of reasonableness."

Second, the deficient performance must have prejudiced the defense so as to deprive the defendant of a fair trial. Prejudice is shown by proving the result would have been different, but for counsel's unprofessional errors.

Ford argued that his trial counsel did not perform a thorough investigation of his background. The U.S. Supreme Court has ruled that the reasonableness of counsels' actions should be evaluated based on "strategic choices made by the defendant and on information supplied by the defendant." The court ruled that counsel should not be faulted for failing to uncover the evidence on their own. Under such circumstances, Ford's trial counsels' investigation would not be deemed constitutionally deficient, if Ford failed to provide him with the potential evidence. There is nothing in the court record to indicate that trial counsel was given the information relating to Ford's background.[6]

Ford's appeals were repeatedly denied by state and federal judges, and a petition to appeal the case to the U.S. Supreme Court was rejected as well. The Georgia Board of Pardons and Parole denied his appeal for clemency, and a county judge also rejected a last minute request to stay the execution.

*   *   *

Cindy Chapman-Griffeth, the mother of 11-year-old Lisa, said in an interview prior to the execution, "I feel like I have been at war, but instead of guns it has been a knife in my heart the whole time." After the execution, as the sun was setting on the grounds of the prison, she said she felt closure but wished that Ford had admitted what he had done and asked her forgiveness.[7]

Chapman-Griffeth described her daughter as a tenderhearted girl who loved people and animals, especially horses, and was always smiling and laughing. A wing at Livingston Elementary School where she attended was named in her honor. The young girl dreamed of becoming a teacher one day. "She liked to learn sign language and speaking to people who were impaired," said Chapman-Griffeth. "She loved unicorns and walking behind her daddy as he plowed the garden, pushing the dirt between her toes. She loved to help me cook and being a big sister. She was also saved [in a religious context] the week before she was murdered at a Bible school."[8]

Martha's brother Paul Chapman described his sister as a quiet, reserved girl who tended to be a follower. "She always looked for the good in every individual," he said. Paul said he met Ford only once, when he came to Georgia in 1985 for a funeral. He remembered noticing his controlling and manipulative behavior during a meal. As a Baptist minister, Paul was used to counseling people. "I took her aside and I told her that he was evil and she needed to put him aside," said Paul. "She told me that she thought he would change. My sister loved life and looked for the good in everyone. She tried to see the good in this man, or this monster, and thought that maybe she could change him. But as we know, that didn't take place."[9]

Turner confessed that "Ford described killing Lisa Chapman in the bathroom at the grocery. Turner said that Ford told him that she was crouched by the toilet staring at him, so he felt he had to shoot her." Chapman-Griffeth said, "She was begging him not to do it in the bathroom where she went to hide."[10]

* * *

When asked what she would say to Ford if given the opportunity, Chapman-Griffeth stumbled. "I don't know what I would say to him," she said. "I'm trying to find peace in my heart and I think this will help. I don't think the man has any remorse, and if he doesn't, I hope he burns 70 times in Hell. He says he's a changed man, but he's never admitted to doing it. Twenty-four years and 32 appeals and he's never admitted it."[11]

Earlier, on the day of the scheduled execution, the Georgia Supreme Court rejected a final appeal to spare Ford's life. The decision was unanimous, though the justices didn't offer a reason. Ford's lawyers argued there were more heinous murders that didn't result in the death sentence, and the hackneyed assertion that execution would be cruel and unusual punishment because of all the time that has passed.[12]

Sitting in the Georgia Diagnostic and Classification Prison near Jackson, 50 miles south of Atlanta, Ford now waited for the inevitable. Ford was 25 when he murdered Matich and Chapman, now as he awaited his own death. He was 49 years old.

He spent his final hours visiting with relatives and friends. He had requested a final meal of fried fish and shrimp, a baked potato, salad, boiled corn, ice cream, cheesecake and soda.[13] As he lay strapped to a gurney with IVs inserted in both arms, Ford said, "I wish to thank all my family and my friends and my loved ones," before his voice trailed off and he began to mumble inaudibly. He declined a final prayer and also an earlier chance to give more extended remarks. He did not ask for forgiveness or apologize for the pain and suffering he caused.[14]

At 7:27 p.m. Ford was administered the three-drug lethal injection. He was dead about 10 minutes after the procedure began.

Paul Chapman said that he has forgiven Ford because that's what God would want him to do. "Some say the death penalty should not be carried out because those were Old Testament laws, but I still believe to this day that he should pay for what he's done, and therefore, if he is put to death, he has received what he deserves," said Paul, adding that it would be easier for him to forgive Ford if he admitted to the murders and apologized for committing them.[15]

Lisa's father Oliver Chapman said he got to hold his daughter for a few moments before she was taken away in a medical helicopter, but she could not speak to him. She died on the way to the hospital. Cindy Chapman Griffeth, Lisa's mother, said she had been encouraged by reports that Ford had become a religious man in prison, but was disappointed when he didn't seem remorseful in his final moments. "I was hoping that he would have a prayer, a sign that he had been saved," she said. "I think the way he went...." She paused, breaking into tears, before she composed herself and continued. "It was too easy for him."[16]

Ford was the first person executed in Georgia in 2010. Georgia courts sentenced 87 killers to death prior to Ford receiving his death sentence. Although the state has executed 49 offenders since 1976, 106 inmates remain on death row.

CHAPTER 26

John Forrest Parker, Alabama.
Executed June 10

Charles Sennett said, "Death is not easy for anybody, right or wrong."[1] Sennett had just witnessed the execution of John Forrest Parker, the man who 22 years earlier killed Sennett's mother in a bizarre murder-for-hire plot. Sennett's father hired Parker, one of his tenants, to commit the murder, and then he committed suicide within days of the killing being carried out.

Elizabeth Sennett died March 18, 1988, at Helen Keller Hospital after she was brutally beaten and stabbed in her home along Coon Dog Cemetery Road in Colbert County, Alabama. Elizabeth Sennett's husband, also named Charles Sennett, was a minister at the Westside Church of Christ in Sheffield, Alabama. He paid Bill Gray Williams $3,000 to kill his wife. Williams paid Kenneth Smith and Parker $1,000 each to commit the murder and kept $1,000 for himself.[2]

According to court records,[3] Elizabeth Sennett was stabbed multiple times in the chest, the back, the base of her neck, forehead, nose and scalp. Parker and Smith hit the victim with a galvanized pipe and then stabbed her while she was pleading for her life.

Williams gave Parker $100 to purchase a weapon on March 17, 1988, and promised to pay him the balance when the job was completed. Instead of buying a weapon, Parker used the $100 for drugs and injected painkillers on the way to Sennett's house.

Parker drove to the Sennetts' residence while Smith, who was in the passenger seat, sharpened Parker's survival knife. Parker parked his car behind the Sennetts' home, told Elizabeth that her husband had given them permission to look at the property as a hunting site. Elizabeth, not realizing the fate that awaited her, permitted the two men to continue with their ruse. The men walked into the woods together. A few minutes passed, and they returned to the house. This time they asked for permission to use the bathroom. While in the bathroom, Parker put cotton socks onto his hands. He then exited the bathroom, jumped Elizabeth and began hitting her.

The two men broke the glass in the medicine cabinet and took a stereo and video cassette recorder to make the assault look like it was done during a burglary. Parker later burned his clothes and threw the stereo off a bridge, and he and Smith threw away the knife. Parker subsequently received the remaining $900 for the murder.

When Sennett arrived home, he found his house ransacked and Elizabeth, lying wrapped in a blanket, close to death. Sennett called Colbert County Sheriff's Investigator Ronnie May at 11:44 a.m. May immediately dispatched a rescue squad and sheriff's deputies to the Sennett's home. May and another deputy arrived at the home about 20 minutes later, and the rescue squad arrived soon thereafter. Elizabeth was transported to the hospital. Resuscitation efforts failed; Elizabeth was dead.

Following an investigation of the crime scene, hairs found in a cap located near Elizabeth's body were consistent with Smith's known hair sample, and fibers from a blanket that had been wrapped around Elizabeth's body were consistent with fibers later taken from Parker's knife. The VCR taken from the Sennett's house was found inside Smith's residence.

* * *

Elizabeth thought her husband had tragically lost his first wife as a young man. Some in the community knew Charles Sennett as a high roller who lived beyond his means. Sennett was also known as a religious man who preached the good word and used his ministry to touch many members of his rural Alabama community. Doris Tidwell knew her minister, Charles Sennett, as someone who took both an emotional and physical interest in her—someone who seemed to need money through no fault of his own. When Sennett asked his lover for $3,000 to repay a bank loan, she gladly gave it to him. Instead, the preacher contracted Williams to kill his wife.[4]

* * *

Parker had a low IQ. He spent most of his school years in remedial classes for intellectually-challenged students. Although he had no previous criminal history, those closest to him believed he was incapable of such violence. Parker's attorneys believed the best they could do for him was to "win" a life sentence. As it turned out, the jury did recommend a sentence of life in prison without the possibility of parole. The presiding judge, Inge Johnson, overruled the jury and imposed a sentence of death.

Thirty-two states have the death penalty; Alabama is one of only three that allow a trial judge to override a jury's verdict of life without parole and impose death. Of these three, Alabama is the only state that elects trial judges in partisan elections. The other two states, Florida and Delaware, have long maintained tight regulations on a trial judge's ability to overrule the jury's judgment. By contrast, no meaningful standards regulate an Alabama trial judge's ability to ignore a jury's recommendation of life without parole.[5]

Since 1976, more than 80 people have been sentenced to death by judges in Alabama even though their juries decided that death was not the appropriate punishment.[6]

Alabama judges are elected and often feel pressure to be tough on crime. Judges can also disregard juries that recommend death sentences and order life in prison, but it almost never happens. In the weeks preceding Parker's execution, the editorial board of the *Birmingham News* asked, how can juries almost always be right when they recommend death, but so often be wrong when they recommend life?

It is not clear why the jury decided death was not a fitting punishment for Parker. Perhaps it had something to do with the fact the victim's husband, who ordered the murder and committed suicide a week after the murder, never answered for his role.[7]

* * *

"This is one of the steps we have to take to get closure and justice," Elizabeth's son Charles Sennett said after the execution. "We still have another step with Smith, but tonight was a step in the right direction." Colbert County Sheriff Ronnie May was the lead investigator on the case. He continued to stay in touch with the victim's sons through the years. "I know they want to start the closure process, and I hope this does it for them," May said after learning of Parker's execution.[8]

Sennett said he and his brother still have unanswered questions. "Why this happened," said Sennett who was 25 and married with two children when his mother was killed. "Daddy took the answers to his grave and so are these boys [Parker and Smith]." Officials who investigated the murder said the underlying motive was that the husband was trying to get out of his marriage and that he was heavily in debt. "This was a devastating situation on these two boys," May said. "To lose your mom in this fashion and then learn that your father orchestrated the entire thing and then he took his own life before he could be punished," added May. "I feel for these two boys and their families, as well as the Parker family."[9]

Sennett said he and his brother met with Parker's mother and father before the execution in Atmore. "They were remorseful for what their son did," Sennett said. "We never hated them. They can't do anything about what their son did. We know they're hurting. The Parker family is a victim to a point and our hearts go out to them."[10]

Sennett said his family wished to express their sympathy to the Parker family and hope they find a way to deal with their loss. "We know what it is to lose a loved one," Sennett said. "The only difference today is that John Parker had 22 years to say goodbye. We did not have that chance to say goodbye to our mom. It is a bittersweet day for both sides."[11]

He said the Parker family will need the support of family and friends, just as his family had for 22 years. "As for the death of John Parker, the pain he did not feel today does not compare to that he inflicted on our mother 22 years ago," Sennett said. "We would like to thank all of our family and friends for the prayers and calls that we have received this week and the last 22 years. Without the support of family and friends, we couldn't make it through."[12]

* * *

Parker appealed to the U.S. Supreme Court late on the day before the scheduled execution after the Alabama Supreme Court voted 7–2 to reject his plea for a stay. Alabama Governor Bob Riley called the prison about 1 p.m. on the day of the scheduled execution to inform corrections officials that he would not stop the execution.[13]

Finally, the U.S. Supreme Court rejected his appeal. According to corrections officials, the request was rejected a few minutes before the execution was scheduled to begin. In the appeal, Parker's attorneys unsuccessfully challenged the constitutionality of an Alabama law that allowed the trial judge to override the jury's sentence recommendation.[14]

As the scheduled execution approached, Parker was moved to a holding cell just a few steps from the death chamber where he would be strapped to a gurney and receive the lethal injection. He spent most of his last day meeting with friends and family members, including his mother and father, Joan and Edward Parker; a friend, Carolyn Watson; and two religious advisers, Ben Sherrod and Taylor Perry. All five witnessed the execution. Parker was calm and spent some of his final hours reading the Bible. Parker had a final meal of fried fish, French fries and iced tea.[15]

Parker's co-conspirator in the physical act of murder, Smith, was also convicted of murder and sentenced to death. Smith remains on death row. Williams, who brought in Parker and Smith to carry out the murder, is serving a life sentence without parole for his murder conviction. The mastermind behind the murder, Charles Sennett, shot and killed himself in his son's backyard. He had been informed immediately after the murder that he was a suspect.

As Parker was strapped to a gurney with IV attached to his arms, he looked to the window where the victim's family sat and used his final words to ask for forgiveness, "I'm sorry, I don't ever expect you to forgive me. I really am sorry."[16]

After sodium thiopental, the drug that causes unconsciousness, was administered, a prison guard called Parker, brushed his eyelashes with a finger and pinched his arm. Medical professionals said that these procedures adopted by the state are commonly used to assess consciousness. A person who is conscious will blink when his eyelashes are brushed and will withdraw his arm when pinched. This process was established to insure that a condemned inmate experiences a minimal amount of suffering when pancuronium, the drug that paralyzes, and potassium chloride, the drug that stops the heart, are administered.[17]

Parker gave most of his possessions to his mother, including a gold watch, a mirror, seven stamps and a box of pictures. He gave a belt and a wallet to two nephews. The Alabama Department of Corrections issued a simple statement saying that Parker was pronounced dead at 6:41 p.m. on June 10, 2010; he died by lethal injection at Holman Correctional Facility in Atmore.[18]

CHAPTER 27

David Lee Powell, Texas. Executed June 15

David Lee Powell spent 32 years on Texas's death row. He was sentenced to death by three different juries. Although he killed a police officer with an AK-47, he did not take the typical route to the death chamber located within the Texas State Penitentiary at Huntsville.

More than 40 years ago, Powell was a highly-regarded student when he arrived at the University of Texas for his freshman year. He came to Austin from his family's small town dairy farm north of Dallas. He was the top student in a graduating class of only 15. He scored nearly perfect on his college entrance exam. Although he was described as shy and naïve, he was the real deal in the classroom. "He was the class nerd; he was a very bright man," former classmate Karen Hair testified at Powell's 1999 trial. "We thought he was a genius. He had very thick glasses, and he walked around with a smile on his face all the time."[1]

Powell was in the UT honors program and after some initial trouble adjusting, his grades and schoolwork improved. Things began to sour during his second year on campus. Powell got involved as an anti-war protester and started using drugs. The once promising student dropped out of school and into a drug-fueled mental illness.

In the years leading up to the murder, Powell's family was alarmed to find the calm, responsible young man replaced by a flighty, fast-talking guy with paranoid delusions. Former friends had trouble recognizing him in his thin, disoriented, disheveled state. "He called me once and said he had to be careful talking to me because the CIA was after him," his uncle Clem Struve said. "I've had mental illness in my family, and I thought he was having a nervous breakdown," Marjorie Powell, his mother, said recently from her Dallas home. "I called a psychiatrist, different people for help." Powell disappeared and no amount of searching could turn him up.[2]

* * *

According to court records,[3] on May 17, 1978, Powell asked his former girlfriend, Sheila Meinert, to drive him from Austin to Killeen, Texas. They went in Powell's red Mustang. Powell had a .45 caliber handgun, an AK-47, and a hand grenade. He also had a backpack containing about 2¼ ounces of methamphetamine. Austin Police Officer, Ralph Ablanedo, was working when he spotted the Mustang and noticed that it did not have a rear license tag. Ablanedo activated his emergency lights and siren and directed the vehicle to pull to the side of the street.

Meinert jumped out of the car and approached Ablanedo. She told him that she had lost her driver's license but showed him her passport. Ablanedo also checked Powell's driver's license and asked the dispatcher to run a warrant check on Meinert and Powell. The dispatcher informed Ablanedo that the computers were not functioning properly but that there were no local warrants for Meinert. Ablanedo cited Meinert for failing to display a driver's license and allowed her and Powell to drive away.

As fate would have it, a moment after Powell drove off, the dispatcher told Ablanedo that Powell had a "possible wanted" for misdemeanor theft. Ablanedo signaled for Meinert to pull over again. Meinert, again, got out of the car. As she was approaching the officer, she heard gunshots and ran back to the car. As Ablanedo approached the Mustang, Powell shot him through the car's back window, knocking Ablanedo to the ground. The first shot was from an AK-47 in semi-automatic mode. As Ablanedo tried to get up, Powell switched the AK-47 to automatic mode and fired a clip, hitting Ablanedo nine more times.

Bobby Bullard, who happened to be driving by on his way home from work, saw Powell shoot Ablanedo. He testified at trial that he saw shots fired from the Mustang that knocked out the back windshield. Bullard saw a man sitting in the middle of the front seat of the Mustang, lying on top of the console. He said that the man who fired the shots had long hair and was wearing a white T-shirt.

Edward Segura, who lived in the area, heard what he thought sounded like machine gun fire. When he went outside, he saw a red Mustang driving away. Segura testified that Ablanedo said that he had been shot. When Segura asked, "who was it," Ablanedo replied, "a girl."

When the dispatcher learned that there was a possible warrant for Powell, as a matter of routine, she sent back-up to assist. Officer Bruce Mills, an occasional partner of Ablanedo, responded as back-up. When Mills arrived at the scene, he found Officer Ablanedo lying on the ground. Although Ablanedo wore a bullet-proof vest, it was not designed to withstand automatic weapon fire. Ablanedo suffered ten gunshot wounds and died on the operating table at the hospital, about an hour after he was shot. He was just 26 years old, married and the father of two young sons.

Velma, Bullard's wife, who came outside after seeing the lights from the police car, Segura, and Officer Mills all attempted to aid Ablanedo while waiting for the ambulance to arrive. All heard Ablanedo say, repeatedly, "that damn girl" or "that Goddamn girl." Mills testified that Ablanedo told him that a girl and a guy were in the car, and that they were armed with a shotgun or machine gun. Mills said that Ablanedo told him, twice, that "he got me with the shotgun."

One shot fired by Powell flattened one of the Mustang's rear tires. Meinert drove the car into the parking lot of a nearby apartment complex. Another Austin police officer en route to the scene with a description of the Mustang from the dispatcher's broadcast, spotted the vehicle in the apartment complex parking lot. As the officer pulled in, he immediately came under automatic weapon fire. He identified the shooter as a male with medium length hair and no shirt firing at him. More police officers arrived, and a shoot-out ensued. Miraculously, no one was shot. Meinert told the police that Powell handed her a hand grenade in the apartment complex parking lot and told her to remove the tape from it. She said that she started peeling tape off the grenade but was hysterical and shoved it back at him.

Officer Bruce Boardman testified that the shooting in the apartment complex parking lot came from a person at the passenger side of the Mustang. He said that he saw that person appear again, making "a throwing motion" over the top of the Mustang, and simultaneously, a female at the driver's side of the Mustang ran away from the car, screaming hysterically and flailing her arms.

After throwing the object, Powell began running away from the scene toward the grounds of a high school across the street. Later, officers found a live hand grenade about ten feet away from the driver's door of a police car. The pin for the grenade was discovered outside the passenger side of the Mustang where the person making the throwing motion had been. The grenade, which had a kill radius of 16 feet and a casualty radius of 49 feet, did not explode because the safety clip had not been removed.

Meinert was arrested in the apartment complex parking lot. She was later convicted for her role in the attempted murder of a police officer. Powell was arrested a few hours later, just before dawn on May 18. He was found hiding behind some shrubbery on the grounds of the high school. Powell's .45 caliber pistol was found on the ground near where he was hiding, and his backpack containing methamphetamine with a street value of approximately $5,000 was found hanging in a tree.

Law enforcement officers searched the Mustang and recovered handcuffs, a book entitled *The Book of Rifles*, handwritten notes about weapons, cartridge casings, the AK-47, a shoulder holster, and a gun case.

Following a search of Powell's residence, officers seized another hand grenade, methamphetamine, ammunition, chemicals and laboratory equipment for the manufacture of methamphetamine, and military manuals. In September 1978, Powell was convicted and sentenced to death for the murder of Officer Ablanedo.[4]

* * *

In 1988, the U.S. Supreme Court ruled in *Satterwhite v. Texas*[5] that the Fifth and Sixth amendments guarantee criminal defendants the right to be told in advance that a psychiatric evaluation may be used to determine their future dangerousness, that they have the right to remain silent, and that their counsel must be informed that the evaluation is taking place.

Under Texas law, a capital defendant may not be sentenced to death unless the State proves beyond a reasonable doubt that "there is a probability that the defendant [will] commit criminal acts of violence that [will] constitute a continuing threat to society."[6]

Because of the similarities between Satterwhite's case and Powell's, the Supreme Court sent Powell's case back in June 1988 to the Texas Court of Criminal Appeals for reconsideration in light of this recent decision.

On review, the Texas court held that Powell waived his right to object to the testimony of two psychiatrists when his lawyers used psychiatric testimony to argue for an insanity defense. Such an argument, the court reasoned, entitles the state to present psychiatric evidence to refute the insanity defense. The Court of Criminal Appeals reaffirmed Powell's guilty verdict and death sentence in January 1989. The case then went back to the Supreme Court which found that, while the Court of Criminal Appeals dealt with the Fifth Amendment issue—the right to remain silent—it failed to answer the Sixth Amendment issue—the right to counsel. In July 1989, the Supreme Court vacated Powell's death sentence.[7]

Powell was resentenced to death. Then the Texas Court of Criminal Appeals vacated the second death sentence in December 1994 because the trial court's instructions to the jury were inadequate. By this time, the law had been changed so that when a death sentence was thrown out, the guilty verdict remained in force, so the state could request a new pun-ishment hearing without having to retry the defendant's guilt.

A new punishment hearing was held, and Powell was sentenced to death for the third time in November 1999. All of his subsequent appeals in state and federal court were denied.[8]

*   *   *

Powell spent his last day alive packing personal property into mesh bags for delivery to his family, none of whom attended his execution—a sad and lonely closing to a once promising life.

He ate a final meal of four eggs, four chicken drumsticks, salsa with four jalapeno pep-pers and lettuce, tortillas, hash browns, garlic bread, two pork chops, grated cheese, sliced onions and sliced tomato, and a pitcher of milk and pitcher of vanilla milkshake to drink.[9]

Powell was executed about 30 minutes after the U.S. Supreme Court refused to hear his eleventh-hour appeal. His attorneys had argued that he would not be a continuing danger to society because he was a model prisoner during his more than 30 years on death row. Juries in 1978, 1991 and 1999 found that Powell was a continuing threat and imposed a sen-tence of death on all three occasions.

When given the chance, Powell offered no final statement to witnesses. He previously apologized to the victim's family by letter. Powell let out a quick gasp and began softly snoring after the drugs were released into his body. He quietly slipped into a lethal slumber and was pronounced dead nine minutes after the drugs were administered. The time of death was 6:19 p.m.[10]

For most of his 32 years on death row, Powell declined to be interviewed by the media. All the while, his lawyers attempted to shift the blame for Ablanedo's murder on to Sheila Meinert. In December 2009, as his appeals began to run out, Powell wrote a letter to the Ablanedo's family. "I am infinitely sorry that I killed Ralph Ablanedo," he wrote. "I shot Officer Ablanedo and I take responsibility for his death. In a few frightful seconds, I stole from you and the world the precious and irreplaceable life of a good man.... There is no excuse for what I did."[11]

Not everyone in Ablanedo's family was impressed with Powell's last minute act of con-trition. Irene Ablanedo, Officer Ablanedo's sister, was a witness at Powell's execution. She was eager to stand at the window next to the death chamber, some five feet away from Powell as he was administered his lethal injection. The pain burned in Irene. "I can't wait for that bastard to take his last breath," she said. "That is what he deserves."[12]

After U.S. Supreme Court outlawed the death penalty, Texas commuted the sentence of every inmate on death row. It wasn't long before Texas was back in the execution business. The legislature passed a new death penalty statute in 1973.

When Powell arrived on death row in 1978, Texas had not yet executed an offender under the new law. Since then, 459 prisoners preceded him to the death chamber, by far more than any other state in the nation. About half that many have had their sentences com-muted or overturned, and 36 have died from other causes. Powell was one of only twelve prisoners remaining on Texas' death row who committed their capital offenses in the 1970's.[13]

Before Powell, the longest time a prisoner served on Texas's death row before being executed was 24 years. Robert Excell White killed a store owner and two customers in a robbery in 1974, and was executed in 1999. Five prisoners have been on death row longer than Powell. Two of them, Raymond Riles and Clarence Jordan, are considered mentally incompetent and ineligible for execution. Ronald Chambers and Anthony Pierce both had their death sentences vacated by the federal courts in 2008, and the state is seeking to have them reimposed. The fifth, Harvey Earvin, is on death row for the 1976 shotgun slaying of a 75-year-old gas station attendant.[14]

* * *

About 150 current and former Austin police officers traveled to Huntsville for the execution—meeting for lunch in a local hotel to watch a video about Ablanedo's life. Most retired officers were wearing black "Journey to Justice" T-shirts. Some wiped tears from their eyes. After being escorted to the prison by Huntsville police, the Austin officers assembled in seven lines—those who had worked with Ablanedo stood at the front—to serve as an honor guard for the slain officer's family.[15]

The officers stood at attention and saluted as Bruce and Judy Mills walked to the prison entrance. Bruce was Ablanedo's colleague and later married his widow and adopted his children; Ablanedo's 87-year-old mother, Betsy; and other family members were greeted and given hugs by Austin Police Chief Art Acevedo.[16]

Acevedo said later that Ablanedo's relatives were overwhelmed by the display of support. "They were very touched," he said, adding that the encounter was emotional for him as well. "When you see his widow and Bruce Mills and his mother start to cry it's hard not to feel their pain," the chief said. "A mother should never have to bury her child." Once the prison doors closed, the officers broke ranks and milled around.[17]

Suddenly, nearby protesters fired up their microphone: "We are here because in one hour the State of Texas is going to murder David Lee Powell," a voice loudly proclaimed—greeted by cheers from many of the police officers. "David Powell, the 27-year-old drug addict, is not the same person as the sober and remorseful 59-year-old man who is being executed today," Nell Warnes, who had visited with Powell since 2004, told protesters later. "From my long-term interaction with David, I am certain that he is no longer a threat to our society."[18]

When it became apparent that Powell was going to be executed, the anti–death penalty protesters kept their distance from the officers and stood silently outside the walls of the Texas State Penitentiary at Huntsville.

CHAPTER 28

Ronnie Lee Gardner, Utah. Executed June 18

Ronnie Lee Gardner died strapped in a chair, a hood over his head, and a white target over his heart. Five rifles, four loaded with a shell and one with a blank, were aimed at his chest just after midnight on June 18, 2010.

Gardner was the first man in 14 years executed in the United States by firing squad. He was the third man to die by firing squad since the U.S. Supreme Court reinstated capital punishment in 1976. Unlike Utah native Gary Gilmore, who infamously uttered the last words "Let's do it" on January 17, 1977, Gardner could muster few words before a black hood was fastened over his head. Asked if he had anything to say during the two minutes afforded him, Gardner said simply, "I do not, no."[1]

*   *   *

Prison officials described Gardner's mood as "reflective" and "calm," in the hours leading up to his execution. Gardner slept, read David Baldacci's *Divine Justice*, looked through his mail and watched *The Lord of the Rings* trilogy. At around 8:45 p.m. Gardner met with a bishop of the Church of Jesus Christ of Latter-day Saints, described as a friend and trusted spiritual advisor. Gardner sat on a bunk in the observation cell and spoke to the bishop through a small port used for handcuffing inmates. Gardner finished meeting with the bishop and attorneys by 9:30 p.m.[2]

Gardner was escorted without incident by prison personnel down the 90 foot hallway to the prison's execution chamber just before midnight, a stark contrast to the fatal escape attempt he undertook 25 years before that resulted in this death sentence.

Soon after Gardner arrived at the death chamber, Utah Attorney General Mark Shurtleff spoke with prison officials by telephone and told them there was no legal reason not to proceed with the execution.

Gardner fasted for 36 hours before his execution. He drank only vitamin water and soft drinks. Gardner ate his last meal two nights before the scheduled execution—a feast of steak, lobster tail, apple pie, vanilla ice cream and a 7UP. Gardner was moved to a smaller observation cell after meeting with family the night before his scheduled execution.[3]

The five executioners, certified police officers who volunteered for the task and remain anonymous, stood about 25 feet away, behind a wall cut with a gunport, and were armed with matching .30-caliber Winchester rifles. One was loaded with a blank so no one knows who fired the fatal shot. Sandbags stacked behind Gardner's chair kept the bullets from ricocheting around the cinderblock room.[4]

Utah Department of Corrections Director Thomas Patterson said the countdown cadence went "5–4–3…" with the shooters starting to fire at the count of 2. Gardner's arm tensed and jerked back when he was hit. As the medical examiner checked for vital signs the hood was pulled back, revealing Gardner's head tilted back and to the right, his mouth slightly open.[5]

* * *

There have been 49 executions carried out in Utah since the 1850s. Forty of those executions were by firing squad. The method has also been widely used around the globe and was long the primary method of execution employed by the military, even in the United States. However, lethal injection has become the primary method of execution used by all of the 32 states that have capital punishment, according to the Death Penalty Information Center.[6]

Utah's territorial government sought permission from the U.S. Supreme Court to use the firing squad back in the 1870s. The Court said that "execution by shooting was not prohibited by the Eighth Amendment's cruel and unusual punishment clause, in that the method did not entail torture or unnecessary cruelty."[7]

The use of the firing squad was also consistent with the 19th century doctrine of the state's predominant religion. Early members of the Church of Jesus Christ of Latter-day Saints believed in the concept of "blood atonement"—that only through spilling one's own blood—could a condemned person adequately atone for their crimes and be redeemed in the next life. The church no longer preaches such teachings and offers no opinion on the use of the firing squad.[8]

Kent Scheidegger of the Criminal Justice Legal Foundation agrees that capital punishment should not amount to torture but says the average person "is not really all that concerned with a murderer experiencing painless death." Public debate is focused more on the larger issue of the death penalty and whether or not the punishment deters crime. "Arguing over the method of execution is kind of a distraction," said Scheidegger.[9]

Deborah W. Denno, a law professor at Fordham University and an expert on the death penalty told the *New York Times* the most humane way to carry out the death penalty is through the use of a firing squad.

Denno said the firing squad is quick, effective and affordable. "It's the most humane procedure," Denno said. "It's only because of this Wild West notion that people are against it."

In 1996, more than 150 media outlets descended on Utah to cover the execution of John Taylor, painting the execution as an Old West-style of justice that allows killers to go out in a blaze of glory that embarrassed the state. There are 10 men on Utah's death row. Three offenders, not including Gardner, have selected the firing squad as their preferred method of execution.[10]

The international publicity that followed the 1996 execution prompted Utah lawmakers to amend the capital punishment law in 2004. The amendment barred the practice of inmates choosing the method of execution. The law now provides that lethal injection is the default method of execution. Inmates sentenced before 2004—like Gardner—could continue to choose their method of execution. In repealing the option, Utah lawmakers said they disliked the negative media attention the firing squad brought to the state.[11]

* * *

Gardner's date with the firing squad was the result of a life of violence and mayhem that devastated countless families. According to court records,[12] in February of 1980, Ronnie Lee Gardner was sent to prison for the first time. He was convicted of robbery. A little more than a year later, Gardner and another inmate escaped from prison. Two weeks after that, Gardner tracked down a man who was sleeping with his girlfriend. During an ensuing gun battle, Gardner was wounded. As a result of the wound, Gardner was arrested and returned to prison.

Gardner was, by then, a career criminal. He served sentences in the Utah State Prison for robbery, burglary and escape. On August 6, 1984, Gardner was taken to the University of Utah Medical Center for a check-up where he overpowered a guard, stole his pistol and escaped for a second time.

In October of 1984, Gardner amped up his criminal behavior. Gardner shot and killed Melvyn Otterstrom as he tended bar at the Cheers Tavern in Salt Lake City. Otterstrom was a husband and father who worked at the Utah Paper Box Company as a controller and moonlighted as a bartender part-time in the evenings. The medical examiner testified in a pretrial hearing that Otterstrom was lying on his back on the floor when he was shot in the face. Darcy Perry McCoy, Gardner's co-conspirator, testified under a grant of immunity in the Otterstrom case that she helped Gardner plan a robbery and waited for him in a car outside Cheers the night of the killing. Immunity means that McCoy would not be prosecuted for her role in the murder.

Gardner was being held under a $1.5 million bond. On April 2, 1985, Gardner was being transported from the Utah State Prison to the Metropolitan Hall of Justice in Salt Lake City for a pretrial hearing related to the murder of Otterstrom. As Gardner and two guards entered the courthouse basement, Darcy Perry McCoy's sister, Carma Jolley Hainsworth, walked up and handed Gardner a gun. She also hid a bag containing men's clothing, duct tape and a knife in a tote bag under a sink in the women's bathroom in the basement of the courthouse.

Gardner and security guards exchanged gunfire. Gardner was shot in the chest and through a lung. He then retreated from the basement hallway. In his attempt to escape, Gardner entered the archives room, where he saw two attorneys, Robert Macri and Michael Burdell, hiding behind the door. Gardner pointed the gun at Macri and cocked the hammer of the gun. Burdell exclaimed, "Oh, my God!" Turning, Gardner shot Burdell, who died in surgery 45 minutes after the shooting.

Gardner then forced prison officer Richard Thomas, who was also in the basement, to lead him out of the archives room to a stairwell leading to the second floor. As Gardner crossed the lobby, he shot and seriously wounded Nicholas G. Kirk, a uniformed bailiff who was unarmed and had just stepped off an elevator. Gardner climbed the stairs to the next floor, where he took Wilburn Miller, a vending machine serviceman, as a hostage. As Gardner exited the building, Miller broke free and escaped. Once outside, Gardner was surrounded by half a dozen policemen with weapons drawn. He was ordered to drop his weapon. He threw his gun to the ground and surrendered to the officers.

* * *

Wayne Jorgensen, a prison officer assigned to guard Gardner at the hospital, testified at trial that Gardner told him he shot Burdell because he thought Burdell looked as if he would attack him. According to Jorgensen, Gardner also declared that he would have killed anyone who tried to stop him from escaping.

The thrust of Gardner's defense was that he was in such pain and physical distress after he was wounded that his shooting Burdell was only a reaction and therefore the killing was unintentional. In preparation for trial, defense counsel spoke with the emergency room doctors who treated Gardner. The doctors told counsel that Gardner was not in shock when he came into the emergency room, did not have excessive bleeding, was lucid and demanding and was aware of the situation.

At trial, Gardner took the stand and testified on direct examination that he had been convicted of various crimes, including crimes of violence. Defense counsel elicited this information because he believed that the prosecution would use those convictions to impeach Gardner, and he wanted to "steal the prosecution's thunder."

Gardner remained a violent predator even while in prison. He captured headlines numerous times for attacks on other inmates. In 1994, he stabbed another inmate with a homemade knife several times and was involved in a standoff inside a prison visiting room where he broke down a glass partition, barricaded the door and had sex with his half-brother's wife as officers looked on helplessly.[13]

Carma Jolley Hainsworth, Gardner's accomplice in his attempted escape, pleaded guilty to aiding in an escape and was sentenced to one to 15 years in prison.

* * *

Members of the victims' families argued both for and against Gardner's death. All said they wanted to end a long nightmare. "This story must be allowed to slip into history," said Jason Otterstrom during the commutation hearing. "Our families need peace."[14]

Supporters of Gardner's victims waited at the Utah State Capitol. The nervous sounds of tapping feet or whispered conversations were all that remained as a small crowd waited for the attorney general to re-emerge. "Ronnie Lee Gardner will never kill again. He will never assault anyone again," Attorney General Shurtleff said to a silenced audience. Gardner was pronounced dead at 12:20 p.m. "Now Ronnie Lee Gardner will be held accountable to a higher power, and I pray he will find more mercy than he showed his victims," Shurtleff said.[15]

"I don't agree with what he done or what they done but I'm relieved he's free," said Gardner's brother, Randy Gardner, after the execution. "He's had a rough life. He's been incarcerated and in chains his whole damn life, now he's free. I'm happy he's free, just sad the way he went."[16]

The execution was witnessed by the media who were separated from other witnesses in observation rooms on opposite ends of the execution chamber. The witnesses sat in the observation rooms behind reflective glass so they could not be seen.

Burdell's family opposed the death penalty and asked for Gardner's life to be spared, but Otterstrom's family lobbied the parole board against Gardner's request for clemency and a reduced sentence. Nick Kirk was a bailiff at the courthouse the day of Gardner's botched escape. Shot and wounded in the lower abdomen, Kirk suffered chronic health problems the rest of his life. Kirk's daughter, Tami Stewart, said before the execution she believed Gardner's death would bring her family some closure. "I think at that moment, he will feel that fear that his victims felt," she said.[17]

Just after midnight, Gardner's family members leaned against each other in a tight cluster and sobbed. As Lynyrd Skynyrd's "Free Bird" played, the group somberly sang along. Some of Gardner relatives whooped and cheered as they released 24 balloons decorated with messages. "I love you, Ron!" some of them screamed, falling into each other's arms. Gardner's daughter, Brandie Gardner, put her hands to her face and sobbed.[18]

Barb Webb, another daughter of Nick Kirk, sobbed when news of the execution came. "I'm so relieved it's all over," she said, hugging her daughter. "I just hope my sister, who just passed away, and my father, and all of the other victims are waiting for his sorry ass. I hope they get to go down after him."[19]

Gardner was the first and only person executed in Utah in 2010. Utah courts sentenced seven killers to death prior to Gardner receiving his death sentence. Although the state has executed seven offenders since 1976, ten inmates remain on death row.

CHAPTER 29

Michael James Perry, Texas. Executed July 10

Michael James Perry lay strapped to a gurney within the death chamber of the Texas State Penitentiary at Huntsville. His final words were, "I want to let everyone here who is involved in this atrocity know they're forgiven by me." Perry did not have a lot of supporters in Huntsville before he spoke. He had fewer supporters after he spoke.

The daughter of one of Perry's victims, who was apprehensive about the death penalty, said execution day "was not a good day no matter what anyone says" and expressed sympathy for Perry's family. But she said his last statement validated the jury's death sentence. "I needed to look into his eyes and see if he was the monster I had made him out to be because he was just a 19-year-old kid at the time," she continued, "When he said that, I knew that he was. I knew that justice had been served."[1]

* * *

Perry had problems from a very early age. At the end of first grade, when he was eight years old, Perry was diagnosed as having attention deficit disorder. At the end of the seventh grade, Perry was diagnosed with oppositional defiant disorder. At the end of the eighth grade, Perry was diagnosed with "conduct disorder." "Antisocial personality disorder" is the adult form of these disorders. Antisocial personality disorder is a psychiatric condition in which a person manipulates, exploits, or violates the rights of others. Symptoms of antisocial personality disorder include repeatedly breaking the law; lying, stealing, and fighting; disregard for the safety of others; and no feeling of guilt.

In junior high, Perry stopped going to school. He frequently ran away from home. Perry stole his mother's jewelry and tried to pawn it, stole his parents' van and ran it into a mailbox, and broke into a neighbor's home to vandalize it.

In September 1997, Perry was sent to Father Flanagan's Boys Town in Nebraska. Three months after his arrival, Perry threatened his house parent, "You know, you people work here. I don't know why you work here. People like me who are going to rape or kill your kids, you know." Perry was promptly sent to the locked facility at Boys Town for four months. Perry was not eligible for mental health care provided at the facility.

Perry's parents, fearing that they would not be able to control Perry, sent him to Casa by the Sea, a secured high school campus in Mexico. Perry graduated from high school, but not from the program at Casa by the Sea. He left on his eighteenth birthday.

Except for some time in the Job Corps, a few months in Houston, and a brief stay with his parents, Perry was essentially homeless after leaving Casa by the Sea. Perry stayed for short periods with acquaintances and in shelters. Moreover, except for the Job Corps, laying tile in Houston and a month at Wal-Mart, Perry did not work after leaving Casa by the Sea.

Perry's incidences of violence continued to pile-up. While in the Montgomery County Jail awaiting trial, Perry was unruly. Perry became belligerent, had to be restrained and tried to bite an officer who was restraining him.

Perry was arrested for deadly conduct after he shot at a house. The night before his arrest for murder, Perry pointed a loaded shotgun at a woman's head and said, "I have already killed somebody; it's not going to hurt me to kill anyone else."[2]

*   *   *

On October 24, 2001, Perry and 19-year-old Jason Burkett went to a friend, Adam Stotler's, home in Montgomery. Adam lived with his mother, Sandra, a nurse.

The reason for the visit was anything but friendly. According to court records,[3] Perry and Burkett decided that they needed one or two new vehicles. They knew that Adam Stotler's mother had "a lot of money" as well as "a newer Camaro and Isuzu Rodeo." They hashed a plan to ask to spend the night at Adam's house. Once everyone was asleep, they would steal the Camaro. Driving Burkett's girlfriend's truck, they went to Adam's house at about 7 p.m. Mrs. Stotler told them that Adam would not be home until 9 p.m.

They drove away, but later decided to go back and steal the car while only Mrs. Stotler was home. They parked down the street and walked back to the house. Burkett knocked on the door and asked to use the phone. Perry grabbed the shotgun and entered the house through the garage. Perry hid in the laundry room and knocked on the back door. When Mrs. Stotler came to answer the door, he shot her with the shotgun. She collapsed to the floor. When he saw that she was still alive and trying to get up, he shot her again.

Perry and Burkett then grabbed some blankets and sheets off the bed to cover her body. Burkett ran down the street and got the truck and loaded her body into the back and covered it with the blankets and sheets. Perry wanted to steal the Camaro, but was unable to find the keys. They drove away in the truck, disposed of the body at Crater Lake, drove to Conroe and picked up Burkett's girlfriend, Kristen Willis.

The group drove back to the Stotlers' house. The plan was to tell Adam that a friend of theirs had shot himself while they were hunting squirrels, and they needed his help. Adam pulled up in an Isuzu Rodeo with his friend, Jeremy Richardson. After Perry and Burkett asked Adam for help, they drove out to a wooded area, while Adam and Jeremy followed in the Rodeo.

According to court records,[4] the four of them got out of their vehicles and walked into the woods while Willis stayed behind in the truck. Adam then suggested that they look for the friend from a different road, so he and Perry drove away in the Rodeo while Burkett and Richardson stayed in the woods.

Adam parked the Rodeo, and the two of them got out. Burkett then approached them with the shotgun, alone. Burkett asked them if they heard gunshots, saying he had fired his shotgun several times to signal his location. In reality, Burkett shot and killed Richardson with those shots.

Burkett then told Adam he would take him to where the others were. Perry walked back to the Rodeo while Adam went with Burkett. Perry saw Burkett shoot Adam, he then covered his eyes and heard another shot. He uncovered his eyes and saw Burkett shoot Adam a third time. Perry then walked over to Adam's body and pulled his car keys out of his pocket.

Burkett and Perry drove the Rodeo back to where Willis was waiting. She became upset with them and drove home. Burkett drove Perry back to the Stotlers'. Perry grabbed Adam's wallet from the Isuzu and took the keys to the Camaro off of his key ring.

As if to demonstrate their callous attitude toward murder, their absence of remorse and lack of empathy, the two men went home, smoked some cigarettes, got cleaned up and went out to a club.

Two days later, Perry was driving the Stotler's Camaro when police observed him violating the traffic code. After a high speed chase, Perry wrecked and fled on foot. He was apprehended and booked as Adam Stotler, whose wallet he was still carrying. He was then released on bond. The next day Sandra Stotler's body was found in Crater Lake.

On October 30, 2010, a Montgomery County sheriff's deputy spotted the stolen Rodeo at a truck stop, with three occupants. The vehicle struck the deputy in the course of fleeing, but the deputy was able to shoot out a rear tire. The vehicle crashed. Perry and Burkett fled on foot, carrying a shotgun. They climbed a fence and ran to a nearby apartment complex, where police arrested them and recovered the shotgun. Perry, who had a deep cut on his arm from the crash, was taken to a hospital for treatment. Officers questioned him at the hospital and obtained a confession[5] which included:

> Once in the house, I hid in the laundry room between the kitchen and garage. I then knocked on the back door, and when Adam's mom came to the back door, I shot her one time in the side near her back with the shotgun. She fell to the floor, and I dropped the shotgun. She then moved or tried to get up or something, and I grabbed the shotgun and shot her one more time. She fell to the floor in front of the laundry room and garage back door. I walked back [to vehicle] to get my cigarettes, and I saw Jason shoot Adam in the left side. I then covered my eyes. I heard a second gunshot and uncovered my eyes. I then saw Jason lean in close to Adam and fire a third shot at close range. I walked over to Adams [sic] body and got his car keys out of his pocket.[6]

* * *

At his trial, Perry claimed that police coerced his confession and ignored his request for a lawyer. "I had a gun shoved in my face," he testified. "At the time, there was quite a bit of excitement. I was under the influence. My arms hurt pretty bad and I was real scared ... my condition in my mind state was that I am going to tell [the detective] anything he wants to hear to get him away from me, to get out of this situation, and that's what I did."[7]

At trial, the defense presented testimony from Perry's biological mother who testified that she used drugs and alcohol until a month or two before Perry was born. Despite this, Perry was full weight and healthy when born. Although no biological relatives had committed murder, Perry's mother testified to a family history of depression, alcoholism, drug use, and thievery. Dr. Gilda Kessner, a clinical psychologist with a forensics background, interviewed Perry and testified that Perry's youthfulness was his greatest risk factor for recidivism. After serving time in prison, Dr. Kessner testified, the likelihood of Perry's becoming violent would drop to zero. The jury didn't buy it.

The jury found Perry guilty of murder. During the sentencing phase, the jury found that Perry posed a continuing threat to society and that there were not sufficient mitigating circumstances to warrant a life sentence. The trial court sentenced Perry to death.[8]

*   *   *

About 90 minutes before Perry was ushered into the death chamber the U.S. Supreme Court rejected a last-minute appeal from his lawyers. They unsuccessfully argued they had new evidence showing Perry was already in jail when Sandra Stotler was murdered. They also contended that Burkett killed Stotler. Prosecutors said a "mountain of evidence" pointed to Perry—most notably that he was seen driving Stotler's stolen car and bragged about the killing before his arrest.[9]

He ate a final meal of three bacon, egg and cheese omelets; three cheese enchiladas; and three cans each of Pepsi, Coke, and Dr. Pepper.[10]

Perry's final words consisted of more than his bizarre offer of forgiveness. Laying on the gurney waiting for the administration of the lethal drugs, Perry continued with his final statement. Looking at his adoptive mother, Gayle Perry, he said, "Mom, I love you," with his voice breaking. "I'm coming home, Dad." Perry's adoptive father died in June. The drugs began to flow. He gave four audible gasps and his breathing slowed. Members of the Stotler and Richardson families watched quietly and intently, while some wiped away tears.[11]

As the drugs took effect, his eyes fluttered and he hiccupped four times. A single tear ran down his right cheek, prompting quiet sobs from his mother, an aunt and friends. The victim's relatives gasped and motioned to each other. Perry was pronounced dead just nine minutes later, at 6:17 p.m. He was the 14th person executed in Texas in 2010.[12]

*   *   *

"Burkett should be up there, too, on the gurney with him," said Charles Richardson, Jeremy's brother, one of the witnesses. "This was friends stabbing friends in the back."[13]

"We can get on with our lives now and have peace," said Stotler's mother, Mary Ann Bockwich. "I just wish Jason Burkett and Kristin Willis were here sitting beside him."[14]

Willis was Burkett's girlfriend at the time of the murders and was present in the wooded area when Adam Stotler and Jeremy Richardson were shot. She testified against Burkett during his trial. Burkett received a life sentence. He was convicted for his involvement in all three murders. He is eligible for parole in 40 years. Ironically, Perry was convicted of only killing Sandra Stotler and received the death penalty.[15]

Neither Perry nor any of his family members ever reached out to the victims' families, Lisa Balloun, Sandra's daughter and Adam's sister, said. "Never. Not once," she said. "He's been blaming and pointing fingers since day one. It just infuriates me; we were the 'bad guys' in this situation."[16]

Montgomery County District Attorney Brett Ligon waited until after the execution to make a public comment. He personally reviewed all the evidence, and said:

> Ethics prevented me from commenting on the ridiculous accusation that Mr. Perry's confession was somehow coerced and the evidence in his criminal case was flawed.... The reality is that Mr. Perry laughed throughout his legal and voluntary confession in which he related gruesome details about the murders of his innocent victims. The remainder of the evidence in the case was as overwhelming as it was disturbing.... Mr. Perry's last words reflected the way he

lived his life: full of hatred, bile and narcissism. I do not relish in the execution of his sentence, but I do not mourn his death. May the victim's families finally have the peace they deserve.[17]

Balloun told her daughters—one was three years old and the other ten months old when Sandra Stotler was murdered—"what a wonderful woman she was" and how Adam was "the best uncle in the world," she said. "Our family is crushed."

For Rosemary Jeffery, Jeremy Richardson's mother, Perry's death has not yet brought the closure she seeks. "It won't be over until Burkett is gone," she said. "Then ... our family can have some rest."[18]

CHAPTER 30

William L. Garner, Ohio. Executed July 13

In the pre-dawn hours of January 26, 1992, William L. Garner gained access to Addie Mack's apartment after stealing keys from her purse while she was receiving treatment at the emergency room of a Cincinnati hospital. Six children, ages eight to 13, were at her apartment alone when Garner used the keys to get inside. He stole some items and set the apartment on fire, killing five of the six children.

Garner took a cab from the apartment to a corner store where he bought Hawaiian Punch, a jelly cake and candy. Eighteen years later, he once again ordered Hawaiian Punch—this time as part of his last meal while awaiting execution at the Southern Ohio Correctional Facility at Lucasville.

* * *

Garner's 2010 date with the executioner began on a cold winter day 18 years prior. According to court records,[1] he was present in the emergency room of University Hospital in Cincinnati, Ohio. Addie Mack was also at the emergency room receiving treatment after a fall. She had left her purse near a pay phone. Garner stole the purse and took Mack's keys, driver's license and wallet. He immediately called a taxicab and asked the driver to take him to Mack's townhouse. At the townhouse were Mack's four children, her niece and a family friend who was also a child.

Garner used Mack's key to gain entry into the townhouse. One of the children woke up, and encountered Garner. He gave her a glass of water and sent her back to bed. He took a telephone, a video cassette recorder, a radio, some video tapes and a television and put them into the cab. He told the cab driver that he had a fight with his girlfriend and she threw him out.

After packing up the cab, Garner returned to the townhouse and set three separate fires. Two of the fires were set in upstairs bedrooms. The third fire was set on the sofa downstairs. He set the fires in spite of the fact that he knew six children were present in the house. Five of the children died from smoke inhalation. Only Mack's oldest child, Rod, escaped the fires, but Denitra Satterwhite, 12, Deondra Freeman, 10, Mykia Mack, 8, Markeca Mason, 11, and Richard Gaines, also 11, all perished.

After setting the fires, Garner jumped in the cab and told the cab driver to take him to a convenience store so he could purchase some snacks, and then to his home. The driver helped him unload the stolen property and carry it into his home. He then gave the cab driver Mack's television to cover the cab fare.

As the police investigated the fires, Mack informed detectives that several items had been removed from her home. Investigators also discovered that two police officers who had received a radio dispatch to respond to an address near the Mack townhouse recalled seeing someone loading several items into a taxicab just prior to the fires.

As a result of a quick and thorough investigation, the cab driver was located and Mack's television was recovered. The cab driver gave police the address where he had taken Garner. Police obtained a search warrant for Garner's home. The police found several items of Mack's property after searching Garner's home. A search of Garner's jacket after he was arrested revealed items stolen from Ms. Mack's purse, including the birth certificates of her children.

Garner gave police a taped statement wherein he admitted starting the fire, but denied any purpose to kill the children. He maintained that he set the fires to cover evidence of the burglary. He stated that he thought the children would smell the smoke, wake up and escape the fires. He made no effort to wake the children. In fact, he sent a child back to bed knowing he was about to start fires in the very bedrooms the children slept.

Garner was indicted on five counts of murder. Each murder count carried three aggravating circumstances for purposes of the death penalty: (1) the killing was committed for the purpose of escaping detection, apprehension, trial or punishment for aggravated burglary; (2) the offense was part of a course of conduct involving the purposeful killing of more than one person; and (3) the offense was committed while he was committing or fleeing immediately after committing the offenses of aggravated burglary and aggravated arson and that Garner acted with prior calculation and design. Garner was also charged with one count of aggravated burglary, two counts of aggravated arson, one count of theft and two counts of receiving stolen property.

Garner filed a motion to suppress—exclude from trial—his statement to police and some of the physical evidence obtained with the search warrant. The trial court ruled in favor of the prosecution and permitted the admission of Garner's statement and all evidence obtained with the search warrant. He pleaded no contest to the theft and the receiving-stolen-property charges. Following a jury trial, Garner was found guilty of five counts of first degree murder. After hearing evidence during the trial's penalty phase the jury recommended the imposition of the death sentence. The trial court accepted the jury's recommendation and sentenced Garner to death on all five murder counts.

*   *   *

Garner was 19 years old when the offenses were committed. He was the youngest of six children, including a twin brother. Shortly after he was born, Garner was returned to the hospital due to "failure to thrive." Failure to thrive is a condition that attaches to some infants whose weight or rate of weight gain is significantly below that of other children of similar age and gender. Failure to thrive has been traced to emotional deprivation as a result of parental withdrawal, rejection, or hostility, as well as economic problems that affect nutrition and living conditions.

Throughout Garner's childhood, he was often without proper food and they had at times to subsist on "sugar bread." At the age of four, Garner would go to the grocery store with his twin brother to carry shopping bags for tips in order to buy food. On some occasions, the children had to steal food to eat. Garner's mother even stole money from the children and "went out with it" instead of buying food.[2]

At one point, Garner's mother put her children into foster homes while she was hospitalized in a psychiatric ward. The children were beaten regularly. An infant sister was killed by one of Garner's mother's boyfriends. Garner's older sister was raped by one of his mother's husbands. Another boyfriend intentionally scalded the feet of Garner's brother, causing permanent disfiguration. Garner, his sister and his twin brother were beaten and raped by an older brother. One of the mother's husbands was an alcoholic. On some occasions, the children were forced to help their mother beat her boyfriends.[3]

No interest was shown in the children's schoolwork or activities. Garner began to do poorly in school when foster care placement separated him from his twin brother.

Psychologists Nancy Schmidt-Goessling and Jeffrey Smalldon found that Garner suffered from organic brain impairment and had an IQ of 76, which is in the borderline range of intellectual functioning. Dr. Smalldon concluded that he had a residual attention disorder, borderline intellectual functioning and a mixed personality disorder with borderline antisocial features.

Psychologist Joseph Schroeder testified on behalf of the state. He opined that Garner had a learning disability and no organic brain damage. His findings were obviously contrary to those of the psychologist who testified on behalf of Garner.[4]

Garner stated that he did not intend to kill the five children. He said he had a secondary motivation for setting the fire. He wanted to draw attention to the children's squalid living conditions. He told police that he had noticed the bedroom "full of girls" and that one of them had asked him for water. He also said he had been in another bedroom where the two boys slept.[5]

*   *   *

Garner arrived in Lucasville on July 12, 2010, the day before his scheduled execution, a place where he was first admitted to death row 18 years earlier. Back then, the Southern Ohio Correctional Facility housed condemned killers who were headed to the electric chair. The prison at the time was the only one in the state to house death row inmates. Much had changed since then.

The electric chair has been replaced with lethal injection. Originally lethal injection was carried out using a three drug protocol and more recently with a single dose of sodium thiopental. Garner, who was sentenced shortly after he turned 20, had been housed at the Mansfield Correctional Facility since 1995, where he lived alone in a 94-square-foot cell. When not in trouble, he was permitted out of his cell for up to 2½ hours per day.[6]

Garner spent his final hours watching television and talking on the telephone with a friend and his twin brother. He visited with his mother and other relatives, as well as with spiritual advisers and his legal team, and took Holy Communion about an hour and a half before the lethal injection procedure began.[7]

As part of his last meal at the Death House, Garner had Hawaiian Punch, as he did the night of the murders. His final meal also included a Porterhouse steak, barbeque chicken and ribs, sweet potato pie, fried shrimp and chocolate ice cream.[8]

It took about 40 minutes for the prep-work and the insertion of two shunts while Garner was in his holding cell. The preparations were broadcast into the witness rooms through video monitors. He then took the 17-step walk to the death chamber and climbed on to the gurney.[9]

While strapped to a wooden gurney, Garner held a dreadlock of hair from a friend in his left hand and read from a hand-written note held up by an official. He apologized to the six family members of victims who were there to witness the execution, separated from Garner by only four feet and a glass window.

"If this will give you closure, I hope it will," he said. Garner thanked the state of Ohio, his spiritual advisers and a friend Stacy Evans the source of the clipped dreadlock he held in his hand as he died. Garner's voice cracked once as he said his goodbyes, but he never lost his composure. "I thought I'd never be free, but I am free now," he said.[10]

Garner glanced over at his niece, a soft smile breaking over his face as the first of the five syringes of sodium thiopental was pumped into his veins. He appeared at peace. If he was scared, he showed no sign.[11]

There was an unusual 10-minute delay before Garner was pronounced dead. During the delay a curtain shielded Garner's body from the view of witnesses, the media in the death chamber and those watching on closed circuit television.

Ernie L. Moore, director of the Ohio Department of Rehabilitation and Correction, said later that when the curtain was pulled—usually signaling the end of an execution and the announcement of the time of death—the coroner said he heard "faint heart sounds" even though there were "no other life signs." Garner was not dead, even though the lethal drug had been flowing through his veins for nine minutes.[12]

No one spoke as Garner lay dying. Garner's body was re-checked for a heartbeat. This time there was none; the curtain was opened, and the execution was over. Warden Donald Morgan broke the silence when the curtain opened at 10:39 a.m. "Time of death, 10:38 a.m."[13]

* * *

Rod Mack, the lone survivor of the fire on January 26, 1992, watched Garner's execution, as did the parents of some of the deceased children. So many family members wanted to see Garner die that prison officials set up a room where three witnesses watched the execution on closed-circuit television. About 10:20 a.m. as the execution began, a storm that had been hanging over the southern Ohio hills was unleashed. There were several loud claps of thunder, and a heavy rain began pelting the prison roof.[14]

Mack and five others were accommodated in the witness room facing the execution chamber. None of the victims' family members spoke to the media after the execution.[15]

"He is finally at peace and that was very important," Garner's older sister, Ross, said after his death. She said she hoped the family members could one day forgive him. "He was ready. Peewee had been ready," Ross said of her brother's execution, "Through the years, we prepared for this day."[16]

CHAPTER 31

Derrick Leon Jackson, Texas. Executed July 20

The Houston Police Department unveiled a new fingerprint system in 1995. The system immediately began to pay dividends. The fingerprints of a state prison inmate, Derrick Jackson, matched prints lifted from a beer can and a glass tumbler in a bedroom at the scene of a 1988 double murder. In 1995, Jackson was serving a 12-year sentence for a robbery he committed in 1992.

According to court records,[1] on September 12, 1988, Alan Wrotenbery, a music teacher, failed to show up for work at Deer Park Elementary School in east Harris County, Texas. The school principal contacted the manager of the Greenway Plaza apartments in central Houston where Wrotenbery lived. After knocking at the door for several minutes, the manager used a master key to unlock the apartment. Once inside, he saw nothing disturbed in the living room or kitchen, but upon proceeding to one of the bedrooms, he found a body covered with blood. The manager, distraught by what he saw, left immediately and called the police.

Police officers found Wrotenbery's body on his bedroom floor. He was wearing only a pair of swimming trunks. In the other bedroom, officers found the nude body of his roommate, Forrest Henderson lying face-down in his bed. Blood was all over the bedroom walls, doors, and curtains.

Police found a bloody metal bar in the hallway and a bloody knife in the kitchen sink. Both victims' wallets were missing, and Henderson's car was gone. It appeared as though the killer was invited into the apartment. There were no markings on the door or lock that would indicate a forced entry.

Wrotenbery's throat was cut. He also received at least three blows to the back of the head with a narrow, blunt instrument, consistent with the metal bar found in the apartment. Henderson had a six-inch skull fracture caused by blunt force, and multiple stab wounds to his chest and upper body. He also had a shallow, non-fatal cut on his neck and defensive wounds on both arms. The victims had been dead at least eight hours before their bodies were discovered.

Police collected blood samples and fingerprints from the crime scene, including a fingerprint from a glass in Henderson's bedroom and a bloody print found on his bedroom door. They also picked up a DNA sample from blood stains on some bathroom towels. Despite this evidence, they were unable to connect the prints or DNA to a suspect.

David Trujillo, who lived next door to the victims, told police that at around 4:45 a.m. the day before the bodies were discovered, he was awakened by the sound of Wrotenbery screaming, "Oh my God! No. No." He also heard what sounded like someone being hit numerous times with a pipe or baseball bat. After 30 minutes of silence, he heard the water running for about 45 minutes. Trujillo never heard Henderson's front door open or anyone leave. Trujillo later told police that he often saw "street trash" entering and leaving the apartment when Henderson lived there alone. Therefore, he was not shocked by what he heard only a few days before. He said that screaming and fighting were common in Henderson's apartment.

On the morning of September 13, Houston police spotted a car going more than 90 mph on the freeway following a burglary at a mall. The car crashed in a vacant lot. The driver fled on foot into an apartment complex and escaped. The car was identified as Henderson's. No other evidence was recovered from it.

It would be seven years before Derrick Jackson would be linked to the murders. Jackson's arrest was not the result of some cold case investigation led by relentless detectives who would not rest until the case was solved. Jackson was arrested seven years later because the police did a pretty thorough crime scene investigation. They found prints and blood, and technology finally caught up to Jackson.

Henderson and Wrotenbery were tenors with the Houston Grand Opera. Wrotenbery also taught music at an elementary school in a Houston suburb. He'd been house-sitting at Henderson's apartment following a divorce until he could find a place of his own. Henderson had just returned to Houston after performing with the opera in Scotland.

On the day of their deaths, they had been rehearsing for an opera production of Georges Bizet's *Carmen*. Wrotenbery returned to the apartment after rehearsals. Henderson visited some Montrose bars. Police claimed that Henderson picked up Jackson in a bar and brought him home. The police characterized Jackson as a predator who targeted gay men.[2]

*   *   *

In 1995, nearly seven years after the murders, the Houston police implemented a new state-of-the-art fingerprint system with an expanded database. The new system matched Jackson with prints lifted from Henderson's apartment.

At trial, an expert in blood-spatter interpretation testified that the bloody fingerprint could only be formed by touching a blood drop while the blood was still wet and could not have been the result of a blood drop landing on an old fingerprint.

A state DNA expert testified at trial that Jackson's DNA type matched DNA isolated from blood stains on a red towel and a beige towel located in Henderson's bathroom. That expert testified that Jackson's DNA type for that specific test conducted on the samples from the two towels would occur once out of every 224 people in the black population.[3] Jackson was African-American.

A second DNA expert, Joseph Chu, testified that he conducted a different kind of DNA test on the blood found on a bathroom towel in the apartment. Chu calculated that the odds that another black person would possess the same DNA profile found on the towel were one out of 7.2 million. That appeared to be conclusive evidence.[4]

In 1995, DNA analysis was still cutting-edge technology but had become ingrained in America's pop culture. DNA evidence took on a prominent role in the so called "Trial of the Century." In *California v. O.J. Simpson*, DNA experts testified about a glove found at Simpson's house, which had blood on it matching Ron Goldman's blood and blood discovered at the crime scene, Nicole Brown's house, which matched Simpson.

Jackson was not as fortunate as Simpson. Johnny Cochran's, "If it doesn't fit you must acquit" kept Simpson out of prison for that crime; however, the jury in Jackson's case, after considering all of the evidence, found him guilty of murder and sentenced him to death.

* * *

Jackson said bad decisions led to burglaries and robberies and ultimately the prison term, but he denied involvement in the killings in spite of the fingerprints and the DNA match.[5]

In an interview from death row leading up to his scheduled execution, Jackson said he didn't want to die but wasn't scared. "It's more a reluctance that it had to come to this," he said. "It's like you have terminal disease for a number of years and finally they say you're not going to be able to live with it any longer so you're going to have to get your affairs together with your family and within yourself."[6]

"It's obvious I'm getting framed," Jackson said in a death row interview. "I'm not your bad guy. People who know me know I'm a good guy."[7]

Jackson said from prison he realized "two people lost their lives and I feel for their families ... I saw the pictures. It was a savage scene," he said, adding that he understood jurors had to "do something when two guys were killed like that." But when they found him guilty, "It kind of blew me away," he said. "I didn't do it."[8]

Michael Bromwich an independent investigator hired to review operations of the Houston Police Department's troubled crime lab, found fault with the way police investigated and pursued Jackson. In his 2007 report reviewing the police crime lab, Bromwich found that a technician apparently manipulated lab findings to bolster the case against the detectives' prime suspect who initially was not Jackson. "The employee neglected to report that Type B blood was found on an apartment door. Only when a charge was later lodged against Jackson, who has Type B blood, was the fact added to the report." The review's findings never got any traction with regard to Jackson's conviction.[9]

In his death row interview, Jackson challenged those fingerprint findings and blasted a series of defense lawyers who, he said, "helped me get down to the execution chamber ... I don't stay up at night and have nightmares," Jackson said. "I pray for myself. I hate the fact that I'm being blamed and will be killed, but it's more sadness than hate."[10]

* * *

Jackson ate a final meal of fried chicken, BBQ ribs, French fries, German chocolate cake, two bananas and ice water. He was then escorted to the death chamber.[11]

He was strapped to a gurney and prepared for the execution by prison personnel. After the IVs were put in place, the warden asked if Jackson had a final statement. Jackson said nothing. He never moved, he did not make eye contact either with his own family or the victim's relatives. He stared at the ceiling of the death chamber. As the lethal drugs began to flow, he gasped several times. Eight minutes later, at 6:20 p.m. he was dead.[12]

"I'm relieved that it's over," Carl Wrotenbery, 80, said after watching his son's killer die. "It's something that had to be done. I did not look forward to it." He said he came to the Texas State Penitentiary at Huntsville from his home in Fort Worth, about 175 miles away, out of a "sense of duty and responsibility" to his family and that he found Jackson's silence at the end "disappointing" but not unexpected. "I didn't expect any pleasure and I certainly didn't receive any," Wrotenbery said.[13]

Jackson's father came to Huntsville with Jackson's two brothers to witness the execution. No eleventh-hour appeal was filed to try to stop the execution. The Texas Court of Criminal Appeals rejected Jackson's final appeal earlier in the week, and the Texas Board of Pardons and Paroles turned down his request for clemency. The elder Mr. Jackson wept while watching his son slowly fade into death.

"Technology caught up with him," said Bill Hawkins, a Harris County district attorney who prosecuted the case. Hawkins said the odds against the DNA match actually belonging to someone other than Jackson were "off the charts."[14]

CHAPTER 32

Joseph D. Burns, Mississippi.
Executed July 21

Joseph Daniel Burns apologized to Mike McBride's family members for the "evil" he brought upon them 16 years ago. "I pray you will one day forgive me, not for myself but for yourself."[1] The evil he brought on the McBrides would soon cost him his life as he laid strapped to a gurney at the death house within the Mississippi State Penitentiary at Parchman.

According to court records,[2] Burns and Phillip Hale went to the Town House Motel on Gloster Street in Tupelo, Mississippi, where Mike McBride was the hotel manager. Phillip Hale and McBride were friends, and Hale had previously introduced Burns to McBride. Hale went in and asked McBride if they could stay there three or four days. McBride said, "Sure," and Hale went out to the truck, got his bag and told Burns to come inside. The two of them "hung out for a while" with McBride. Burns and Hale then went to get something to eat and watch a movie.

On the way back from the movie, Burns and Hale decided to rob McBride. They agreed that Hale would hit McBride, and Burns would take the money. When they got back to the motel, Hale hit McBride and knocked him to the ground. Hale left the room, and when he returned, Burns was stabbing McBride in the back of the neck with a knife, a fork and a Phillips screwdriver while McBride pleaded, "Why me?"

McBride's body was found in his living quarters at the Town House Motel. McBride died from a combination of blunt force injuries to the head and neck caused by the numerous blows to the head and back of the neck inflicted by Burns and exsanguination, loss of blood, from the injuries to his face and neck.

After the stabbing, Burns and Hale wiped away their fingerprints, grabbed $3,000 from the safe and took off. Burns had broken the lock off of the safe with a pair of pliers.

After the murder, Burns and Hale returned to a trailer in Verona where they were living with Janie Taylor and Brandi Sides. Burns went into Janie's room, whom he was dating at the time, woke her up, told her what they had done, counted the money and divided the money evenly between himself and Hale.

Hale then went to his brother Jeff's shop, but he was out of town. Burns showed up later and informed Hale that he had thrown the "stuff" behind the trailer park where they lived.

Hale later told his brother that he and Burns killed McBride. Burns also told Hale's brother what had happened. The following weekend, Burns, Hale and Jeff went to Tunica to the casinos and spent the money they had stolen from McBride. The three returned to Tupelo with only about $200.

Hale and Burns were not arrested until August of 1995. The Tupelo Police Department arrested them pursuant to an investigation that ensued after two anonymous phone calls were received by Crime Stoppers.

While Burns was placed in Lee County Jail, he began corresponding with a female prisoner, Contina Kohlheim. In the letters Burns sent Kohlheim, he wrote about killing a man. "Look about the guy I killed, me and Phillip were dealing with a lot of dope—and Phillip was giving our dope to this guy. He owed us $58,000. I told Phillip to ask him one more time to pay us, but he never did. So that night we went to the town house, and I killed his ass." In the other letter Burns sent Kohlheim, he wrote, "I took a man's life now I'm looking at the Death Penalty."

The letters were signed from "JoJo," or "Love JoJo." Burns gave the letters to a male trustee who, in turn, gave them to a prison guard who then gave them to a female trustee to deliver since the male prisoners were not allowed to go to the female side of the jail. Kohlheim turned the letters over to the police.

Following a request by the district attorney's office, the corrections staff obtained a handwriting sample from Burns under the pretense of having him write down a list of requested visitors. A comparison was then made between the letters written to Kohlheim and the known writing sample of Burns.

An expert determined that there was a strong probability that the signatures on both letters were Burns'. The expert further determined that the content of both letters were probably written by Burns. There was also a fingerprint analysis done on the letters. Burns' fingerprints were found on both letters obtained from Contina Kohlheim.

*   *   *

The murder of Mike McBride was not Joseph Burns' first brush with the law. Court records show that Burns had been convicted of burglary and larceny in 1987. He also had an earlier conviction, but that record is sealed because he was a juvenile at the time.

Burns' attorney during the 1987 case was Roger Wicker, who went on to be a U.S. Senator from Mississippi. Burns was sentenced to five years but given a chance to enter into the state's Regimented Inmate Discipline Program (RID). The RID Program was Mississippi's version of a boot camp prison diversion program. The Department of Corrections describes RID as an intensive para-military program intended to rehab inmates in a short time period.[3]

On the day of Burns' scheduled execution, Governor Haley Barbour denied his request for clemency. "I will not substitute my judgment for that of the courts, which have considered the matter," Barbour said. Mississippi allows the death penalty in cases where a person is convicted of murder along with another felony, such as robbery.[4]

Burns was scheduled to die at 6 p.m. on July 21, 2010, by lethal injection.

*   *   *

Mississippi became a state in 1817. Since that time, according to the Mississippi Department of Corrections,[5] the state has used several forms of execution. Hanging was the first method of execution used in the state and continued to be utilized until October 11, 1940. On that date, Hilton Fortenberry, convicted of murder in Jefferson Davis County, became the first prisoner to be executed by electrocution. Between 1940 and 1952, the old oak electric chair was moved from county to county to conduct executions. During the 12-year span, 75 prisoners were executed.

In 1954, a gas chamber was installed within the gates of the Mississippi State Penitentiary in Parchman. It replaced the electric chair, which today is on display at the Mississippi Law Enforcement Training Academy. Gearald A. Gallego became the first prisoner to be executed by lethal gas on March 3, 1955. During the course of the next 34 years, 35 death row inmates were executed in the gas chamber. On June 21, 1989, Leo Edwards was the last person executed by gas in Mississippi.

In 1984, Mississippi amended its law to provide for lethal injection. In 1998, the Mississippi legislature removed lethal gas as a form of execution.

*   *   *

During the afternoon of the day scheduled for Burns' execution, the U.S. Supreme Court ordered the state to delay the execution while justices reviewed issues raised by Burns' attorneys, including whether Burns was denied a mental evaluation. State officials agreed to the delay. However, less than a half hour after the originally scheduled time for execution, the stay was lifted. Burns' death sentence was reinstated.

Soon after the denial was announced, witnesses were escorted to the execution site. Burns had spent the day in a cell near the death chamber. He visited with his mother, three sisters and two daughters.

Commissioner Christopher Epps said he visited with Burns early on the day of execution and again in the afternoon. "He is resigned he will be executed today, and I think he is ready."[6]

Burns did not eat breakfast that morning. He was given a plate of sausage, biscuits and eggs, but Commissioner Epps said he declined the food. For lunch, Burns ate salami with bread, cheese, pickles, lettuce and juice. He had an afternoon snack of roast beef and turkey sandwiches and a Coca-Cola.[7]

Burns did not initially request a last meal but later changed his mind. He was offered the standard meal all other inmates are given for dinner—red beans and rice, corn, greens, cornbread, cake and iced tea.

"He didn't see a big deal in not requesting a last meal," Commissioner Epps said. "It's the first time I can recall an inmate didn't request one," Epps said after he questioned Burns about not making a last meal request. Although the Department of Corrections requires that last meals be prepared by the regular staff, Epps related that it's not uncommon to see some pretty unusual and even extravagant requests.[8]

Strapped to a gurney with IV tubes in his arms, he recited the 23rd Psalm. After the final line—"And I will dwell in the house of the Lord forever"—he added, "You can believe that because that's where I'm going. All right, devil, let's do your work. That's it," he said as corrections officials cut off the microphone.

After a short time he closed his eyes and was still. Although he apologized to the McBride family, he continued to complain to prison officials, right up to the time of his execution that Phillip Hale played a greater role in McBride's death.[9]

During the original trial, Hale faced a jury and testified against Burns and blamed the murder on him. Now, while Burns was about to face his creator, once again he continued to lay some responsibility at the feet of Hale.

His mother and a sister were on hand as witnesses. They did not go to the media center to speak after the execution.

*   *   *

McBride's brother-in-law, Greg Gordon of Tupelo, read from a statement in which he asked for prayers for both families. Gordon said it was only through those prayers that the McBride family could forgive Burns for what he did. "It is only through God's love, mercy and grace that we were able to forgive and pray for Burns," Gordon said. "Today, justice was served for that senseless act," he said.[10]

Burns was serious about his final statement. It was reported that he rehearsed the statement of contrition for hours before he was put to death. Burns had a renewed hope when he learned of the Supreme Court's request for a stay of execution, but at 6:16 p.m. the court cleared the way for Burns' execution, and he was dead in less than an hour.[11]

Joining Gordon in the witness observation room was McBride's nephew, Josh Criddle; three members of media selected as witnesses; and Governor Haley Barbour's representative, State Senator Merle Flowers. Also in the room was a representative of the Mississippi Department of Corrections Division of Victims Services.

The representative actually held Gordon's hand throughout the execution, which took about 10 minutes from beginning to end. The victim's representative said, "The true reason for the execution is not for the offender but justice for the victim."[12]

Burns was pronounced dead at 6:50 p.m. at the Mississippi State Penitentiary at Parchman.

Commissioner Epps appeared at a press conference following the execution. "It is our agency's role to see that the order of the court is conducted in a manner which is professional and with decency and dignity. That has been done and the cause of justice was championed today," said Epps as he does following every execution carried out in Mississippi.[13]

CHAPTER 33

Roderick Davie, Ohio. Executed August 10

In the spring of 1991, 19-year-old Roderick Davie was working at the Veterinary Companies of America (VCA) in Warren, Ohio. He had been working for VCA, a distributor of pet and veterinary supplies, for about a year. He was cordial with his fellow workers and his work history was unremarkable. However, he was fired in April of that year after a fight with the building's owner.

After being fired, Davie was unemployed and living with his girlfriend and their two-year-old daughter. He lived in Warren, a hard-scrabble steel town in northeast Ohio, a short distance from Youngstown. In the early 1990s, jobs were hard to come by in northeast Ohio.

A little more than two months after his firing, Roderick Davie showed up at VCA. Early in the morning on June 27, 1991, William John Everett, a truck driver, and Tracey Jefferys, a secretary, were already at work. Both were friends and former co-workers of Davie. Around 7:20 a.m. another truck driver, John Coleman, arrived at VCA. Everett was surprised to see Davie in the warehouse, and the two talked briefly.

*   *   *

According to court records,[1] Everett finished loading his truck and walked into the lunch room. Everett heard someone come up from behind him. When he turned around, he saw Jefferys standing next to him, crying and shaking, and Davie holding a black .38 caliber revolver with a six-inch barrel.

Davie told Jefferys and Everett to walk into the warehouse and "get down" on the floor. Davie yelled at Coleman, who was loading his truck, to come over as well. When Coleman came over, Davie told the three to lie face down on the floor. After the three complied, Davie said, "So, you all work for VCA, huh?" and began shooting. He shot Coleman and Everett.

Everett was struck in the back of the head, left shoulder, and left arm. Jefferys got up and ran. Davie ran after her yelling, "Come here, bitch." Davie caught up with Jefferys, grabbed her by the arm and dragged her back. Davie then looked at Coleman, "So you ain't dead yet, huh, brother?" Davie then shot Coleman again.

Davie walked over to Everett and took his wallet out of his left rear pocket. He unloaded the gun and turned to Jefferys, "You're lucky, I'm out of bullets." Once again, Jefferys started to run this time she sought refuge in the lunch room. Davie ran after her, and Jefferys started to scream. Davie was beating Jeffreys to death. After three or four minutes, the screaming stopped. Everett got up and saw Davie standing with his back toward him in the doorway of one of the offices. Everett ran out of the building through one of the loading docks to the VCA parking lot.

When Davie realized that Everett had survived the shooting and left the building, he jumped into a truck and drove straight at Everett as he scrambled across the parking lot. Everett saw Davie in the truck and managed to go across the street and jump over the end of a bridge. The truck hit the side of the bridge and stopped.

Everett crawled to a wall of the bridge and hid. Davie jumped over the bridge and began striking Everett with a stick, but Everett managed to get the stick from him. Davie found a larger stick and proceeded to beat Everett with the larger stick. Suddenly, Davie stopped, looked up at the top of the bridge, and took off.

A police officer went down under the bridge to help Everett who was wounded and bleeding. Everett told the officer that two more people had been shot at the VCA. Shortly thereafter, an ambulance arrived, and police proceeded to VCA and found the lifeless bodies of Coleman in the warehouse and Jefferys in the lunchroom.

At around 8:30 a.m. Carl Miller the chief bailiff for the Warren, Ohio, Municipal Court received a telephone call from Dwayne Thomas, a guy known around town as Styx. He told Miller that he had some information regarding the murders at VCA and that he and Davie were at Davie's house. Miller had known Styx for about five years and believed him to be reliable. After the telephone call, Miller, along with police detectives, proceeded to Davie's house. Styx was placed in the police cruiser along with Davie. As the police cruiser was backing out, Davie asked the officers if he could drive by the VCA warehouse. The police declined.

While at Davie's house, the police recovered his clothing. Blood found on the clothing was later determined to be consistent with Jefferys' blood. Inside the pockets of the blue jeans, police found a checkbook belonging to Jefferys and some .38 caliber spent shells. A forensic investigator determined that the spent shells had been fired from the gun found in the truck Davie used to pursue Everett.

Detectives interviewed Sonya Barnes, Davie's girlfriend and mother of his two-year-old daughter. With Barnes' consent, the detectives searched the house and found a black pouch belonging to Jefferys on the kitchen table. Barnes' father found a wallet belonging to Everett on the top of the refrigerator.

Barnes said that Davie came home before 8:00 a.m. that morning wearing "a green like khaki green short sleeve shirt, with a red T-shirt under it, and jeans." Davie told her, "I'm in trouble. Some people have been shot," and then he said he shot them. Thereafter, Davie took a shower and put some of his clothing in a plastic bag which he took outside.[2]

At trial, Barnes changed her story. She tried to cast suspicion on Styx. She testified that "[Davie] told [her] to say that he did it, for reasons unknown to [her]." Barnes also claimed that Styx asked Davie for money the morning of the murders, and that Styx pulled a .38 revolver on Davie.

Davie testified on his own behalf at trial. He did more than cast suspicion on Styx; he implicated him as the shooter and killer of Jefferys. Davie said that he went to the VCA to see if he could borrow some money from Jefferys and Everett to pay Styx the money that he owed him for a drug deal that had gone bad.

Davie claimed that, on several occasions including the previous night, Styx threatened him. Styx and Davie went to VCA together. Davie intended to ask his friends to loan him some money.

According to Davie, he heard gunshots and saw Jefferys run into the office with Styx running behind her. Davie went to help Jefferys, but Styx pointed the gun at him and told him to stay out of it. Davie went back into the offices where he could hear Jefferys screaming, and then he heard silence. When Davie walked back into the lunch room, he saw Jefferys lying on the floor. He lifted the chair off of her, determined that she was not breathing, hugged her and then laid her down. Then, he took Jefferys' car keys which were lying on the lunch room table and drove home.

The Trumbull County, Ohio, jury did not believe Davie's version of the murders. He was convicted of the murders of Coleman and Davis and the attempted murder of Everett and sentenced to death.

*   *   *

The *Youngstown Vindicator* provided a vivid portrait of Davie's last day. Governor Ted Strickland followed the recommendation of the Ohio Parole Board and denied clemency to Davie. Early on the day before his scheduled execution, Davie was transported from the Ohio State Penitentiary at Youngstown to the Southern Ohio Correctional Facility at Lucasville, home of Ohio's execution chamber. He spent most of his final day in a holding cell that sat just 17 steps from the death chamber.

Davie, who converted to Islam while in prison went by the name Abdul-Hakiym Zakiy, was allowed to have a Quran, a miswak—a twig used by Muslims for teeth cleaning—and cap. He spent his final hours talking to family members on the phone, praying and singing.[3]

He declined lunch, saying he was fasting. During the evening, he was allowed contact visits with his brother and sister-in-law. Davie did not request a final meal. He broke his fast with a prison-issued vegetarian meal, including vegetarian nuggets, sweet potato, cauliflower, pineapple, cookies and grape drink.[4]

He slept briefly after 1 a.m. He spent much of the night and early morning on the phone with family members, including his daughter. Davie declined to speak with his attorney during his final hours. He ate a snack cake, wrote a letter about 4:30 a.m. and then showered and dressed in clean clothing before cell-front visits with his brother and sister-in-law.[5]

Prison officials said medical teams checked Davie's veins twice and found no complications as they prepared him for execution. A spokeswoman for the Ohio Department of Rehabilitation and Correction said that Davie appeared calm in his final hours.[6]

A prison log of his activities while in the Death House noted that his visits with family went well, with Davie laughing at times. He became emotional closer to the time of his execution, however, holding hands and praying with prison chaplains.

Prison staff took about 10 minutes to insert an IV in both arms while Davie was strapped to a gurney. Davie apologized to Jefferys' mother, who rocked back and forth and held the hand of a victim advocate. "To Ms. Jefferys, I'm sorry," Davie said, part of a tattoo peeking out from the medical tape and tubes that covered his left arm. "I don't know if it means anything, Ms. Jefferys, but from the bottom of my heart, I mean that. I'm sorry."[7]

Randy Coleman, whose brother was hired after Davie was fired, held a photograph of three men as Davie apologized to his family. Next to him, another of his brothers looked straight ahead at the gurney.[8]

He added later, looking at William Everett who was shot, chased by a truck and beat with a stick under a bridge, "John, I hope you can let it go man and forgive me. You hear me, John?"[9]

Davie said he was done and the warden took the microphone. His lips continued to move like he was reciting a prayer. He turned toward the window separating him from the witnesses and closed his eyes. A curtain was closed over the window, separating the witnesses from Davie. The room was silent, except for the rustling of cellophane as Everett opened a piece of candy.[10]

The victims' witnesses watched quietly, holding hands at times. Davie was pronounced dead, the result of a single lethal dose of sodium thiopental, at 10:31 a.m.

* * *

William John Everett and Sandra Richmond, Jefferys' mother, wanted Roderick Davie to know they were there. "None of this is easy," said Everett, the lone survivor of Davie's attack. "But it's what has to be done. I want him to see me. I want him to know I'm there, that I'm in the room. I need to do that for myself and for John and Tracey."[11]

Sandra Richmond said her daughter "wasn't even supposed to be at work" that day. "She went in to work as a favor to her boss," Richmond said. "That's the kind of person she was—always helping out and doing for people."[12]

Richmond said she doesn't believe that anything, even watching Davie executed, could bring closure to her family or to the families of his other victims. "It's like closing the chapter on everything that has happened to this point," she said. "It's the next step in a process and the final step in this part of it. But nothing will ever close it completely. Tracey was my baby, my only daughter. Nothing will bring closure to that or what [Davie] did."[13]

Everett and Richmond said they had not seen Davie since he was convicted of the crimes. "There's been no reason to see him, no reason to talk to him," Richmond said. "Why should we? He has shown no remorse, no sorrow, nothing ... it's something that will never go away," Everett said. "Nothing can ever make it go away. It happened and it's something that's always there."[14]

Everett said he has never understood Davie's reasons for attacking him and the others. "I tried being nice to him," he said. "I showed him how to play pool. Tracey was kind to him. She was just a sweet person. None of us did anything to him. He didn't even know who would be there that day. So what? You lose your job and that's what you do? It makes no sense."[15]

"It's his sentence," Everett said. "It's what the court sentenced him to, to die. This is justice being served. That's why we're here—to see justice."[16]

CHAPTER 34

Michael Jeffrey Land, Alabama.
Executed August 12

Michael Jeffrey Land spent 16 years, six months and 23 days on death row. Land's supporters were quick to say that he had been a success in prison. He overcame a youth spent plagued by mental health problems. He created a prison laundry system, he earned his GED and held various positions of responsibility in prison.[1] However, his criminal activity also landed him in prison on more than one occasion prior to his stint on death row.

Candace Brown was known to frequent prisons, not as an offender, but as part of her ministry, to reach out a hand of comfort to those in prison. She was also the mother of a two-year-old son. The 30-year-old was working at a bank, attending Birmingham-Southern College and pursuing her prison ministry.

Land and Brown's paths crossed while he was in the county jail and she was visiting the jail to minister to another inmate. Although Brown became acquainted with Land, she was concerned that he might have been involved in a recent burglary of her home.

* * *

On a spring evening in May of 1992, Candace Brown drove to her mother's home to pick up her son. Still concerned about the burglary at her home five days earlier, Brown's mother and brother followed her home to make sure she was safe.

The following morning, May 19, Brown's landlord went to her residence to let workers on the property for the installation of a fence. According to court records,[2] the landlord noticed that a window located near the back door had been broken, the telephone wires had been cut, and that the window on the driver's side of Brown's car had been shattered. After knocking on the front door and receiving no response, he notified the police.

When officers from the Birmingham Police Department arrived at Brown's residence, they observed a pane of glass lying on the ground with a shoe imprint. The imprint had a distinctive tread design bearing the lettering "USA." The landlord opened the house for the police officers, who found Brown's two-year-old, Michael, alone and unharmed. The officers also found a note pinned to the bulletin board with the name and telephone numbers of Land and his mother, Gail Land.

Following up on the lead, police went to a shopping mall in Hoover, Alabama, where Land was working on a roof repair project. The police detectives informed Land that they were investigating the disappearance of Candace Brown, and he agreed to answer some questions at the police station.

Land admitted that he knew Brown from prison visits but said he had not seen her in more than a week. During the interview, a detective noticed that the tread design on the bottom of Land's tennis shoes appeared to match the print the police found on the window glass at Brown's house. The interview ended and, as Land was about to leave detectives asked to see his shoes, the detectives immediately saw what appeared to be bloodstains. The detectives asked Land to removes his shoes and clothes, and they gave him a jail uniform to wear.

Land offered at least two alibis, both involving girlfriends, but neither amounted to anything after the police followed up with the women.

The police then told Land that he needed to tell the truth about the disappearance of Brown. Confronted with the inconsistencies in his statement, Land agreed to make a second statement.

In his second statement, Land said that he had met two men, whom he named "Tony" and "Edward," at a gas station late the night that Brown disappeared. These two men had asked him if he knew an "easy mark" for a burglary. Land stated that he suggested Brown's house and that Tony and Edward paid him $20 to cut and remove the glass to a window in Brown's house. Land said that the three of them entered the kitchen through the window.

Land said that, after they entered the house, Brown walked into the kitchen. At that point, one of the two men slapped her, knocking her to the floor and causing her nose and mouth to bleed. Land went on to explain, as Brown fell, she grabbed his hand and, he said, in doing so she may have gotten some blood on his gloves. When Detectives told Land that no blood was found in Brown's house, Land said that the two men had cleaned the blood up with paper towels and then had placed the towels in his pants pocket. Land told police that after Brown was injured, he became frightened, left the house and did not know what happened to her after that.[3]

The next day Brown's body was discovered in a limestone quarry near her residence by a group of high school students who were hiking. She had been shot in the back of her head with a .45 caliber automatic handgun.

The police obtained a search warrant for Land's car. In the trunk police found a .45 caliber semi-automatic handgun. Also, found in Land's car was a pair of wire cutters. Both items would play a prominent role in determining Land's fate.

* * *

At trial, the evidence against Land was overwhelming. A State expert testified that the wire cutters found in Land's car had made the cuts on the telephone wire leading into Brown's residence. Two types of glass fragments found on a pair of gloves seized from Land's car were consistent with the glass in the shattered window of Brown's car and with the glass in the broken window near the rear entry of Brown's house. Land's tennis shoe sole had the same distinctive design as the shoe print found on the removed pane of glass at Brown's house.[4]

The bullet recovered from Brown's head and a bullet that was test-fired from the .45 caliber handgun found in Land's car matched. Land's gun killed Brown. Finally, a DNA profile of a semen stain found on Brown's blouse matched Land's known blood sample; and that only one in 20,620,000 white males would have those same DNA characteristics. The police also identified blood on Land's shoes as matching the victim.

Land was convicted of two counts of murder for the death of Brown. The jury found him guilty of murder during a burglary, and guilty of murder during a kidnapping, both aggravating circumstance for purposes of the death penalty. By a vote of 11–1, the jury recommended that he be sentenced to death. Alabama is one of only two states—Kentucky is the other—that permits less than a unanimous vote by a jury to impose the death penalty. The trial court followed the jury's recommendation and sentenced Land to death.

*   *   *

Governor Bob Riley turned down Land's request for clemency only days before the execution. In a lengthy clemency petition, Land's attorneys had asked Governor Riley to spare his life because he had turned his life around in prison. Assistant Attorney General Clay Crenshaw asked Riley in a letter to reject Land's plea for clemency "because of the horrible nature of his crime."[5] Riley agreed, saying he would not alter the decisions of jurors and the courts:

> Mr. Land committed a calculated, cold-blooded, brutal murder that took the life of Candace Brown, an innocent mother of a two-year-old son, almost 20 years ago. Mr. Land was tried and convicted by a jury of his peers, a jury that voted to recommend he be sentenced to death. The trial judge concurred and imposed the death penalty. This conviction and sentence have been upheld by the Alabama Court of Criminal Appeals and the Alabama Supreme Court, and the inmate's request to delay his execution has been denied by the U.S. District Court of Northern Alabama and the 11th U.S. Circuit Court of Appeals. The United States Supreme Court denied Mr. Land's petition for writ of certiorari earlier this year. This office has reviewed Mr. Land's petition for clemency as well as letters from the victim's family. I see no reason to overturn the sentence imposed by the jury and judge, and upheld by the higher courts.[6]

Land spent most of his execution day visiting with his mother, Gayle Gossett; a former Birmingham police officer; and family, his stepfather, brother, and grandfather.

A prison spokesman said Land got his last meal out of vending machines at the visitation yard. He ate a meatball sub sandwich, a double pork chop sandwich and a Philly cheesesteak sandwich, with an orange soda and orange juice.[7]

Land was strapped to a gurney in the death chamber. He had IVs secured in both arms. He was moments away from death as he spoke quietly to a prison chaplain, who held his hand and prayed for a few moments. The lethal drugs were administered and the chaplain stepped away. Land's hands relaxed and he seemed to lose consciousness. A guard came over and rubbed Land's forehead, but he made no response and was pronounced dead minutes later.[8]

Efforts by Land's attorneys to get the Alabama Supreme Court and the U.S. Supreme Court to halt the execution failed. He was executed less than an hour after the U.S. Supreme Court rejected his final appeal. The Alabama Supreme Court turned down a plea to stop the execution earlier in the afternoon. When the warden asked Land if he had any final statements, Land replied "No, thank you though."[9]

Candace Brown's son, Michael, was two years old when his mother was killed. On August 12, 2010, Michael, now 19 years old, was sitting in an observation room about to watch his mother's killer die. He was accompanied by his grandparents, John and Brenda Brown, and three uncles. The Browns left after the execution without talking to the media.

Land lay dead within the walls of the Holman Correctional Facility at Atmore; it was 6:23 p.m.

*   *   *

John Brown said his daughter's death left an emptiness in their family. "It's been a tragedy for us," he said. "You never expect to outlive your child. She was our only daughter." He said he has no animosity toward Land's family. "I know they are going to hurt," he said, but he went on to state that it was important that the decision of the jury and judge be carried out. "He went in my daughter's house; he cut the phone lines, and he took her out and shot her," he said. "All of this was done by his choice."[10]

Brown remarked that the greatest loss is that suffered by his grandson, who he and his wife raised after the slaying. "He never really got a chance to know his mother," Brown said. "He has been deprived of the relationship they were building."[11]

Brown said that his daughter loved to laugh and joke and was a faithful Christian. "I'd like for them to remember her in those ways and the fact that she was a Christian," he said. "That means more to me than anything."[12]

"We've always sought justice for our daughter, and that is what we're seeking, justice," Brown said. "Eighteen years is what we've waited. We aren't going down there to gloat; I am going down there to represent my daughter." Brown's father said that her life revolved around her son and helping others. "She loved him to death. She lived for him," Brown said. "She was so proud of him, and we were so proud of her."[13]

CHAPTER 35

Peter A. Cantu, Texas. Executed August 17

Jennifer Ertman and Elizabeth Pena were friends who attended Waltrip High School together in Houston, Texas. The girls spent a warm summer day in 1993 swimming at a pool located on the grounds of a friend's apartment. At about 11:15 that night, they left the apartment to head home. Jennifer, 14, and Elizabeth, 16, were trying to beat their 11:30 p.m. summer curfew.

They knew they would be late if they took the normal path home, down two busy Houston streets, so they decided to take a well-known shortcut down a railroad track and through a city park to Elizabeth's neighborhood.[1]

That decision cost them their lives. Three of the six men involved in their deaths would also die, but by lethal injection in the death chamber of the Texas State Penitentiary at Huntsville.

*   *   *

On the night of June 24, 1993, a group of teenage boys gathered at T.C. Jester Park in Houston to participate in a gang initiation ritual. According to court records,[2] 17-year-old Raul Villareal was being initiated into the Black and White gang, led by 18-year-old Peter Cantu. The other gang members were: Derrick Sean O'Brien, 18; Jose Medellin, 18; Efrain Perez, 17; and Roman Sandoval, 17. Two 14-year-olds, Frank Sandoval and Venancio Medellin, brothers of two of the gang members, were also present.

The gang initiation required Villareal to fight each of the gang members until he either fought them all or passed out. He lasted through three fights before briefly losing consciousness. Following the gang ritual, the members drank beer, while they walked toward some nearby railroad tracks.

At about the same time, Elizabeth and Jennifer started down the railroad tracks as a shortcut home.

The girls were walking along the tracks when they encountered the gang members. When Cantu saw them he and the other gang members went after the girls. Jennifer got away, but someone grabbed Elizabeth and dragged her down off the hill. When Elizabeth screamed, Jennifer ran back to try to help her, but Cantu grabbed her and pulled her down the hill as well. At this point, Roman and Frank Sandoval decided to leave. Roman told Cantu that he was not interested in either raping or killing girls.

The older boys began raping the two girls. This went on for about an hour while 14-year-old Venancio watched. He went back and forth between his brother and Cantu, urging them to leave, but Cantu told him that he should "get some," so he joined in on raping Jennifer. The girls were still being raped when Cantu whispered to Venancio, "We're going to have to kill them."[3]

When everyone was finished, Cantu ordered the gang members to take the girls into the woods. He told Venancio to stay behind, saying he was "too little to watch." Various gang members began strangling the girls. Cantu kicked Elizabeth in the face with his steel-toed boots, knocking out several of her teeth. Several of Jennifer's ribs were broken from being kicked. All of the gang members took turns stomping on both girls' necks to make sure they were dead.[4] Finally, Cantu robbed Jennifer of her rings, necklaces, and cash.

Later that night, Perez, Villareal, and Jose Medellin met at Cantu's house. He lived with his older brother and sister-in-law, Joe and Christina Cantu. They talked about the rapes and killings. Medellin said that they "had fun" and that their activities would be seen on the TV news. Cantu acknowledged his involvement to his sister-in-law. He also split up the jewelry and money he took from the girls.

Four days after the girls disappeared, Christina Cantu convinced her husband to call the police. She told him that she felt sorry for the families and wanted them to be able to put their daughters' bodies to rest. Joe Cantu then placed the call to the Houston Police Department's "Crimestoppers" tip line, identifying himself as "Gonzalez." He told the police that the girls' bodies could be found in T.C. Jester Park at White Oak Bayou.[5]

* * *

Six months before Jennifer and Elizabeth were murdered, three of their killers murdered another young woman, Patricia Lourdes Lopez. Patricia was a 27-year-old mother of two young children. On her way home from a football game, Patricia ran out of gas and was parked on the side of the freeway. She walked to a nearby convenience store and telephoned someone to come and help her. As she was leaving, she was stopped by Joe Medellin, Peter Cantu and Sean O'Brien, who asked her to buy them some beer since they were underage. They said they would buy her some gas and get her on the road again if she did. She bought the beer and went with the group, unwittingly heading to her death.

Instead of taking her back to her truck, the three men took her to a back parking lot in Melrose Park in Houston, where they took turns raping her before stabbing her to death. A drunken O'Brien had told Patricia that if she did not cause him to have an erection through oral sex, he would kill her. The medical examiner stated that Patricia was probably on her knees in front of her murderer when she was stabbed, based on the angle of the wounds. She had been stabbed, slashed in the abdomen, throat and back and strangled.[6]

* * *

A jury found Peter Cantu guilty of murder in February 1994 and sentenced him to death. The Texas Court of Criminal Appeals affirmed the conviction and sentence in January 1997. All of his subsequent appeals in state and federal court were denied.

Four of the other gang members that night were also convicted of the crimes against Jennifer and Elizabeth and sentenced to death. Derrick Sean O'Brien was executed on July 11, 2006. Jose Medellin was executed on August 5, 2008. Raul Omar Villareal and Efrain Perez were sentenced to death, but a 2005 U.S. Supreme Court decision outlawing the death penalty for juveniles saved their lives. Venancio Medellin, who was 14 at the time, was convicted of aggravated sexual assault and sentenced to 40 years in prison.[7]

*   *   *

The case that saved the lives of Villareal and Perez was *Roper v. Simmons*.[8] In *Roper*, the U.S. Supreme Court found that a national consensus had developed against the execution of juveniles and struck down the procedure as a violation of the Eighth Amendment prohibition of cruel and unusual punishment.

Christopher Simmons was one of 81 people, nationwide, sitting on death row for murders they committed as juveniles. Raul Omar Villareal and Efrain Perez would have been two of the other 80 death row inmates

In 1993, Simmons was 17 years old when he broke into the home of Shirley Crook. Simmons, along with an accomplice, tied up Crook and tossed her, still alive, off a bridge into Missouri's Meramac River. While planning the crime, Simmons assured his accomplice they would not be punished because they were juveniles.

At trial, the evidence was overwhelming. The jury returned a guilty verdict and sentenced Simmons to death.

Prior to the *Roper* decision, two more states, South Dakota and Wyoming, had outlawed the execution of juveniles. That brought the number of states abolishing juvenile executions to 31; one more than had abolished the death penalty for the mentally disabled prior to *Atkins v. Virginia*.[9] At the time, New Hampshire, Pennsylvania and Florida were considering legislation that would abolish juvenile executions.

In addition, a Virginia jury chose not to impose the death penalty on Lee Boyd Malvo, age 17 at the time of his crimes, for his admitted 2002 participation in ten thrill kills that paralyzed the region surrounding the nation's capital. Perhaps Malvo's sentence influenced the court's decision to consider *Roper*. However, Malvo's sentence did not influence the sentence of his adult accomplice, John A. Muhammad, who was executed in Virginia on November 10, 2009. Muhammad's execution took place only 68 months after his conviction, considerably quicker than the national average of 13 years.

The high court may have been wary of starting down the slippery slope of juvenile culpability. The American Bar Association (ABA), among other organizations, ardently espoused new scientific research, which indicated that brain development continues well into adulthood. In particular, the frontal and prefrontal lobes that govern impulsive behavior and the ability to anticipate consequences can be late in developing.

An ABA publication entitled *Adolescence, Brain Development and Legal Culpability*[10] suggested, "Adolescents are less morally culpable for their actions than competent adults and are more capable of change and rehabilitation. The ultimate punishment for minors is contrary to the idea of fairness in our justice system, which accords the greatest punishments to the most blameworthy." Further studies have suggested that juveniles may lack the brain capacity to control impulses and make informed decisions. As a result juveniles may be less blameworthy for their conduct than adults.

If a juvenile is less culpable for purposes of capital punishment, are they less culpable for purposes of life in prison or any adult punishment? The concern was centered on the culpability argument. A successful culpability argument may be the first step in a process that will ultimately result in juveniles not being held accountable for vicious, heinous crimes that, regardless of age, they have and continue to commit. This argument has now seeped into the debate regarding juvenile life without parole.

As Justice Antonin Scalia wrote in his dissent in *Atkins*, is there an established correlation between mental acuity and the ability to conform one's conduct to the law in such a rudimentary matter as murder?

In 2012, the U.S. Supreme Court took the next step in juvenile accountability. In *Jackson v. Hobbs*, 567 U.S. ___ (2012), and *Miller v. Alabama*, 567 U.S. ___ (2012) the court ruled that a mandatory sentence of life in prison without the possibility of parole imposed upon a juvenile violates the Eighth Amendment ban against "cruel and unusual punishment."[11]

Mandatory sentences prevent judges from exercising discretion. "It prevents taking into account the family and home environment that surrounds him—and from which he cannot usually extricate himself—no matter how brutal or dysfunctional. It neglects the circumstances of the homicide offense, including the extent of his participation in the conduct and the way familial and peer pressures may have affected him," Justice Elena Kagan wrote for the majority.

In *Roper*, the court noted the infrequency in which the death penalty was applied to juvenile offenders. At the time only 20 states had laws permitting the imposition of the death penalty for juveniles. However, only six of those states had executed a juvenile since the decision in *Stanford v. Kentucky*,[12] the 1989 High Court decision permitting the execution of juveniles aged 16 and 17 years of age.

In addition, since *Stanford*, five states had abolished the death penalty for juveniles altogether. *Roper* also acknowledged international opinion; "The United States is the only country in the world that continues to give official sanction to the juvenile penalty. It does not lessen fidelity to the Constitution or pride in its origins to acknowledge that the express affirmation of certain fundamental rights by other nations and peoples underscores the centrality of those same rights within our own heritage of freedom."[13]

Instead of the bright line standard, 18 years of age, created by *Roper*, the public might have been better served by leaving the door open for executing the exceptionally mature juvenile offender who otherwise qualifies for the death penalty. In a concurring opinion in *Roper*, at least one member of the Missouri Supreme Court recognized that there is absolutely no difference between 17 years and 364 days and 18 years of age.

* * *

Cantu ate his last meal in Huntsville. It was a conservative selection of enchiladas, fajitas and a cinnamon bun.[14]

Cantu was prepared for execution out of the view of witnesses. He was restrained on a gurney in the antiseptic room used for more executions than any other room in America, the death house at the Texas State Penitentiary at Huntsville. Cantu had IVs secured in both arms. At 6:09 p.m. the lethal injection drugs were pumped into Cantu's body. He let out a final breath, and eight minutes later, he appeared to fade into a lethal slumber. He made no final statement. He did not apologize or ask for forgiveness. In his final moments he showed no remorse and expressed no empathy for the families of his victims.

For those watching the execution, it was a death too good for the man who brought a violent and terrifying end to the lives of two teens 17 years ago. "Put it this way: I wish my daughter could have died the way he died today. Wasn't no pain. These girls went through an awful lot of pain when they died," said Adolfo Pena, father of Elizabeth. "He deserved to die, and 17 years later he died. Not soon enough."[15]

Pena, his wife Melissa at his side, said it did not matter to him that Cantu offered no words of contrition, or any words at all. "There's nothing he would have said to me that would have made any difference," said Pena, who was wearing a white T-shirt with a photograph of the two girls printed on the front. "Seventeen years is a long time to have something eating on you like that. We think about those girls every day."[16]

Randy and Sandra Ertman did not speak with the media after the execution. Longtime friend Jim Stacey, speaking on their behalf, said they were ready to put the crime and its aftermath "as far behind them as possible," and left Huntsville immediately after the execution. "Randy and Sandy have been through enough—there's nothing left for them to say," Stacey said. "There's no way to ever get closure from this. Maybe some satisfaction, but never closure."[17]

Ertman rejected an invitation from Cantu's lawyer to come to his office and read a letter of apology from Cantu. "It's a little late," Ertman said. "I told him to stick it. Hell, no." He did speak with the Associated Press after the execution and he did not hold back. "He [Cantu] should have been hung outside the courthouse," Ertman continued. "I don't mean this in a gruesome way, but if they want to make the death penalty a deterrent up in front of [Houston] City Hall, they've got all these beautiful trees. They should have hung them. If they hung all five of them, that would be a deterrent."[18]

"I'm sure a lot of people will get closure from this because it affected a lot of people," said Pena, acknowledging the support his family and the Ertmans have received over the years. "They are still behind us. I don't believe anybody ever in their lifetime is going to forget this. It affected more than just Melissa and me and Randy and Sandy."[19]

The murders of Jennifer and Elizabeth became one of the most notorious crimes in modern Houston history. A memorial was erected to them at Waltrip High School where they attended. A memorial for them was also placed at T.C. Jester Park. The gruesome deaths would evoke painful memories and strike fear into Houstonians for many years.[20]

Maria Frausto didn't know Jennifer or Elizabeth or their families, but she said she often says a small prayer when she jogs past the memorial in T.C. Jester Park. "It's good that they won't be forgotten," Frausto said. "They are still in our hearts and prayers."[21]

CHAPTER 36

Holly Wood, Alabama. Executed September 9

On the evening of September 1, 1993, Holly Wood entered the residence of Annie Gosha looking for Gosha's daughter, Ruby. Wood and Ruby had a child together. When Wood found Ruby lying in bed asleep, he put a 12-gauge shotgun to her head and pulled the trigger.

Wood wanted to kill Ruby. This was not the first time he tried. According to court records,[1] he told his cousin, Calvin Salter, he had attempted to stab Ruby in the heart but that Ruby had used her arms to protect herself, and a lethal stab wound was averted.

Ruby told her mother that one night, approximately two weeks before September 1, Wood came up behind her, while she sat in her car, and cut her on the arm, causing her to lose the function of two fingers.

Dr. Alfredo Paredes, a medical examiner with the Alabama Department of Forensic Sciences found, after Ruby's death, a recent cut and recent bruises on the victim's palm and on the back of her left hand, two recent trauma-induced scars on her right forearm, a recent scar on her left forearm, and a recent scar on her left upper arm. The wounds appeared to be defensive.

* * *

The court records[2] in Wood's case further establish that Ruby and her children were living with her mother, Annie Gosha, at her house in Troy, Alabama. Before moving in with her mother, Ruby had lived with Holly Wood in Enterprise. Their turbulent relationship had recently ended.

On September 1 at around 5:00 p.m. Wood arrived uninvited at Mrs. Gosha's house, purportedly to bring Ruby some cigarettes and diapers for their child. Wood and Ruby argued, and Ruby told Wood to "go on and leave me alone, take your cigarettes and diapers and give them to somebody else because it is over between us."

Mrs. Gosha told Wood to leave her property and to never come back. As Wood left the house, he told Ruby that he would "get" her someday. That "someday" was only hours away.

Later that evening Wood picked up his cousin Calvin Salter. Wood was driving his father's pickup truck. They drove over to Troy, Alabama, with Salter driving. Once in Troy they drove past the Gosha residence. While near Ruby's house, an automobile driven by a man named "Amp" went by, and Wood told Salter to follow Amp's car. Wood said that if he caught Ruby and Amp together, he would kill Ruby.

Wood and Salter followed Amp's car until it passed the Gosha residence. Wood then directed Salter to drive slowly toward the Gosha house, and when they neared the house, Salter stopped the truck. Wood then took a 12-gauge shotgun from the gun rack of the truck, stuck it down his pant leg and covered it with his shirt. He got out of the truck and walked toward the Gosha house.

Salter parked the truck at a nearby apartment complex and made a telephone call at a public pay telephone. He heard a gunshot and returned to the truck. When he arrived back, Wood was sitting in the truck. Wood said, "Let's go."

*　　*　　*

It was about 9:00 p.m. when Mrs. Gosha and Ruby retired to separate bedrooms. Mrs. Gosha was lying in bed watching television when she heard a "pop" or what sounded like a "firecracker shot." She went through Ruby's bedroom into the kitchen, where she saw that the outside door was open. When she returned to Ruby's bedroom, she found Ruby lying in bed. Ruby had been shot; there was a gunshot wound near her eye and one near her cheek. Mrs. Gosha telephoned the police and an ambulance.

*　　*　　*

As Wood and Salter drove back to Luverne, a small town in southern Alabama, Wood told Salter that he had shot Ruby while she was sleeping. Wood told Salter, "I shot that bitch in the head, and [blew] her brains out and all she did was wiggle." Wood threw some 12-gauge shotgun shells out the window. He knew Ruby was dead and that the police would be coming after him.

Wood was arrested at his father's house in Luverne. Wood was in the presence of police officers from that point forward and none of the police officers discussed any details of Ruby's murder with Wood.

Salter was interviewed by police and led them to a wooded area near Wood's father's house where they found the shotgun under some leaves. Salter also told police that a few days before the murder; he went with Wood to Ruby Gosha's house to deliver some diapers to Ruby. Ruby and her mother both told Wood to leave. Salter said that later that same day, he and Wood saw Ruby at a shopping center. According to Salter, Wood spoke with Ruby at that time, but Salter did not know what they talked about.

As the police were transporting Wood from the Luverne Police station to the Troy Police station and without any questioning or prompting from the police, Wood stated the following, "You motherfuckers must think I am crazy. What do I look [like] going in somebody's house shooting them in the head while they are asleep?" Wood somehow knew details of a crime he denied committing and facts of a murder never described to him.

*　　*　　*

A forensic scientist for the Alabama Department of Forensic Sciences examined the shotgun recovered in the woods and the shotgun shell wadding and lead shot pellets found in the victim's head. The wadding are actually the pellets that are fired in mass from a shell through the shotgun barrel. The wadding pattern can give an investigator some idea how far the shooter was from the victim.

The forensic scientist testified that the wadding was a 12-gauge type and was consistent with the type of columns and wadding used in Remington shotgun shells and with the type of ammunition used in the recovered shotgun. He also determined that the pellets recovered from the victim's head were consistent in size and weight with "number 6 shot from a shotgun shell."[3]

The case wound its way through the Pike County District Court, leading to a Grand Jury indictment and a trial in the Pike County Circuit Court. Wood was convicted of first degree murder and sentenced to death.

Wood exhausted all his state remedies—the Alabama Court of Criminal Appeals, the Alabama Supreme Court, Federal Court and ultimately getting his day before the U.S. Supreme Court. He argued all along that his constitutional rights had been violated and for the most part, all along the courts disagreed.

At one point a Federal District Court Judge tossed out the death sentence on the basis that Wood's lawyer failed to tell jurors Wood had an IQ of less than 70 and had been classified as mentally disabled.

Then the 11th U.S. Circuit Court of Appeals in Atlanta reinstated the death penalty. The Court found that Wood "failed to show that the lawyer was unconstitutionally ineffective." The U.S. Supreme Court agreed with the circuit court early in 2010.[4]

Wood's clemency petition included reports from state psychiatrists who determined that Wood was mentally disabled and that his reading, spelling and arithmetic skills are in the second- to fourth-grade range. The petition suggested that Governor Bob Riley should stop the execution because his attorneys failed to tell jurors that Wood was mentally disabled during the sentencing phase of his trial.

Governor Riley turned down Wood's request for clemency hours before he was scheduled to die by lethal injection at Holman Prison. "For his brutal crime, he was tried and convicted by a jury and the jury recommended he be sentenced to death. This conviction and death sentence have been upheld by higher courts, and I see no reason why this office should overturn the sentence," Riley said in a statement after rejecting Woods request for clemency.[5]

Wood now looked to the U.S. Supreme Court as the hour of his execution drew near. A request for a stay of execution was pending before the U.S. Supreme Court. Wood's attorneys contended their client was mentally disabled with an IQ below 70. Wood's attorneys also argued that his trial counsel failed to inform the jury of his mental disability. Wood's petition stated, "It is undisputed" that Wood had an IQ below 70, which would place him in the range necessary to be classified as mentally disabled.

Wood's attorneys argued that *Atkins v. Virginia*,[6] the U.S. Supreme Court decision that bars the execution of the mentally disabled should prevent his execution. Early in 2010 the U.S. Supreme Court, by a 7–2 vote, rejected his claim that his trial attorney was ineffective, *Wood v. Allen*.[7] The argument failed to convince the justices in January 2010 and it did not convince the justices on the eve of Wood's execution.

The Alabama Attorney General's Office filed a brief asking the Supreme Court to allow Wood's execution to proceed, arguing that Wood has been on death row for 16 years and that his claims have been considered previously by federal and state courts. The attorney general's office also said that before his arrest, Wood held several jobs and was able to function in society. It also argued that Wood showed mental acuity in the way he planned and carried out the killing of Gosha.[8]

The High Court rejected Wood's last minute appeal to stay his execution.

*   *   *

Wood met with family and friends at the Holman Correctional Facility at Atmore. He requested no special last meal, and the department of corrections did not reveal what he ate before his execution. Two sisters and a brother of Gosha, along with a son and a daughter, witnessed the execution.[9]

He had no last words. Two of his sisters witnessing the execution screamed, cried and prayed loudly. Wood's two sisters, Johnny Pearle Wood and Mae Ole Wood Herndon, were screaming and beating on the glass separating them from their dying brother, the two sisters hollered, "Oh, my God.... Oh Lord have mercy ... my brother, my Lord, oh my God, my brother ... don't leave [us] like this."[10]

Prison officials say Wood died by lethal injection at 6:21 p.m. on September 9, 2010. He was the 37th person executed in the United States in 2010 and 1,225th person executed in the modern era of the death penalty.

Wood's sisters were calmly escorted from the death chamber by prison guards, leaving a note with the guards for the Associated Press. The note said that Alabama Gov. Bob Riley should have stopped the execution because their brother was "mentally disabled." The note continued: "The law failed to protect the mentally disabled ... the legal system in Alabama is flawed."[11]

Gary McAliley, the Pike County District Attorney summed up the legacy of Holly Wood during an interview prior to the execution, "He was a most dangerous person, and we're very fortunate he doesn't hurt more people."[12]

CHAPTER 37

Cal Coburn Brown, Washington. Executed September 10

Cal Coburn Brown was moments away from being executed by lethal injection at the Washington State Penitentiary in Walla Walla. He used those final moments to protest what he perceived to be sentencing disparities, saying that criminals who had killed many more people, such as Green River killer Gary Ridgway, were serving life sentences while he received a death sentence.

Ridgway murdered at least 48 women in Washington during the 1980s and 1990s, earning the nickname when his first five victims were found in the Green River. "I only killed one victim," said Brown. "I cannot really see that there is true justice. Hopefully, sometime in the future that gets straightened out."[1]

Brown's selfish and cruel final words, absent an apology to the family of the "one victim" he killed, made the need for his execution all the more obvious to the witnesses in attendance. Brown had a savage disposition toward women and, only by the sheer resilience of some of his victims, was not a multiple murderer.

* * *

On the morning of May 23, 1991, Holly C. Washa was at the Wyndham Garden Hotel near the Seattle-Tacoma Airport where she had just quit her part-time job. She was a 21-year-old Nebraska native who came to Seattle to follow her big-city dreams.

According to court records,[2] as Washa was driving out of the parking lot in her 1985 Oldsmobile, Brown pointed to one of her tires giving her the impression that something was wrong. Washa pulled her car to the side of the road. Brown then forced his way into her car, grabbed her by the hair and stuck a knife in her face.

They went through the drive-up window at a Seafirst Bank and cashed some of Washa's checks. Then they went to the Seattle waterfront area where Brown tied Washa's hands behind her back with her purse strap and pushed her into the passenger seat of her car. He then purchased some handcuffs at a gun shop while leaving Washa tied up in the car.

Brown drove Washa to the Shadow Motel where he was renting a room. He demanded that she take her clothes off and tied her to the bed with his neckties and her purse strap. He cut up her shirt and stuffed it into her mouth for a gag. Whatever his intent, he changed his mind and moments later ordered her to get dressed and took her to get something to eat. While at a Burger King drive-through, he pointed a knife at Washa in a threatening manner, putting her in imminent fear of harm. After they returned to the motel room, he ordered her to remove her clothing and lie face down on the bed. He also told her not to scream or make any sudden movements.

Brown engaged in sexual intercourse with Washa for about two hours, during which time he noticed she was looking at the door and possibly thinking of escape. He decided it was time "to have a little control ... make her a little more scared of me." He then tied her up, this time face up, in a spread eagle position, with her hands behind her back and her mouth gagged, and whipped her with a belt about a half a dozen times.

Brown allowed Washa to get dressed again, tied her hands behind her back, and they drove to restaurant for pizza. When they returned to the motel, he again forced her to undress and tied her to the bed this time in a face down, spread eagle position with her hands tied behind her back. He then had sexual intercourse with her again. At about 11:00 p.m. that evening, he telephoned Susan Schnell, a woman he recently met, to reconfirm their weekend plans in Palm Springs, California. After that, he crawled into bed with Ms. Washa, who was still bound and gagged, and he slept.

The next day, Friday, May 24, 1991, Brown forced Washa to drive him to her apartment where he hoped to find checks belonging to her roommates that he could forge.

When they returned to the motel, Brown again tied Washa to the bed face down with her hands handcuffed behind her back and her mouth gagged with a washcloth. This time he tortured Washa. He penetrated her vaginally and anally with an aftershave lotion bottle. He shaved her pubic hair and held a hot hair dryer close to her vagina, breasts and stomach. He also shocked her by using an electric cord which was detached from its appliance but still plugged into the wall.

At about 8:45 p.m. on the evening of May 24, 1991, Brown left for the Seattle-Tacoma Airport to catch a plane to California. He forced Washa into the trunk of her car with her hands handcuffed behind her back and drove to the Doug Fox Travel Agency parking lot where he momentarily parked the automobile. Because shuttle buses were driving around the lot, Brown was concerned that someone might discover Washa since "she could just bang and clang and crunch and scream and be out very quickly." He then went to the trunk and cut her throat with "three swipes" and stabbed her several times in the chest and abdominal areas. Because Washa's blood began leaking from the trunk of the automobile, he moved from the travel agency lot to the Budget Park and Ride lot near the airport.

Later, Brown told the police he killed Washa because he did not want to leave any witnesses alive. He also told them he kidnapped her because he needed money to get to California and "didn't like the idea of waltzing into a bank with my face, you know, all over the place." He also stated he was "going to rob somebody and let 'em go but then I just realized ... after I did it that it would just be the same as waltzing into a bank and have my picture taken." He described his actions toward Washa during the final day of her life as "torture" and acknowledged that the electric shock must have been particularly painful for her.

When Brown got to California, he and Susan Schnell spent Sunday, May 26, 1991, touring the Palm Springs area together. She was driving her burgundy red 1981 Corvette sports car. Upon returning from dinner around midnight, they began kissing and fondling. Brown performed oral sex on Schnell and then offered to give her a back rub. He straddled her while she lay face down on the bed.

Suddenly, as Schnell lay on the bed, Brown violently jerked her arms back and told her not to scream. When she did, he slit her throat. As she continued to scream, Brown restrained her with handcuffs and brought the knife around to her chest and threatened her with it. She saw the knife. He told her he just wanted her money. Brown repositioned Ms. Schnell on the bed and tied her to it, using her pantyhose. He shaved her pubic hair and, raped her vaginally and orally. He then ordered her to write him a check for $4,000.

Brown's conduct toward Schnell was very similar to his conduct toward Washa. Schnell appeared to be heading for the same fate.

Brown became concerned about Schnell's bleeding and told her he was going out for medical supplies. He tried to gag her with a sock and restrain her arms above her head, but abandoned the effort when she began coughing up blood. Her feet, however, remained handcuffed to the bed. While he was gone, with her arms free, she was able to reach the telephone and call the desk clerk. Palm Springs police arrived and took a description of Brown from Schnell.

She was taken to the hospital for emergency surgery. She survived and testified as a witness in the King County trial.

After being arrested by the Palm Springs police, Brown was interviewed by two police detectives. A total of three interviews took place between May 27 and May 28, 1991, with the first two initiated by the detectives and the third initiated by Brown.

During each of his statements he related in calm, deliberate, clear, graphic and specific detail a narrative of his activities, with few questions from the detectives, who allowed him to relate his story. His statements were characterized as confessions.

He told the detectives where the killing took place in Washington and where Washa's automobile could be found. The Palm Springs police immediately contacted King County police who dispatched police officers to the Budget parking lot near the Seattle-Tacoma Airport where they located the 1985 blue Oldsmobile in space 266 with Washa's body in the trunk. Brown still had the keys to Washa's car in his possession.

* * *

Brown's violence dates back many years. Brown had an extensive criminal record, including a 1977 conviction in California that involved a knife assault on a woman in a shopping center. In 1984, Brown was sentenced as a dangerous offender for his attempted assault of a 24-year-old woman in Corvallis, Oregon. Brown, a freshman at Oregon State University at the time, had been introduced to a woman through a mutual friend. Brown appeared at the woman's home wearing a hat and carrying a backpack. He persuaded her to let him in claiming he had a sprained ankle. When she turned her head to call him a cab, Brown flung a 43-inch leather strap over her head to choke her, but the thong caught on her lip.

The victim recalled the thong instantly tightening, and she was yanked off her feet backwards. She rolled to her side and saw him wild-eyed staring into her face. He held her, she screamed and a police officer who happened to be nearby arrested him. Police found a large knife and a roll of two-inch wide duct tape in his backpack. The woman's two young sons were home during the attack.

Brown served the minimum seven-and-a-half-year sentence for the Oregon attempted assault conviction and was released on parole from the Oregon State Penitentiary on March 25, 1991, after receiving a favorable psychiatric evaluation.

Upon Brown's release, he was placed under the supervision of a parole officer that specialized in the supervision of sex offenders. The parole officer was given a letter from the district attorney who had prosecuted Brown. In the letter, the District Attorney stated that not only did he consider Brown to be one of the most dangerous criminals whom he had ever prosecuted, but also that "unless he has undergone a remarkable transformation in prison, he will remain a potential mutilator and killer of women."

During the first two months of his parole, Brown enrolled once again at Oregon State University and met with his parole officer. Toward the end of that period, the parole officer could not get in touch with Brown and on May 23, 1991, requested that an arrest warrant be filed for Brown. On the very same day, Brown carjacked Holly Washa.[3]

* * *

After pleading guilty in California and receiving a sentence of life in prison, Brown was tried in Washington. A jury convicted Brown of first-degree murder and sentenced him to death.

In 2007, when the U.S. Supreme Court agreed to hear an appeal from Brown, Holly's family expressed their frustration. "Here he is, all these years later, enjoying the life that some people don't have," said Ruthcile Washa, the grandmother of Holly Washa. "The death penalty will give us peace of mind that he won't get out and do this to someone else."[4]

Brown had a prior execution date in March 2009 but received a stay of execution only hours before he was scheduled to die. The Washington Supreme Court by a 5–4 vote stayed the execution. Holly Washa's family flew to Washington from Nebraska to watch Brown die in 2009. "We'll come back ... we'll come back," Holly's father John Washa said at the time.[5]

For his final meals Brown chose to have biscuits and gravy for breakfast and skipped lunch. For dinner, which is served between 4 and 6 p.m. Brown chose to have pizza, apple pie and root beer.[6]

Brown was given two hours of time outside and spent most of his time talking with his attorneys. His mood was one of impending resignation as to what's going to happen. Governor Christine Gregoire denied Brown's request for clemency.[7]

Holly's father, brother and two sisters again made the trip from Nebraska to witness the execution. Prosecutor Dan Satterberg also witnessed the procedure. Brown did not apologize to the family of the victim but said he understood their emnity for him. He said he forgave that hatred, held no hostility toward them and hoped the execution would give them closure. He also said the prison staff had been most professional and that he had no complaints about his treatment on death row for the last 17 years.[8]

After his comments, Brown, who was lying on his back strapped to a gurney, looked up at the tubes sticking out of the wall and connected to his body. When the drug was administered, his chest heaved three times and his lips shuddered, then there was no movement. Brown's attorney and members of his family were not present at the execution, though he spoke with them by phone.[9]

"It's been so long that we have had to deal with all of this; now that it's over, I don't have to think about him anymore," a tearful Becky Washa, Holly's sister, said after the execution.[10]

The execution of Brown was the first time the state has used just one drug in a lethal injection. The execution was carried out "professionally, humanely and was dignified," according to the state Department of Corrections. At the time, Washington and Ohio were the only states to use a single drug, sodium thiopental, to execute condemned inmates. In other states, lethal injection is done with a three-drug protocol, a method that has come under fire from defense lawyers and groups opposed to the death penalty. "Our preparation, and from what we have learned from the state of Ohio, we had every confidence the one-drug protocol would be efficient and swift," said a corrections spokeswoman.[11]

After making the nearly three-minute statement from the prison's death chamber which ended with, "Thank you, God bless you, God bless my family." Brown was administered five grams of sodium thiopental intravenously.[12]

Witnesses said Brown died only minutes after the drug was administered. He was pronounced dead by prison officials at 12:56 a.m. Brown was the first person executed in Washington since August 2001.

Prosecutor Satterberg, who witnessed the execution along with members of Washa's family and several news reporters, characterized Brown's death as "quick and painless." He added, "He's among the worst of the worst criminals ever in the state of Washington."[13]

Brown was the first and only person executed in Washington in 2010. Washington courts sentenced four killers to death prior to Brown receiving his death sentence. Although the state had executed five offenders since 1976, ten inmates remain on death row.

CHAPTER 38

Teresa Wilson Lewis, Virginia. Executed September 23

In the autumn of 2002, Teresa Lewis met Rodney Fuller and Matthew Shallenberger at a Wal-Mart in rural Pittsylvania County, Virginia. Prior to the Wal-Mart encounter, Lewis did not know either of the men. After a conversation, Shallenberger and Lewis exchanged telephone numbers and began to communicate frequently. Lewis was married at the time and living with her husband in a mobile home in southern Virginia near the North Carolina border.

Soon after the chance meeting, Lewis and Shallenberger began a sexual relationship. On one occasion, Lewis and her 16-year-old daughter, Christie Bean, met Shallenberger and Fuller at a parking lot in Danville. Christie, who had never met Fuller previously, had sexual intercourse with him in one car while Lewis and Shallenberger engaged in sexual intercourse in another vehicle. On a later date, Fuller and Shallenberger went to the Lewis' home where she performed a "lingerie show" for the men and had sexual intercourse with both men.[1]

Lewis used sex and the promise of insurance money to coax Shallenberger and Fuller into killing her husband, Julian Lewis. The first attempt was foiled, but unfortunately they were not deterred.

* * *

According to court records,[2] in the early morning hours of October 30, 2002, Shallenberger and Fuller, armed with shotguns, entered Lewis' mobile home through a rear door that Lewis had left unlocked as planned. Shallenberger woke Teresa, who had fallen asleep next to Julian. She left Julian in the room asleep. She went into the kitchen where she waited while Shallenberger shot Julian several times. As Julian lay mortally wounded but still alive, Teresa came in and grabbed his pants and wallet.

While Shallenberger was taking care of Julian, Fuller went into Julian's son, CJ's, bedroom and shot him several times with a shotgun. After shooting CJ, there was some uncertainty as to whether he was dead, so Fuller took Shallenberger's shotgun and returned to shoot CJ two more times. After retrieving some of the shotgun shells, Shallenberger told Teresa that he was sorry she had to go through something like this, hugged and kissed her and then left.

Lewis remained in the mobile home with the victims for about 45 minutes after the last shots were fired. She made at least two telephone calls, but did not call the police or an ambulance. At approximately 3:55 a.m. the 9–1–1 Center recorded a call from Lewis reporting that a single intruder had entered her home at approximately 3:15 or 3:30 a.m. and shot her husband and stepson.

When the police arrived, Lewis directed them to the master bedroom. They found Julian badly wounded, but still alive and talking. He "made slow moans and uttered, 'Baby, baby, baby, baby,'" according to the police. Julian told the officers his name and, when asked "if he knew who had shot him ... responded, 'My wife knows who done this to me.'" Julian died shortly after police talked with him.

Lewis told investigators that she and Julian had talked and prayed together before he went to bed that night and that she told him she was going to the kitchen to pack his lunch for the next day. A lunch bag was found in the refrigerator with an attached note stating, "I love you. I hope you have a good day." She also drew a picture of a "smiley face" on the bag and wrote, "I miss you when you're gone."

Soon after the murders, Lewis did something that would be indicative of her involvement in the murder of her husband and stepson.

Late in the morning on the day of the killings, Lewis called Mike Campbell, Julian's supervisor, at work. She told Campbell that Julian had been murdered and asked for Julian's paycheck. Campbell told Lewis that she could pick it up after 4:00 p.m. that day. Campbell later told police that Julian brought his lunch to work in a blue and white cooler and did not use lunch bags.

Also on the day of the murders, Lewis spoke with Army Reserve Lieutenant Michael Booker, CJ's commanding officer. CJ was in the Army Reserve and about to be deployed. Lewis informed Lt. Booker that she was the secondary beneficiary of CJ's military life insurance policy. When Lt. Booker told Lewis that she would be entitled to the life insurance, Lewis responded, "That's fine; Kathy, CJ's sister, can have all of his effects as long as I get the money."

On the day of the funerals, Lewis called Kathy prior to the services and told her that "she had just left the hairdresser's and had gotten her nails done, and that she had bought a beautiful suit to wear to the funeral."

In addition to her attempts to obtain Julian's paycheck, Lewis also made an attempt to withdraw $50,000 from Julian's Prudential Securities' account by presenting a forged check made payable to her at the bank. The bank employee refused to cash the check because the signature did not match Julian's signature in the bank's records.

*   *   *

On November 20, 2002, Lewis was indicted by a grand jury for murder for hire of Charles J. Lewis, murder for hire of Julian Clifton Lewis, Jr., conspiracy to commit murder, and robbery of Julian Clifton Lewis, Jr.

In a strange turn of events, Lewis pled guilty to all charges. Before accepting the pleas, the circuit court questioned Lewis and made a determination that her guilty pleas were made voluntarily, intelligently and knowingly.

The court also considered a competency assessment of Lewis made by Barbara G. Haskins, M.D., a board-certified forensic psychiatrist. Dr. Haskins opined that Lewis had the capacity to enter pleas of guilty to charges of capital murder and had the ability to understand and appreciate the possible penalties that might result from her pleas.

After considering the evidence adduced during the sentencing hearing and the written summary of the Commonwealth's evidence, the circuit court found that Lewis's conduct was outrageously or wantonly vile, horrible, or inhuman and sentenced her to death for both murders.[3] The court also sentenced her to 20 years for each conspiracy charge, and life in prison for the robbery charge.

*   *   *

On the scheduled day of execution, Lewis was moved to the Greensville Correctional Center, site of Virginia's death house. She ate a final meal of fried chicken, sweet peas with butter, German chocolate cake and Dr. Pepper.[4]

Lewis' attorneys never argued that she was innocent or that she should not be punished. They contended she did not deserve to die because she was borderline mentally disabled, with an IQ of 72, and was manipulated by a smarter, more diabolical co-conspirator. Her supporters also suggested it was wrong for her to be sentenced to death when the trigger men, Shallenberger and Fuller, both received life sentences, although Shallenberger committed suicide while in prison.

Prison chaplains and fellow inmates supported Lewis, saying she created a ministry of sorts in prison and was a source of strength for other women looking for a maternal figure. Some prisoners said she sang gospel music, calming the ward.[5]

Governor Rob McDonnell, who had supported legislation to expand the use of the death penalty, denied a first clemency request, then a second renewed plea. He said in a statement that no medical expert had determined that Lewis was mentally disabled as defined by Virginia law.[6]

As Lewis entered the death chamber, she appeared serious and fearful. She looked around the room as she was escorted to the gurney. Her arms, legs and torso were quickly strapped down by five execution team members, and at 8:58 p.m. a blue curtain was drawn, blocking the view from the witness room as intravenous lines used to administer the drugs were inserted.[7]

At 9:09 p.m. the curtain opened and Lewis was asked whether she had a last statement. She asked if "Kathy" was present, presumably referring to Kathy Clifton, the daughter and sister of the two murdered men. Clifton had said earlier that she and her husband would attend the execution. Family witnesses view from a private room; corrections officials did not respond to Lewis' question. "I just want Kathy to know I love you and I'm very sorry."[8]

The first of three drugs were injected into the prostrate Lewis. Her left foot had been moving as if she was tapping it, but the movement quickly stopped.[9] A guard reassuringly tapped her lightly on the shoulder as she slipped into unconsciousness.[10]

*   *   *

In Virginia, the first drug is sodium thiopental, which renders the offender unconscious. The second, pancuronium bromide stops the breathing. The final chemical, potassium chloride, stops the heart. She was pronounced dead at 9:13 p.m. and the curtains were redrawn, again blocking the view.[11]

There are approximately 3,261 killers on death row in the United States. Only 61 of those offenders are women. Lewis became only the 12th woman executed in the United States and the first executed in Virginia this century.[12]

Nearly three years would pass before another woman, Kimberly McCarthy, was executed, during the summer of 2013 in Texas.

According to the *Washington Post*[13] the other 11 woman executed in the United States since 1976 are:

1. Margie Velma Barfield, by lethal injection on November 2, 1984, in North Carolina. Barfield confessed in court to poisoning four people, including her mother. She was convicted in 1978 of using ant and roach poison to kill her fiancé, a tobacco farmer.

2. Karla Faye Tucker, by lethal injection on February 3, 1998, in Texas. Tucker and a friend killed a man and woman in 1983. Tucker used a pickax.

3. Judy Buenoano, by electrocution on March 30, 1998, in Florida. She was executed for the arsenic poisoning of her husband in 1971. She also drowned her paralyzed son.

4. Betty Lou Beets, by lethal injection on February 24, 2000, in Texas for fatally shooting her fifth husband. Beets also was convicted of shooting and wounding her second husband and was charged, but never tried, in the shooting death of her fourth husband.

5. Christina Riggs, by lethal injection on May 2, 2000, in Arkansas for suffocating her two children.

6. Wanda Jean Allen, by lethal injection on January 11, 2001, in Oklahoma. She was condemned for killing her lesbian lover. She also served two years for fatally shooting a childhood friend.

7. Marilyn Plantz, by lethal injection on May 1, 2001, in Oklahoma. She was convicted of hiring two men to beat and burn her husband.

8. Lois Nadean Smith, by lethal injection December 4, 2001, in Oklahoma. Smith killed her son's ex-girlfriend.

9. Lynda Lyon Block, by electrocution on May 10, 2002, in Alabama for the 1993 murder of a policeman.

10. Aileen Wuornos, by lethal injection October 9, 2002, in Florida. Wuornos was a prostitute who killed six men.

11. Frances Newton, by lethal injection September 14, 2005, in Texas for the fatal shootings of her husband and two children.

* * *

Lewis' case generated passion and interest around the world. The European Union asked Governor McDonnell to commute her sentence to life, citing her mental capacity. Iranian President Mahmoud Ahmadinejad cited the case at an appearance in New York. Bestselling author John Grisham also fought for her clemency.[14]

About a month before the execution, Lewis was interviewed at the Fluvanna Correctional Center for Women, where she was imprisoned for seven years because the state's death row accommodates only men. She said that she prayed and read her Bible. She had nightmares about the murders and said that she thought of Julian Lewis and C.J. Lewis each day. "I wish I could give Kathy the world and take away her hurt," Lewis said. "I can't even imagine the pain she's been through all these years."[15]

Her attorney, James Rocap III, said Lewis was peaceful before going to her death and had been praying and singing in the days leading up to her execution. "We thought that we were supposed to be helping her, while she was actually helping us," Rocap said.[16]

After the execution, Rocap said: "Tonight the machinery of death in Virginia extinguished the childlike and loving spirit of Teresa Lewis." He said she met with both of her children yesterday and wrote letters to both of them.[17]

Prosecutors believed that Lewis was the mastermind behind the murderous plan, giving her co-conspirators money to buy the weapons and orchestrating an earlier failed attempt to have her husband killed. "Instead of pulling a trigger on a gun, she pulled a couple of young men in to pull the trigger for her," said David Grimes, the Pittsylvania County Commonwealth's Attorney.[18]

CHAPTER 39

Brandon J. Rhode, Georgia.
Executed September 27

Brandon Rhode was scheduled for execution at 7 p.m. on September 21, 2010. Rhode, as with all offenders facing imminent death, was to be under constant observation by two guards. Something went wrong at the Georgia Diagnostic & Classification Prison at Jackson. Rhode attempted suicide by making deep cuts in both arms and his neck with a razor blade. The razor blade had been hidden in his cell and apparently, with a blanket obscuring the view of prison guards, he tried to end his life before Georgia could.

He was rushed to a hospital where he was assessed for critical care as a result of losing a substantial amount of blood. He was treated, sutured and returned to prison. His lawyer met with him at the prison on the afternoon of the September 21. He was held in a restraint chair. His lawyer described him as being "in severe pain and discomfort," his face "haggard, pallid and jaundiced."[1] The Georgia Supreme Court issued a stay of execution until 2 p.m. on September 23. Rhode's death warrant did not expire until September 28. His execution would be rescheduled or delayed four more times in order to carry out the execution and avoid the expiration of the death warrant.

Rhode's lawyers sought to stop his execution by challenging the state's failure to protect Rhode from self-inflicted harm, disputing his competency to be executed, and questioning whether he was mentally fit to understand and appreciate the punishment he faced.

"He has been subjected to the surreal and incomprehensible: Heroic measures taken to stabilize his life by the prison staff that would then execute him," defense attorney Brian Kammer said in one court filing. Kammer urged the court to push back the execution again so experts could evaluate whether Rhode was mentally competent to be executed, or understood why he was being punished. "The threat of execution has pushed Mr. Rhode's limited coping skills to the breaking point," spurring him to slash himself with blades he hid from guards while under a blanket.[2]

One by one, the courts refused to intervene to delay the execution beyond September 28. A stay beyond the 28th would have effectively postponed the execution because the death warrant would have expired. The state of Georgia was determined to carry out Rhode's execution without the delay of issuing another death warrant.

A trial court conducted a two-day hearing to determine if Rhode was competent to be executed. The court, by way of a 14-page order, ruled that Rhode was indeed competent to be put to death by lethal injection. On September 27, the Supreme Court rejected Rhode's appeal of the trial court's ruling. The state Board of Pardons and Paroles refused to reconsider its denial of clemency of a week earlier. The federal courts also refused to intervene.[3]

*   *   *

At the time of the crime, Rhode, who was 18 years old, and his accomplice, Daniel Lucas, who was 19 years old, were burglarizing the home of Steven and Gerri Ann Moss. It was April 23, 1998. The Moss home was located in rural Jones County, in central Georgia. They fled when Rhode discovered an alarm system. They returned later that day to burglarize the home again.

According to court records,[4] while Rhode and Lucas were ransacking the Moss home searching for valuables, 11-year-old Bryan Moss arrived home and saw Rhode and Lucas inside the house through a front window. Bryan grabbed a baseball bat and heroically burst through a back door to take on the intruders.

Bryan was subdued at gunpoint by Rhode. He was forced on to a chair, while Rhode and Lucas discussed his fate. Lucas fired a single shot at the boy, inflicting a non-fatal shoulder wound. At that point 15-year-old Kristin Moss, Bryan's sister, returned home. Lucas took Bryan into a back bedroom. Rhode met Kristin at the door, sat her in a chair, and shot her twice in the head with a handgun, a .357 magnum.

Lucas then shot Bryan six times with a .25 caliber pistol. The children's father, Steven Moss, was then ambushed by Rhode when he arrived home. He shot Steven four times with the .357 magnum. Before leaving, Lucas obtained a .22 caliber pistol from Rhode's automobile and shot Bryan and Kristin again.

Within about 20 minutes, a total of 13 shots were fired at the three victims. Eight out of the 13 shots entered either the head or chest of the victims; any of those eight wounds would have caused death.[5]

Gerri Ann Moss, the victims' wife and mother, told investigators that she had seen her husband at about 3:30 p.m. at her job, he had left and was going home. She found her massacred family when she got home from work.[6]

Chad Derrick Jackson, Rhode's roommate, told police that he observed Rhode and Lucas handing rifles and other items out of Jackson and Rhode's bedroom window and loading them into Rhode's car late in the evening on the day of the murders. Jackson also testified that Rhode and Lucas admitted to him the next day that Lucas first shot Bryan in the shoulder, that Lucas then shot Bryan while Rhode simultaneously shot Kristin, that Rhode next shot Steven Moss and that lastly, Lucas shot each victim to ensure that they were dead.

Danny Ray Bell, who also lived in the same house as Rhode, testified that Rhode and Lucas spoke to him between the two burglaries and that Bell advised Rhode not to return to burglarize the same home. Bell testified that, at the time of this conversation, Rhode had a .357 magnum in his waistband. According to Bell, when Rhode returned from the second burglary, Rhode said that he had "messed up big time" and needed to dispose of some weapons and other items. Rhode admitted to Bell that Lucas shot a young boy and that he shot a girl and a man.

Rhode made a statement admitting he fired two times at Kristin with the .357 magnum, and he led law enforcement officers to two locations where he and Lucas had stashed weapons and other items. A forensic expert matched two of the guns that were found, a .357 magnum and .25 caliber handguns to bullets retrieved from the crime scene and the victims' bodies.[7]

Rhode and Lucas were tried separately, several months apart. During trial, Rhode testified that he shot Kristin twice and dropped his gun. He said Lucas picked up the gun and shot Steven Moss. Lucas told investigators a different story. He said he shot 11-year-old Bryan Moss six times while Rhode shot Kristin and Steven Moss in the next room.

The jury found Rhode guilty of three counts of murder, three counts of felony murder, two counts of burglary, and one count of kidnapping. He was sentenced to death after the jury concluded that death sentences were warranted for the murder of three members of the Moss family.

Lucas, Rhode's co-defendant, was also convicted of murder, burglary and kidnapping. He too was sentenced to death. As of the end of 2013, Lucas remained on death row at the Georgia Diagnostic and Classification State Prison.

*   *   *

Suicide attempts on death row are rare. In March 2010, Ohio inmate Lawrence Raymond Reynolds, Jr., overdosed on an antidepressant hours before he was to be transferred to the state's death chamber. He recovered in a hospital and was executed a week later.

In Texas, David Long was executed in December 1999 after overdosing on antidepressants authorities believe he hoarded in his death row cell. Long's attorneys sought to postpone the execution, but a judge refused a reprieve, saying that because Long previously was judged competent to be executed, there was a presumption of competency.[8]

Prosecutor Fred Bright called the clemency hearing, Rhodes' "final hour." Prosecutors and defense attorneys presented statements before a five-member state parole board, who would decide whether to proceed with the execution or commute Rhode's sentence to life without parole.[9]

The board heard statements from Rhode's loved ones and attorneys on the morning of the hearing, and the prosecution gave statements to the board during the afternoon session.

"Seven people spoke on behalf of the Moss family, including Gerri Ann Moss, who spoke via phone," said Bright. "She spoke last." Bright received the decision just before 3:30 p.m. on the day of the hearing. He said it was "fairly quick." The execution would proceed.[10]

After several postponements, Rhode's execution had been set for 7 p.m. on September 27, 2010. Although rescheduled four times, the execution did not go off as planned. It was pushed back several hours as corrections officials waited for the U.S. Supreme Court to decide on Rhode's final plea for a stay of execution. The court rejected his appeal late in the evening.

After 9 p.m. medics tried for about 30 minutes to find a vein to administer the three-drug lethal injection within the death chamber of the Georgia Diagnostic & Classification Prison, located 45 minutes south of Atlanta.

Rhode declined a special last meal request and instead ate the standard institutional meal of chicken and rice, carrots, turnip greens, mixed beans, cornbread, bread pudding and iced tea.[11]

As Rhode laid trapped to a gurney in the death chamber, he declined to speak any last words or have a final prayer. Rhode's eyes darted around the room before the lethal drugs began coursing through his veins. Within minutes he was staring blankly at the ceiling of the death chamber. Moments before Rhode was pronounced dead, he turned his head, exposing a bandage over the part of his neck he slashed. It took 14 minutes for the lethal dose to kill him.[12]

He was dead by 10:16 p.m.

*   *   *

Jones County assistant district attorneys Gregory Bushway and Keagan Goodrich witnessed the execution. Bushway prosecuted the case with District Attorney Bright, who was not able to be at the prison.[13]

Bright had not changed his opinion of Rhode. When the case was prepared for trial, a plea bargain was not offered. Bright wanted the death penalty. "I vividly remember in the guilt-innocence portion of the trial, when the jury had been out five hours, the attorneys asked me about a manslaughter plea. My response was, 'Read my lips; I'm not even interested in offering life without parole.'"[14]

Gerri Ann Moss lost her son, daughter and husband at the hands of Rhode and Lucas. She said, "Nothing will be able to put this to rest. Nothing ... I guess I'm mad because I have to live like this." Twelve years after their deaths, people are still working hard to remember the Moss family in every way possible, even if it is not always easy. "It's such a great loss to society and I just remember them being so kind and sweet and they always, always, always were thinking of others," said Gerri Ann prior to the execution.[15]

"Kristin was beautiful, popular, athletic. Bryan was, just, he was my best friend, protector, he protected everyone, he was just everyone's friend, and Steven made you laugh," said family friend Rebecca Nobel on the eve of the scheduled execution.[16]

"They're giving back the love that they received from us, and it's beautiful," said Gerri Ann from her home in California.[17] A candlelight memorial was hosted by friends of the Moss family the night before the execution. Moss did not attend Rhode's execution.

CHAPTER 40

Michael W. Benge, Ohio. Executed October 6

Michael W. Benge was violent, unemployed and addicted to crack. Those three things converged on February 1, 1993.

Benge was 31 years old, and his relationship with his girlfriend had turned sour as a result of his drug use. He stole her jewelry and other things for money to buy crack. Benge began to batter his girlfriend. The aftermath of the beatings became so obvious that his girlfriend skipped family gatherings to avoid embarrassment. With no money to feed his addiction, he bludgeoned his girlfriend to death to get access to her ATM card.[1]

The execution of Michael Benge made headlines. He was the eighth person executed in Ohio in 2010. Benge's execution marked the highest number of executions for a single year since Ohio reinstated the death penalty in 1999. Ohio executed more people in 2010 than any other state with the exception of Texas. The Lone Star State has accounted for nearly one-third of all executions nationwide during the modern era of the death penalty. Texas executed 17 men in 2010.

* * *

Before dawn on February 1, 1993, a car belonging to Judith Gabbard, Benge's girlfriend, was found abandoned on the west side of the Miami River in Hamilton, Ohio. The vehicle was found near the bank of the river with the front passenger-side tire stuck in a gully. According to court records,[2] after the vehicle was towed away, the tow truck operator observed blood on the front bumper and passenger side of the car and notified the police.

The police returned to the area where the car was found and discovered the body of Gabbard in the Miami River. Her body was weighted down with a large piece of concrete which had been placed upon her head and chest. The police found her checkbook, some cash and jewelry. The police realized immediately that this was not a robbery. The police retrieved a tire iron from the river, approximately 12 to 15 feet from where Gabbard's body was found.

The police arrested Benge the next day. As detectives approached Benge, he dropped Judith Gabbard's ATM card. Benge was taken to the police station for questioning. After being read his Miranda warnings, he agreed to talk with detectives. Benge told the police that two black men in a Bronco had chased him and Gabbard to the river and that their car had gotten stuck.

Benge claimed that one of the men injured Gabbard and took her ATM card while the other held him at gunpoint, demanding the ATM code. When Benge refused to tell him, the man returned the ATM card to him. Benge escaped by jumping into the river. As he swam away, he heard Gabbard screaming as the men beat her.

The story was unbelievable, and the police detectives told him they did not believe it. Benge told them that he thought he should talk to a lawyer. The questioning ceased once Benge invoked his right to counsel.

However, a short time later, Benge told police he wanted to talk. He signed a Miranda warning card indicating that he waived his Miranda rights, although he had already invoked his right to counsel. Benge gave the police a tape-recorded statement in which he recounted a different version of what happened the night before.

Benge told police that he had driven to the riverbank with Gabbard so that they could talk. He said that they had argued over the fact that he was addicted to crack cocaine. Gabbard also accused him of being unfaithful to her. Benge said he got out of the vehicle to urinate. At that point, he said Gabbard drove at him trying to run him down, but the car got stuck in the mud. Benge said that he became enraged, pulled Gabbard out of the car, and began beating her with a metal pipe he found lying on the ground. Benge said he threw her body into the river, face down, disposed of the weapon and swam across the river.

He did not recall whether he put any rocks or cement on her body. Benge said he went to the home of his friend, John Fuller, to get dry clothes. He told police that Fuller's fiancée, Awantha Shields, provided him with dry clothing.

Benge was indicted on one count of murder with death penalty specifications that included an offense committed for the purpose of escaping detection for another offense and an offense committed during the commission of an aggravated robbery. He was also charged with aggravated robbery and gross abuse of a corpse.

*   *   *

At trial, Awantha Shields testified that in the early morning hours of February 1, 1993, Benge arrived at her house wearing wet clothes. Benge asked her if she had ever killed anyone. He told her that he and his girlfriend had "got into it" earlier, that it blew over, and that they went to the riverbank. He then told her that they had started fighting again and that he hit her in the head no more than ten times with a crowbar, put rocks over her head and pushed her in the river. Benge told her that he had killed his girlfriend to get her "Jeanie" card, a reference to her ATM, which, for a crack addict, miraculously produces money from a machine.[3]

He also said that if the police questioned him he would lie and say that a couple of black guys jumped him and his girlfriend and beat his girlfriend up. He also told her that he had given her ATM card to a guy named Baron to get $200 to buy crack cocaine but that he never saw the money.

Prosecutors used his two statements against him. The first one to show that he gave conflicting statements and the second to show he admitted killing Gabbard.

Benge took the stand on his own behalf and reiterated what he had told police during his second interview, including that Gabbard had tried to run him down and that he was in a rage when he killed her. Benge also claimed that he had permission to use Gabbard's ATM card and did not rob her. On cross-examination, he admitted losing his job in January 1993 due to his crack cocaine habit and that he had no income at the time he killed Gabbard.[4]

Benge was convicted on all counts and specifications. The jury recommended that he be sentenced to death, and that recommendation was accepted by the trial court. The court of appeals affirmed Benge's convictions and death sentence.

* * *

Benge raised a number of issues on appeal. A couple of issues pursued by his legal team had an interesting twist. There was also an interesting issue that counsel did not pursue. The issue not pursued was addressed by the U.S. Supreme Court in 2010 and may have resulted in a different outcome for Benge.

When Benge was first brought to the police station, he was questioned by police. When police confronted him and indicated that they thought he was lying, Benge invoked his right to counsel pursuant to *Miranda v. Arizona*.[5] The interrogation ceased at that point.

Benge then asked to talk to police again. This is a troubling issue. Once Benge invoked his right to counsel it seems clear that the police should not have reengaged without counsel being present. However, this issue was never raised during Benge's appeals.

* * *

In 2010, the U.S. Supreme Court In *Maryland v. Shatzer*[6] set a bright-line standard for reengaging an accused in police questioning after invoking the right to counsel. Michael Shatzer was in prison when the police questioned him about the sexual assault of his son. After being read his Miranda warnings he invoked his right to legal counsel and the interrogation was terminated. Thirty months later the police returned to interview him. Shatzer was, again, Mirandized and confessed to assaulting his son. Shatzer's confession was used to convict him of sexual assault.

Justice Antonin Scalia wrote in *Shatzer*, there should not be an "eternal" bar against further police questioning after a suspect requested an attorney. The thirty-month break in custody was enough. However, Scalia went further. Those suspects who have been released from custodial interrogation for at least 14 days could be returned to custody and, if they did not again invoke counsel, could be interrogated. Any incriminating statement could be used at trial.

* * *

Would Benge's admission be excluded under *Shatzer*? Was it worth pursuing on appeal? We'll never know.

The second issue was raised unsuccessfully by Benge. In the midst of a lunch recess during trial as Benge was being escorted out of the courthouse, a relative of the victim tried to attack him on the courthouse steps. Deputies prevented the attack and arrested the attacker. Benge's counsel moved for a mistrial, which the court denied. Prior to overruling the motion, the trial judge questioned the jurors, outside the presence of the attorneys and Benge, to determine whether anyone witnessed the altercation and whether there were any grounds for finding bias on behalf of a juror or jurors.[7]

One alternate juror, who neither deliberated nor voted, heard yelling and screaming but did not see the attack. This juror told the judge that it would not interfere with his impartiality.

The following day, a different juror expressed concern over whether precautions would be taken to ensure the jury's safety while leaving the courthouse. Once again, the court overruled defense counsel's motion for a mistrial. The court offered to further question jurors but defense counsel declined the offer.[8]

Ohio appellant courts have held that the trial court determines, as a question of fact, whether an outburst outside the courtroom would deprive a defendant a fair trial by improperly influencing the jury. The trial court found no influencing of the jury and denied Benge's request for a mistrial.

Benge also contended that he had a right to be present at all proceedings and that he was deprived of that right by being excluded from the trial court's discussions with the jurors. The Fifth Amendment to the U.S. Constitution, enforceable against the states through the Fourteenth Amendment, affords a criminal defendant the right to be present at all stages of his or her trial, including voir dire proceedings used to determine a juror's fairness and impartiality.[9]

Clearly, Benge's constitutional rights were violated by the court's ex parte conference with jurors. Interestingly, the Ohio Supreme Court ruled that it was an error to exclude Benge's counsel from discussions between the trial judge and jurors. However, the error was harmless because Benge had not shown how his presence would have benefitted him or how he was prejudiced by his absence.

*   *   *

In seeking mercy, Benge's lawyers argued he was physically abused by a stepfather and stepbrother and began abusing substances when he was 11—first alcohol, then marijuana and eventually cocaine. They said his brain was impaired as a result.[10]

Governor Ted Strickland was not moved by Benge's plea for mercy. Benge's last chance to dodge execution evaporated when Strickland agreed with the Ohio Parole Board's unanimous recommendation against using executive clemency. He had exhausted his legal appeals, all the way to the U.S. Supreme Court. Benge's death was imminent.[11]

Neither Benge's two children nor his mother witnessed his execution. They and other family members spoke with him by phone the day before and visited him the morning of the scheduled execution. Benge's last meal consisted of a large chef salad with ham, turkey and bacon bits, bleu cheese and ranch dressing, barbecue baby back ribs, two cans of cashews and two bottles of iced tea.[12]

Gabbard's daughter appeared nervous, kicking her foot and clutching a bottle of soda in her hand as Benge was prepared for execution. Gabbard's daughter, son and brother were present for Benge's execution.[13]

Benge's final words were those of contrition, "I can't apologize enough and I hope my death gives you closure," Benge said in his last statement. "That's all I can ask. Praise God and thanks." He continued as he laid strapped to a gurney at the Southern Ohio Correctional Facility at Lucasville, "As for Judy's family, I've caused you all more pain than you all can endure in your lifetime. I just hope someday you can find peace in your hearts," he said.[14]

Benge chose to have his attorney, Randall Porter, as a witness. The two exchanged a nod before the lethal dose of sodium thiopental began to flow. Benge continued to talk to officials in the room until he closed his eyes several minutes after his last statement.

The family was otherwise quiet during the procedure, which ended with Benge's death at 10:34 a.m.[15]

After the execution, Kathy Johnson, Gabbard's sister, said, "It makes us feel there was justice for my sister. That's what this was all about." When asked about Benge's last words, she said, "I don't feel like Mike Benge was remorseful. He has blamed everyone else but himself."[16]

Johnson went on to say that she didn't believe Benge was truly sorry. "He's blamed his family, he's blamed my sister, he's blamed my family. He has never taken responsibility for his own actions." Wearing a pin with her sister's picture as she spoke, Johnson said that at least now her sister, the oldest girl among nine siblings, could rest in peace.[17]

CHAPTER 41

Donald Ray Wackerly II, Oklahoma.
Executed October 14

One evening in early September 1996, Donald Wackerly told his wife that they needed money and that he would do "whatever it took" to get some. He wanted to impress upon his wife just how serious he was. As he sat in their Muldrow, Oklahoma, home he wore latex gloves and loaded his .22 caliber rifle, wiping off each bullet before loading it into the chamber.

The next day, Wackerly and his wife, Michelle, left Muldrow and drove to a dam on the Arkansas River in rural Sequoyah County right along the Arkansas border. There, they spotted a lone truck parked near a levy and an older gentleman fishing nearby. Wackerly parked his Jeep a few feet from the blue Toyota pickup truck and instructed his wife to walk down to the levy to see if any other people were around. She walked down to the levy, talked to the fisherman for a few minutes, and returned to her husband to confirm that they were alone. Wackerly then instructed his wife to sit and wait.[1]

*   *   *

Forty-five minutes later the fisherman, Pan Sayakhoummane, a 51-year-old Laotian who lived in Fort Smith, Arkansas, returned to his truck. According to court records,[2] as he approached, Wackerly raised the hood of his Jeep and asked for a jump to revive a dead battery. Michelle Wackerly knelt behind the Jeep.

Wackerly raised his .22 caliber rifle and shot Sayakhoummane about seven times in the head, back, chest, arm, wrist and hand. Michelle stayed hidden until she heard a thump, Sayakhoummane's body hitting the ground.

When Michelle stood up, she saw Sayakhoummane's body lying flat on the ground as her husband struggled to get a fishing pole from underneath his body.

Wackerly then took action to dispose of Sayakhoummane's body and truck. He drove the truck a short distance down a dirt road while Michelle followed in the couple's Jeep. Wackerly took a tackle box from the truck before asking his wife to wait while he drove Sayakhoummane's truck into the river. The truck's bumper caught on the river bed so the truck remained only partially submerged. Finished with his efforts to dispose of the evidence of the killing he just committed, Wackerly returned to his wife and the couple proceeded to a Sonic Drive-In restaurant for dinner.

Later that night, Wackerly sifted through the contents of Sayakhoummane's wallet and cut up all the identity cards he found. He placed the shredded cards in a Ziploc bag and threw them away, along with Sayakhoummane's wallet. The other property he had stolen—

Sayakhoummane's tackle box and fishing reels—he stashed in a spare room. Wackerly later sold the reels to a local pawn shop for sixty dollars.

The day after the murder, a passerby spotted the partially submerged pickup truck near Lock and Dam 14, about 15 miles from Fort Smith. Sayakhoummane's body was in the bed of the truck.

An initial investigation produced no leads. Three months later the only witness came forward. Michelle Wackerly went to Oklahoma state investigators and told them about the murder. She was now estranged from her husband. Based on her statement, an agent retrieved Sayakhoummane's fishing poles from the woods near the river and located his reels at the pawn shop, where the shop's owner confirmed that it was Donald Wackerly who had sold them. Agents also searched Wackerly's apartment and found Sayakhoummane's tackle box, a pair of latex gloves, a .22 caliber rifle, and a box of ammunition with some bullets missing. The weapon and ammunition were consistent with the bullets removed from Sayakhoummane's body.

Wackerly was charged with first-degree murder and robbery. At trial, the State relied on the testimony of Michelle Wackerly, the physical evidence corroborating her account, the testimony of the pawn shop owner and the testimony of Michelle Wackerly's brother, Curtis Jones, who recounted that Wackerly had confessed to him that he had killed a man at the dam.

* * *

In the end, the jury convicted Wackerly of both the murder and robbery charges. The case proceeded to the trial's penalty phase, at which time the prosecution argued that two aggravating circumstances made Wackerly death penalty-eligible. The first aggravating circumstance was that the murder was committed in a manner aimed to avoid or prevent a lawful arrest or prosecution. The prosecution would argue that Wackerly put Sayakhoummane's body in the truck and attempted to submerge the truck in the Arkansas River. The second was future dangerousness and the likelihood that Wackerly would commit future criminal acts of violence that would constitute a continuing threat to society.

Evidence produced during the penalty phase of Wackerly's trial proved that he committed an armed robbery of a Webber Falls, Oklahoma, convenience store nine days after killing Sayakhoummane.

Michelle Wackerly stood guard at the store's entrance while Wackerly, wearing a hunting mask and carrying a pistol, ordered the store's cashier to give him money. When the cashier declined, Wackerly held his pistol within inches of the cashier's forehead and repeated his demand. This time, the cashier complied. As Wackerly walked with cash in hand toward the exit, he heard a banging from the back of the store. Thinking it was a second employee; he turned back to the register, pointed his gun at the cashier, shouted "I'll kill both of you" and sprinted away.[3]

Wackerly presented three witnesses during the penalty phase. Sue Spinas testified that he performed farm labor for her, that he was a reliable employee and that she would hire him again if given the opportunity.

A second witness, Donna Lomax, Wackerly's half-sister, testified that Wackerly was spoiled by his parents and never disciplined, and, as a result through no fault of his own, he generally seemed unprepared for life. Ms. Lomax also testified that, when he was 14, Wackerly was the driver in a car accident in which his passenger died. He never took responsibility for causing the death, Lomax related, again contributing, in her estimation, to his general unpreparedness for adulthood.

Finally, Diana Branham, Wackerly's step-sister, testified that her seven-year-old son had a great relationship with Wackerly.

The court instructed the jury that there was evidence presented on the following mitigating circumstances during the penalty phase of trial:

1. The defendant did not have any significant history of prior criminal activity;
2. The defendant is likely to be rehabilitated;
3. The defendant's troubling emotional and family history;
4. The defendant loves his family;
5. The defendant's family loves him;
6. The defendant was a steady, reliable employee for Sue Spinas;
7. The defendant's execution would have a devastating effect upon his nephew.[4]

At that point the jury began deliberating Wackerly's fate. If the jury found that the aggravating circumstances outweighed the mitigating circumstances, then the jury could sentence Wackerly to death. The aggravating circumstances must receive the unanimous support of the jury; mitigating circumstances need only be supported by one juror.

Jurors were further directed by the court that they "may consider sympathy or sentiment for the defendant in deciding whether to impose the death penalty," and that they could impose a non-capital punishment even if they found the aggravating circumstances outweighed the mitigating circumstances.

Even with the deck stacked in favor of the defendant, the jury sentenced Wackerly to death for murder and life in prison for robbery. In doing so, the jurors unanimously found that both statutory aggravating circumstances supported the death penalty, and these points outweighed any mitigating circumstance.

* * *

As his scheduled execution approached, Wackerly's counsel filed a motion in federal court seeking to have his Buddhist spiritual adviser inside the death chamber with him during the execution. A federal judge dismissed that case the day before the execution after an agreement was reached with prison officials to allow Buddhist monks to perform several rituals on Wackerly's body after his death.[5]

Wackerly's attorney, Michael Salem, said the agreement is not optimum for his client but would be adequate. "At this point, given the circumstances and the shortness of time, this is reasonable," Salem said. Wackerly would be allowed to recite a mantra of ultimate compassion until he dies, Salem said. The Buddhist spiritual adviser and others in an adjacent observation room would also be allowed to chant.[6]

As part of his Buddhist practice, Wackerly believed in reincarnation and the teaching that the thoughts and feelings at the time of death can affect the circumstances of rebirth, according to court documents filed on his behalf. "As I understand Buddhist tradition, the good feeling and good spirit in the heart and mind at the time of death is related to their belief of a good reincarnation," said Salem.[7]

"The idea here is to allow this ritual," Salem said. Oklahoma Assistant Attorney General Dan Weitman appeared in court on behalf of prison officials and said he accepted the agreement.[8]

* * *

Wackerly maintained his innocence, telling the Oklahoma Pardon and Parole Board a month before his scheduled execution that he was visiting his parents in Fort Smith when Sayakhoummane was killed, that his ex-wife implicated him after he became abusive toward her and that "she wanted me out of the picture." Wackerly said his ex-wife gave him the tackle box and other items taken from the victim and claimed they came from her brother, who hoped to settle a debt with Wackerly.[9]

Two of Wackerly's sisters, Donna Lomax and Dianna Davis, released a statement after the execution thanking friends and family for their support over the years, saying they would miss their brother and also addressed the Sayakhoummane family. "We would like to thank our family and friends for their support of us, as well as Donnie, over the years. Their kind words and prayers have helped to sustain us through this very difficult process. We have been blessed beyond measure by the outpouring of love shown to our family. Donnie loved his family dearly and we certainly love him. We will miss our brother very much and pray he is in a better place. The Sayakhoummane family will forever be in our hearts and our prayers."[10]

Three of Sayakhoummane's relatives witnessed Wackerly's execution, but did not talk with the media after the execution.

Wackerly's last meal was a medium stuffed-crust pizza from Pizza Hut with mushrooms, bell peppers, black olives and jalapenos, a Dr. Pepper, coconut cream pie, and a chocolate shake.[11]

His last words were uttered as he lay strapped to a metal gurney in the Oklahoma State Penitentiary at McAlester. He had a sheet covering him from his feet to his chest as he chanted, "Om mani padme hum," along with two Buddhist monks who were in the witness room, separated from the death chamber by a plate glass window. The chant is described as the Buddhist "mantra of compassion." Prison officials believe that it was the first execution in state history accompanied by Buddhist religious elements.[12]

As the execution began, Wackerly acknowledged his attorneys and winked at a relative before he started chanting. The execution by lethal injection began at 6:06 p.m. and within seconds, Wackerly's chants faded to whispers, the heavyset Wackerly exhaled powerfully and became quiet. He was pronounced dead six minutes later.[13]

After Wackerly's death, two Buddhist Monks were escorted into the death chamber and allowed to perform several rituals consistent with Buddhist principles, the agreement reached between Wackerly's attorneys and the state of Oklahoma. The ritual lasted about 15 minutes. Wackerly's body was then turned over to a state medical examiner.

CHAPTER 42

Larry Wayne Wooten, Texas.
Executed October 21

Larry Wayne Wooten preyed on the elderly. He lived in Paris, Texas, the county seat of Lamar County on the border of Texas and Oklahoma, about 105 miles north of Dallas. Wooten would leave an indelible mark on Paris as he repeatedly victimized the older residents of this small, rural community.

Wooten's first conviction came in 1982, when he pled guilty to a charge of burglary with the intent to rape a 73-year-old woman in Paris. Police found Wooten in the elderly woman's bed, asleep and naked. Wooten was placed on probation for seven years.

Just two years later, Wooten was arrested after fleeing from police, having tried to break into the same elderly woman's home. Wooten was apprehended by police with a martial arts knife in his pocket. A search of the woman's home revealed that the telephone line had been cut, a screen and window had been broken and the back door had been pulled off its hinges. Wooten pled guilty, and was sentenced again to probation, this time for ten years.[1]

In 1991, Wooten's probation was revoked when he pled guilty to robbery. The robbery finally landed him in prison. He was sentenced to 10 years and was released on parole after only 2½ years.

Kerye Ashmore, the former Lamar County District Attorney, said that Wooten was a person of interest in the murder of another elderly woman in Paris who was killed in 1996.[2]

Wooten's final elderly victims lost their lives.

* * *

Wooten knew 80-year-old Grady Alexander and his 86-year-old wife, Bessie. He did odd jobs and ran errands for the Alexanders. In fact, Wooten was once married to their niece, and the elderly couple had in the past loaned Wooten money, never realizing that the money was to feed his drug habit.

According to court records,[3] on September 3, 1996, Grady Alexander and his wife Bessie, were found dead in their home. They had been beaten with a cast-iron skillet and a pistol. They had both been stabbed and had their throats slit. Bessie was beaten with a pistol with such force that the grips and portions of the trigger mechanism of the pistol broke off. Both were nearly decapitated. Grady and Bessie had defensive wounds, as well, indicating a brutal struggle for their lives.

Prosecutors said Wooten robbed the couple, taking their savings of $500 so he could buy cocaine. On the night after the savage murders Wooten went on a cocaine binge with a woman who told police that when she met up with Wooten, he was wearing blue-striped overalls and that he had a "wad of money" in his front pocket. She told police that there was blood on the overalls, and Wooten had blood on his hands and fingernails.[4]

DNA evidence that matched Wooten to the murders included blood found on the couple's kitchen floor and Wooten's overalls that were stained with Grady Alexander's blood.

* * *

During the trial, the prosecution presented evidence that Wooten knew the Alexanders. He had been invited into their home as a result of his marriage to their niece, Ruby Black. A motive for the killings was provided when Ruby testified that the Alexanders always had a large sum of cash at home. Ruby told the jury that Wooten would sometimes spend his entire paycheck on cocaine. She also admitted that she had loaned him money that he ultimately spent on cocaine. It was for this reason that she stopped loaning Wooten money. Ruby also encouraged the Alexanders not to loan him any more money.

At the trial, the prosecution presented blood evidence found on the victims' kitchen floor. A DNA analysis showed that it included Wooten's blood. Grady Alexander's blood was discovered on a pair of Wooten's pants which were found near an area where Wooten had bought drugs around the time of the murders.

The prosecution ended its case with the testimony of a forensic psychiatrist who said that the Alexander murders were particularly disturbing because of Wooten's wholesale failure to express any remorse, the "overkill," and the fact that Wooten knew his victims.

The psychiatrist also found Wooten's history of "impulsive criminality" to be disturbing; and that Wooten "hasn't mellowed out with age." Based on this, considering Wooten's chronic substance abuse problems and the fact that he apparently had no desire to stop using cocaine, the psychiatrist concluded that Wooten would indeed be a future danger to society, both in prison and on the street.[5]

Wooten said he didn't kill the couple. He acknowledged that he knew them and formerly worked doing odd jobs on their behalf. He claimed he went to their home in Paris, found the bodies and fled.[6]

Although Wooten was offered a plea bargain of life in prison, he decided to roll the dice and go to trial. His lawyers and hired experts were convinced that a successful challenge to the DNA evidence could be mounted to create a reasonable doubt about Wooten's guilt.

Wooten's gamble cost him his life. A Lamar County jury found him guilty of murder and sentenced him to death.

* * *

Wooten appealed his conviction to the Texas Supreme Court. Wooten's attorneys argued he would not have turned down a plea bargain if he knew about additional DNA evidence that didn't become available until after his trial began. Wooten turned down a plea agreement of life in prison after DNA experts working for his trial attorneys believed the blood evidence did not reliably connect him to the crime. However, after the trial began, additional lab results showed the DNA evidence was stronger than originally thought.[7]

Wooten's troubled plea may have had a different result in 2012. The U.S. Supreme Court extended the Sixth Amendment right to a fair trial to include competent legal representation during plea negotiations.

The cases were *Lafler v. Cooper*[8] and *Missouri v. Frye*.[9] In Cooper, the court considered whether an attorney's advice to his client to reject a favorable plea bargain based on an incorrect understanding of the law was ineffective assistance of counsel. In Frye, the court considered whether counsel's failure to disclose the terms of a favorable plea offer is a violation of the Sixth Amendment right to a fair trial.

The court could no longer ignore that plea bargaining is the grease that keeps the criminal justice system lubricated. With more than nine out of ten cases resolved by plea, the court had finally extended constitutional scrutiny to a process that occurs in nearly every single case. Competent legal counsel during plea negotiations is deservedly a constitutionally protected right.

According to court records in Wooten's case,[10] District Attorney Ashmore said he never misrepresented the strength of the DNA evidence. Central to the prosecution's case was DNA analysis of blood evidence found at the murder scene and elsewhere that would be—if reliable—virtually conclusive of guilt. The trial court directed the prosecution to turn over all DNA analysis and evidence in its possession. The prosecution furnished a preliminary DNA report to defense counsel in May 1997 and a further accounting of DNA evidence in January 1998. Defense counsel obtained their own experts who, on the basis of the evidence available at the time, believed the prosecution's DNA evidence to be unreliable.

It was at this point that the prosecution presented Wooten's attorney with a plea deal: if Wooten pled guilty, he would receive a life sentence. If he chose to go to trial he would remain eligible for the death penalty. With his experts telling him that the prosecution's DNA analysis was faulty, Wooten rejected the offer and his case proceeded to trial.

Once jury selection was under way, however, additional data emerged from the DNA laboratory, which made it clear that the laboratory had unintentionally failed to turn over all available DNA evidence. This late-coming data also revealed the prosecution's DNA evidence to be significantly more reliable than initially apparent. Wooten's counsel moved for a continuance to permit their experts time to complete their evaluation. The trial court denied that motion, jury selection ended, and Wooten's trial began.

Defense counsel still assumed that they would be able to attack the veracity of the DNA evidence, albeit less convincingly. After opening statements were made and some witnesses were called, more evidence came in from the laboratory that suggested the strategy was probably misguided.

The trial court granted a twelve-day continuance to permit a full analysis of the new DNA findings by the defense experts. The in-depth analysis indicated that any apparent evidentiary flaws were illusory or had been corrected.

The 5th U.S. Circuit Court of Appeals ruled that both sides are at risk in a plea offer and there's no constitutional right to a plea bargain. The Court of Appeals affirmed Wooten's conviction and his death sentence.[11]

In prior appeals, Wooten had claimed he should not be executed because he is mentally disabled. In October of 2003, Wooten filed an application for state writ of habeas corpus, alleging that he was mentally disabled and his execution would violate the 2002 U.S. Supreme Court decision in *Atkins v. Virginia*, banning the execution of the mentally disabled. In January of 2004, the Texas Court of Criminal Appeals remanded Wooten's claim back to the trial court to determine whether he was mentally disabled.[12]

Wooten was tested and the results were presented to the trial court. Wooten's IQ was in the range of 77 to 84. An IQ of 70 is considered the threshold for mental disability, but it is not considered a bright-line standard, or cut-off, for the death penalty. Wooten's mental disability claim did not hold water; the court found that the evidence did not support his claim.

* * *

In an interview from death row about a month before his execution, Wooten claimed that he did not kill the Alexanders. He said he went to their home, found their bodies and then fled. "If I call the cops, they'll think I done it. I walked away. I didn't tell anybody. I thought they would pin it on me, and that's exactly what they did."[13]

The presiding judge at Wooten's trial, Judge Eric Clifford responded to a request from the Board of Pardons and Parole in the following manner, "As far as my memory goes, this crime is probably the most heinous crime ever committed in this area. Please be advised that I see no reason why the sentence should be modified in any way, and I highly support the sentence being carried out as originally ordered."[14]

Wooten's petition for clemency was denied by Governor Rick Perry and his final appeal to the U.S. Supreme Court was refused on October 4, 2010. Wooten's death by lethal injection was inevitable.

Wooten visited with his two sisters and his attorney in the final hours before his scheduled execution at the Texas State Penitentiary in Huntsville. He ate a final meal of 10 fried chicken legs, 10 chicken wings, mashed potatoes, greens, rice pudding, tea and banana pudding.[15]

No family members of the Alexander family attended the execution. Wooten's two sisters, who witnessed the execution, cried and prayed. Between 10 to 15 anti–death penalty protesters stood about a block away outside the prison with one woman using a bullhorn saying, "The state of Texas has committed another murder."[16]

During his brief final statement, Wooten did not mention the Alexanders. His last words were, "Warden, warden, warden? Where is the warden at? I have nothing to say so you can send me home to my heavenly father." He cried as the drugs were administered and let out one final gasp as the lethal injection took effect. Nine minutes later, on October 21, 2010, at 6:21 p.m. he was dead.[17]

Larry Wooten was the 17th, and final, Texas inmate executed in 2010. Texas would once again be the most prolific state in terms of executions. Texas has accounted for more than one out of every three executions carried out in the United States since the death penalty was reinstated. Wooten was the 464th person executed in Texas since 1982 and the 225th person executed during Governor Perry's tenure.

Kerye Ashmore, the attorney who prosecuted Wooten back in 1998, called him a "scary guy" with a history of violence. There was no doubt in his mind that Wooten deserved the death penalty. "If you are going to have a death penalty, this is the kind of people you want to have the death penalty for."[18]

CHAPTER 43

Jeffrey T. Landrigan, Arizona.
Executed October 26

Some inmates, facing death in a matter of minutes, will say nothing. Some will pray. Some will apologize or ask for forgiveness. What Jeffrey Landrigan did in Arizona, as he lay strapped to a gurney at the Arizona State Prison Complex in Florence, was as incredible as it was sad.

Landrigan was a native of Oklahoma. Oklahoma entered the union as the 46th state in 1907. Since that time and even before, Oklahomans have lived for Saturday afternoons in the fall, when the Oklahoma Sooners took to the gridiron.

By the time Landrigan's date with the executioner arrived, the University of Oklahoma (OU) had won seven National Championships, had five Heisman Trophy winners and had won over 800 games. Bud Wilkinson, Barry Switzer and Bob Stoops had given fans much to cheer about.

In a strong voice with a heavy Oklahoma accent, Landrigan's last words were, "Well, I'd like to say thank you to my family for being here and all my friends, and Boomer Sooner," referring to the University of Oklahoma Sooners.[1]

*   *   *

According to court records,[2] Landrigan murdered Chester Dyer in 1989 in Phoenix, after escaping from an Oklahoma prison where he was being held as the result of a murder conviction.

Dyer was known as a promiscuous homosexual who frequently tried to "pick up" men by flashing a wad of money. This would invariably occur after he cashed his paycheck. Dyer told a friend "Michael" that he had recently met a guy named "Jeff," with whom he wanted to have sex. Dyer's physical description of Jeff was consistent with the description of Landrigan.

Dyer called Michael several times on Wednesday, December 13, 1989. During the first call, Dyer said he had picked up Jeff, that they were at the apartment drinking beer, and he wanted to know whether Michael would come over to "party."

Approximately 15 minutes later, Dyer called a second time and said that he was in the middle of sexual intercourse with Jeff. Shortly thereafter, Dyer called to ask whether Michael could get Jeff a job. Jeff spoke with Michael about employment, and asked if he was going to come over. Michael declined the invitation.

Dyer failed to show up for work the following day, and calls to him went unanswered. On December 15, a co-worker and two others went to Dyer's apartment and found him dead. Dyer's body was fully clothed with his face down on a bed. There was a pool of blood under Dyer's head and an electrical cord was tight around his neck. There were facial lacerations and puncture wounds on his body. A half-eaten sandwich and a small screwdriver lay beside the body. Blood smears were found in the kitchen and bathroom. A partial shoeprint impression was found in sugar on the apartment's tile floor.

Cause of death was ligature strangulation. The medical examiner found that Dyer was probably strangled after being rendered unconscious from blows to the head with a blunt instrument.

When Landrigan was first questioned, he denied knowing Dyer or ever having been to his apartment. When arrested, however, he was wearing one of Dyer's shirts. Several fingerprints taken from the scene matched Landrigan's. The impression in the sugar matched his sneaker, down to a small cut on the sole. Tests also revealed that a small amount of blood had seeped into the sneaker. A blood match was found on the shirt worn by Dyer.

Landrigan's ex-girlfriend testified that she had three telephone conversations with him in December of 1989. During one of those, he told her that he was "getting along" in Phoenix by "robbing." Landrigan placed the last call to her from jail sometime around Christmas. He said that he had "killed a guy ... with his hands" about a week before.

Landrigan was offered a plea deal to second-degree murder but opted to go to trial. Landrigan was uncooperative and disruptive during his trial. On June 28, 1990, a jury found him guilty of burglary, theft and first-degree murder. At sentencing, Landrigan did little to help himself. In fact, his conduct may well have sealed his fate. Counsel attempted to present the testimony of Landrigan's ex-wife and birth mother as mitigating evidence, but at Landrigan's request, both women refused to testify. When the trial judge asked why the witnesses refused, Landrigan's counsel responded that "it's at my client's wishes." When counsel tried to explain that Landrigan had worked at a legitimate job to provide for his family, Landrigan interrupted and stated "if I wanted this to be heard, I'd have my wife say it."

When counsel characterized the murder Landrigan committed in Oklahoma as having elements of self-defense, Landrigan interrupted and clarified: "He didn't grab me. I stabbed him." Responding to counsel's statement implying that a stabbing involving Landrigan while in prison in Oklahoma involved self-defense because the assaulted inmate knew Landrigan's first murder victim. Landrigan interrupted to clarify that the inmate was not acquainted with his first victim, but just "a guy I got in an argument with. I stabbed him 14 times. It was lucky he lived." At the conclusion of the sentencing hearing, the judge asked Landrigan if he had anything to say. Landrigan made a brief statement that concluded, "I think if you want to give me the death penalty, just bring it right on. I'm ready for it."[3]

Landrigan was sentenced to death. For good measure he was also sentenced to an aggravated term of 20 years in prison on the burglary and six months in the county jail for theft.

*   *   *

Prior to the murder in Arizona, Landrigan was convicted of murder in Washington County, Oklahoma. He was originally sentenced to death and later resentenced to 20 years to life.

The conviction stemmed from the 1982 fatal stabbing of his best friend, Greg Brown, who was about to become a father and wanted Landrigan to be his boy's godfather. Brown and Landrigan, along with some friends, were smoking marijuana and drinking whiskey at a trailer park in Dewey, Oklahoma, when the killing occurred.

According to court records,[4] Landrigan, along his with wife and son, arrived at the mobile home of Gordon Aiken at about 8 p.m. Soon after they arrived, Landrigan and Aiken went to purchase a fifth of whiskey. On their way back to the trailer park, the group picked up Landrigan's brother-in-law, Robert Martinez. When they returned to the trailer, Landrigan, Brown and the others began drinking whiskey and smoking marijuana.

Landrigan and Brown began calling one another "punk" and began arguing whether Landrigan could beat Brown in a fight. As Landrigan started to leave, Brown pushed him against the trailer wall, and told him, "if you want to settle the argument, we can take it outside." Brown went outside, followed by Landrigan.

Landrigan was holding a knife behind his back. Aiken rushed to a bedroom to find his rifle. Landrigan lunged at Brown and stabbed him in the chest. Aiken returned to the living room with the rifle. Someone in the trailer took the rifle, pointed it at Landrigan and told him to "back up or I'm going to blow your head off." Landrigan escaped between two cars as Brown collapsed on the ground.

Landrigan ran to a friend's machine shop and told him he had "wasted a guy." He later told Washington County Undersheriff Jim Eppler, "Jim, I tried to kill the mother fucker. I don't take that shit off nobody. I cut him twice. I think I cut him twice."

Landrigan testified on his own behalf at trial. He said that as the men continued to drink, he could see that what began as friendly teasing was now making Brown angry. He testified that, as he was leaving, the victim grabbed him by the throat and threatened to "whip my ass." Landrigan said the men went outside. He explained how he attempted to go back into the trailer, but someone inside pointed a shotgun in his direction. He jumped at Brown, but did not know he had a knife in his hand when he hit Brown.

Landrigan was found guilty of first-degree murder and sentenced to death, but the conviction was overturned on appeal and Landrigan entered a plea to second-degree murder and a 20-year to life prison term.

Despite his murder conviction, Landrigan was put on a minimum-security work crew, from which he once fled to have sex with a woman he had met in a park. On November 11, 1989, he walked away for good, escaping from prison. He headed for Yuma, Arizona, where he hoped to find his birth mother.[5]

*   *   *

A temporary restraining order staying Landrigan's execution had been imposed by a U.S. District Court judge in Phoenix and affirmed by the 9th U.S. Circuit Court of Appeals. The court imposed the order as it tried to force Arizona to disclose where and how it had obtained its supply of sodium thiopental, one of three drugs used in Arizona executions.

Sodium thiopental is a barbiturate that renders the condemned person unconscious so he or she cannot feel suffocation or pain induced by the second and third drugs administered during execution. The drug was in short supply. Hospira, Inc., a Lake Forest, Illinois, based company, the sole U.S. manufacturer and only apparent supplier of sodium thiopental approved by the U.S. Food and Drug Administration, has ceased production of the drug.

Landrigan's attorneys wanted assurances that Arizona's sodium thiopental had been lawfully obtained and would be effective, so as not to constitute cruel and unusual punishment in violation of the Eighth Amendment. The state resisted disclosing the information, citing a state law concealing the identities of executioners and all people with "ancillary" functions needed to carry out the execution.[6]

In the final days leading up to Landrigan's scheduled execution, intensive legal maneuvering by his defense team included a request to re-examine DNA evidence as well as disclosure of how the state legally obtained the sodium thiopental. Simultaneous arguments were raised in both state and federal courts.

The U.S. Supreme Court disposed of the disclosure issue with a one-page, 5–4 decision agreeing that Arizona prosecutors were not obligated to disclosure where the drugs were obtained. "There was no showing that the drug was unlawfully obtained, nor was there an offer of proof to that effect," the court order said. Justices Ruth Bader Ginsburg, Stephen Breyer, Sonia Sotomayor and Elena Kagan dissented, voting to keep the stay in place. Justices Anthony Kennedy, Clarence Thomas, Samuel Alito, Antonin Scalia and John Roberts were in the majority, lifting the stay.[7]

In spite of the Supreme Court's decision, Arizona Attorney General Terry Goddard revealed that the drug had come from Abbott Pharma in the U.K. Later, the British government intervened and banned the export of sodium thiopental for purposes of future executions.[8]

* * *

Landrigan was born into a family of criminals. His birth father, whom he never met face to face, died on death row in Arkansas, his grandfather was shot to death by police while robbing a drugstore, and even before a court found that he killed Dyer, he had already been convicted of another murder.[9]

Landrigan was born March 17, 1962, to a woman who had used drugs and alcohol all through her pregnancy. His birth name was Billy Patrick Wayne Hill, and his father abandoned him when he was a month old. His mother later abandoned him at a day-care center when he was eight months old. He was put up for adoption in Oklahoma. As an adolescent, he abused drugs and alcohol and spent time in juvenile-correctional facilities.[10]

He was imprisoned for murder, and while in prison he nearly killed another inmate. Landrigan told prison officials, "I stabbed him 14 times."[11]

* * *

Landrigan's execution came quickly after the U.S. Supreme Court ruled that his execution could proceed. Two days before the scheduled execution Governor Jan Brewer announced that she would not grant a reprieve to Landrigan. Landrigan's last meal consisted of steak, fried okra, French fries, strawberry ice cream and a Dr. Pepper.[12]

A curtain that blocked the witnesses' view of Landrigan was opened at 10:14 p.m. on October 26, 2010. The witnesses were sitting in observation rooms that are separated from the execution chamber by glass partitions.

Landrigan looked quizzically at the 27 people gathered to witness his death. He smiled to friends and family, his lip curling slightly under his reddish mustache. He gave his final statement invoking the Oklahoma Sooners and then looked around and smiled again. Then, as the first drug—sodium thiopental—took effect, he slowly closed his eyes. A medical technician entered to check that he was fully sedated. Then the execution continued.[13]

Landrigan spent 20 years on death row. The judge who presided over Landrigan's trial for murder in Arizona described him in this way, "Mr. Landrigan appears to be somewhat of an exceptional human being. It appears that Mr. Landrigan is a person who has no scruples and no regard for human life and human beings and the right to live and enjoy life to the best of their ability, whatever their chosen lifestyle might be. Mr. Landrigan appears to be an amoral person."[14]

His violent and murderous ways had come to an end.

Landrigan was the first and only person executed in Arizona in 2010. Arizona courts sentenced 127 killers to death prior to Landrigan receiving his death sentence. Although the state has executed 24 offenders since 1976, 135 inmates remain on death row.

CHAPTER 44

Phillip D. Hallford, Alabama.
Executed November 4

Eddie Shannon was murdered on the same night that his sister's body was being shown at a funeral home in Chipley, Florida. Shannon lost a sister, and within just a week, his family would lose him. Angelina Johns, Shannon's stepmother said, "It was very devastating for our family."[1]

Melinda Hallford Powell was 15 years old and pregnant in 1986. Her father, Phillip Hallford, had been sexually assaulting Melinda for eight years. One night, her father forced her to lure her boyfriend, Eddie Shannon, to a secluded area where Hallford shot Shannon to death and threw his body over a bridge into the Choctawhatchee River.

After Shannon was killed, Hallford made a necklace out of the casings from the bullets that were used to murder Shannon. Hallford forced Melinda to wear the necklace. "You can't imagine what it was like. I was kind of a zombie after that," Melinda said.[2]

* * *

According to court records,[3] during the early morning hours of April 13, 1986, Hallford used Melinda to lure the 16-year-old Shannon to an isolated area near an abandoned bridge over the Choctawhatchee River in Dale County, Alabama. Dale County is located in a rural southeast Alabama.

Hallford forced Melinda to telephone Shannon and ask him to meet her near the secluded bridge. She made the call around midnight on April 12 and arranged to meet Shannon as she had been instructed by her father. Then, Hallford, Melinda, and Hallford's 15-year-old stepson, Sammy Joe Robbins, drove to the bridge. Hallford and his stepson got out of the vehicle and hid in the nearby brush. Melinda remained in the car.

Around 1:00 a.m. Shannon walked over to the vehicle and began talking with Melinda. Hallford approached, turned Shannon around and, as the two struggled, Hallford shot Shannon through the roof of his mouth with a .22 caliber pistol. Just after the shot was fired, Shannon said, as he slumped to the ground, "What did you shoot me for?"

Hallford replied, "For fucking around with somebody else's pussy." He grabbed Shannon by the feet and dragged him toward the bridge. As he was being dragged, Shannon was crying and saying, "Oh my God, you shot me," and "Oh, Jesus Christ, you shot me."

At one point, Shannon regained his balance, and Hallford forced him toward the river while holding him by the hair. Hallford shot Shannon two more times and threw his body in the river before he returned to his car. Together Melinda, Sammy Joe, and

Hallford drove back to their home. Hallford and Sammy Joe returned to the crime scene before daylight with a jug of water and a brush and washed away blood spots on the bridge.

After daylight, Hallford and Sammy Joe again returned to the murder scene to see if Shannon's body had floated to the surface of the river. If it had, they intended to sink the body by shooting it with a shotgun.

The next day, Hallford built a fire in a drum in his backyard and burned Shannon's wallet and its contents, which included a photograph and a military identification card. While burning the wallet, he told Melinda that Shannon "was a cheapskate because he didn't have any money in his wallet." He also showed her a picture of a girl he had taken from the wallet and told her that Shannon had not been faithful to her.

Shannon's badly decomposed body was discovered in the river by two fishermen on April 26, 1986. An autopsy disclosed three wounds caused by .22 caliber bullets. The bullets were recovered from the victim's head. One bullet entered the roof of the mouth, one in front of the left ear, and one in the forehead. Any of the fired bullets could have caused death.

After the discovery of Shannon's body, when the police investigation began to focus on Hallford, he fled to Florida with Melinda.

*   *   *

Hallford was arrested in Escambia County, Florida, on May 23, 1986, and was extradited to Alabama. He testified on his own behalf at trial, denying any knowledge of the crime or even knowing the victim. He attempted to establish an alibi for his whereabouts on the night of the killing by casting suspicion on his stepson, Sammy Joe Robbins.

Melinda testified during the penalty phase after her father was convicted of murder. She was the only witness for the State of Alabama. She described her sexual relationship with Hallford that began when she was seven or eight years old. Melinda testified that she and her father were engaged in an incestuous relationship when she became romantically involved with Shannon and that her father was jealous of Shannon.

During Melinda's testimony Hallford's attorney objected. Hallford's attorney contended that the judge erred when Melinda's testimony, regarding a sexual relationship with her dad, was heard by the jury.

The colloquy with Melinda went as follows[4]:

QUESTION: Melinda, last spring, was Eddie Shannon your boyfriend?
ANSWER: Yes, sir.
QUESTION: Last spring—late in 1985, did you have a sexual relationship with your father?
DEFENSE COUNSEL: Your Honor, I'm going to object. That's leading and highly prejudicial and I ask for a mistrial.
THE COURT: I overrule. Motion for mistrial denied.
PROSECUTING ATTORNEY: Did you?
ANSWER: Yes, sir.
QUESTION: Did that relationship involve sexual intercourse?
ANSWER: Yes.
DEFENSE ATTORNEY: Your Honor, I'm going to object. He's leading and this is not material to the sentencing phase of the trial.
THE COURT: I overrule your objection.

Hallford's attorney argued that the admission of the testimony "incest" and "sexual misconduct" violated the exclusionary rule which prohibits the introduction of prior criminal acts for the sole purpose of suggesting that the accused is more likely to be guilty of the crime in question. However, when Melinda testified, Hallford had already been found guilty of murder. She was testifying during the penalty phase, the point in a capital trial when the jury determines the sentence, life in prison or the death penalty.

Alabama law provides for liberal admission of evidence during the penalty phase, more than would be admissible during the guilt stage of a murder trial. At the penalty phase, evidence may be presented as to any matter that the court deems relevant to sentence and shall include any matters relating to aggravating and mitigating circumstances. The aggravating circumstances provide a basis for imposing the death penalty. The mitigating circumstances provide a basis for imposing a sentence of life in prison. The jury is bound to impose a sentence that reflects which circumstance outweighs the other. For instance, if the aggravating circumstances outweigh the mitigating circumstances, the death penalty must be imposed.

In Alabama, any evidence which has probative value and is relevant for purposes of sentencing will be permitted during the penalty phase of trial regardless of its admissibility under the exclusionary rules of evidence, provided that the defendant is accorded a fair opportunity to offer rebuttal.[5]

The jury determined that the killing was "an execution type slaying, evincing a cold blooded, calculated design to kill." A killing of this nature falls within the category of heinous, atrocious, or cruel. Hallford was convicted of murder and sentenced to death.

The Alabama Court of Criminal Appeals found that Melinda's incestuous relationship with her father prior to the killing was relevant and of probative value in the sentencing aspect of the trial. It was relevant to negate any claim by Hallford that he had no significant history of prior criminal activity.

In addition, the Court of Appeals found that Hallford had testified during the guilty phase of the trial that he had given his children, including Melinda, a home and had taken care of them when no one else would. This testimony was before the jury for their consideration with regard to sentencing. The testimony of the incestuous relationship was also admissible for the purpose of negating Hallford's testimony, which had been offered in an effort to portray himself as a good father and therefore a person of good character.[6]

Hallford's appeals were rejected and his execution was scheduled for November 4, 2010.

* * *

Two people attended the execution on Hallford's behalf, his Philadelphia attorney Andrew Kantra and private investigator Glori Shettles. Hallford had several visitors in the hours before his death, which included his mother, Mertie Boyett, his brother and sister-in-law, Ronald and Eara Hallford, a spiritual advisor as well as Shettles and Kantra. Hallford lost a bid for a stay of execution by the Alabama Supreme Court just hours before he was set to die by lethal injection at Holman Correctional Facility at Atmore.

Hallford's attorney filed an eleventh-hour appeal for a stay of execution with the U.S. Supreme Court. The High Court denied the request. Governor Bob Riley also refused to grant clemency. Riley said Hallford committed a "heinous, premeditated" act that a jury and courts have found deserves the death penalty.[7]

Hallford did not request a final meal, but instead had cheese crackers, nacho cheese Bugles, a ham-and-cheese sandwich and a Dr. Pepper from vending machines. Hallford gave several personal items he kept in his cell to his mother, which included a black watch, a Bible, an address book and a poster board painting.[8]

Prior to the execution Melinda expressed her frustration with the process and her unrepentant father. "I don't understand how someone can do the things that he's done," she said. "He's had a long list of excuses and denials. I wish he would 'fess up before he dies and tell everybody the truth."[9]

Those invited to witness the execution sat silent in observation rooms overlooking the execution chamber as the curtain opened indicating that the execution of Phillip Hallford was imminent. Officials at Holman Correctional Facility began the execution process promptly at 6 p.m.

In the moments before his death when given the opportunity for any last words, he only replied with the word, "no." He spoke briefly with the chaplain for Holman Correctional Facility, along with a corrections officer. Prison officials began to administer the injection. Lying quietly strapped to a gurney, the bald, heavyset Hallford appeared calm. He closed his eyes, stopped moving and quietly slipped away. He was dead at 6:26 p.m.[10]

*   *   *

Shannon's stepmother, Angelina Johns, said in a statement that "what Phillip Hallford did to my stepson Eddie Shannon was unforgivable," Johns said. "Eddie Shannon was an innocent 16-year-old just beginning to live his life."[11]

Shannon's family received what they called "long overdue justice" as Hallford took his last breath.[12]

David Ferguson, Shannon's brother, also attended the execution.

Johns' written statement included, "Speaking for my husband and I, we are glad justice has finally been done, and we can close this chapter."[13]

Johns also said in the statement that Shannon did not deserve to lose his life at the young age of 16. "Mr. Hallford had no reason for taking this young man's life, particularly on the same night we had his sister laying in state at a Chipley, Florida, funeral home," Johns said in the statement. "We lost two young lives within a week."[14]

Melinda, who now lives in North Carolina and is married with three children, said she had lived "a nightmare" for years at the hand of her father. She said she was "relieved" to hear that Hallford was dead. "Now he's not going to hurt anybody else." She said her father never admitted to sexually abusing her. Melinda said she hoped her father would admit to what he did to her and to Shannon before he died. Told that Hallford had nothing to say, Melinda said, "I'm sorry to hear that."[15]

CHAPTER 45

John David Duty, Oklahoma.
Executed December 16

John David Duty was in an Oklahoma penitentiary serving three life sentences after being convicted of armed robbery, kidnapping, first degree rape and shooting with intent to kill. It was December of 2001 and Duty decided he that he had served enough time in prison, he had been in prison since 1978, and at the age of 49 he was not prepared to spend another 30 years in prison.

Duty did not try to escape or even commit suicide. He decided he would murder his cellmate, ask for the death penalty and have the state of Oklahoma put an end to his miserable existence in the state penitentiary system. Duty's diabolical plan involved treachery, murder and the heartless effort to compound the suffering of his victim's family.

* * *

In December 2001, according to court records,[1] Duty was placed on the disciplinary "H-unit" at the Oklahoma State Penitentiary at McAlester in Pittsburg County located in a rural southeastern portion of the state. He was sent to restrictive housing after committing a misconduct, a violation of prison regulations. On December 13, 2001, prison officials placed 22-year-old Curtis Wise in the same cell with Duty.

On the evening of December 19, Wise was duped into engaging a "ruse" so that Duty would be moved to administrative segregation. Wise pretended he was Duty's hostage. Duty promised Wise some cigarettes in exchange for his cooperation in Duty's plan. Wise was placed on his stomach on the cell floor while his hands were tied behind his back and his feet were bound.

Instead of waiting for prison guards to find Wise and remove Duty to another administrative unit, Duty strangled Wise to death with a bed sheet. Duty induced Wise's cooperation so that he could carry out—without resistance—his actual plan, murder.

About an hour later, Duty sat down and wrote a cold blooded letter to Wise's mother. The letter included the following:

> Mary Wise, Well by the time you get this letter you will already know that your son is dead. I know now because I just killed him an hour ago. Gee you'd think I'd be feeling some remorse but I'm not. I've been planning since the day he moved in last Friday. Tonight I finally pulled it off. Would you like to know how I did it? Well I told him I wanted to use him as a hostage. Hell he went right for it, thinking he was gonna get some smokes out of the deal. Well I tied him up hands and feet, then I strangled him. It's not like the movies, it took a while. But I really did him a favor as he was to [sic] stupid to live. I mean he didn't know me 5 days and he let me tie him up like that, Please! Besides he was young and dumb and would've just been in

and out of prison his whole life. So I saved him all the torment. I've been in 24 years, wish someone would have done me the same favor back then. I guess you're thinking I'll be punished for this. Well not likely in this county. The DA's here are weak bitches and don't give a damn about deaths of inmates. We're all just scum to them. Besides I'm doing 2 life sentences so they can't hurt me. But you can call them and tell them about this letter, but it wouldn't do you any good. Well I'm gonna close for now and I'll tell police in the morning about Curtis.[2]

A police investigator interviewed Duty the morning after the murder. Duty told the investigator he wrote the letter to Wise's mother and mailed it. The investigator alerted the warden and the letter was intercepted before it left the prison.

At some point after the murder, Duty wrote a second letter, this one to the district attorney's office taunting Pittsburg County prosecutors. He asked "whether you intend to file murder charges against me or not." Duty wrote:

Now I have a proposition for you. I'm willing to come over there right now and plead guilty to a Murder 1 charge. But that's only if you do it immediately. After that you can just spend the money for a jury trial. But here's my deal. I do it only for a death sentence. I'm never getting out of here with the time I'm doing. And with all my bad behavior in here I'm never going to make parole. So there's no time you can give me that would harm me in the least way. And because of my violent record you can't say I don't deserve the death penalty. I've killed another inmate, taken hostages 3 times, and assaulted a guard. Plus other various things to[o] numerous to mention. You may think me crazy for this, and yes I'm [sic] guess I am a bit crazy or I'd not have done [the] things I've done. But I'm totally sane and know what I'm doing, and am prepared to face my punishment which I rightfully deserve. Now if you don't do this you're only telling me it's ok for me to kill again [and] again because you're not gonna do anything to me. And if that's what it takes to get you to do something then I'll be more than happy to do it. Only next time it will be a guard or staff member, as I know you'll prosecute me then. So the ball is in your corner, are you going to do your job or do you allow me to continue on doing mine.[3]

Duty was charged with first degree murder. The State sought the death penalty alleging four aggravating factors: (1) Duty was previously convicted of prior violent felonies; (2) the murder was especially heinous, atrocious and cruel; (3) Duty was a continuing threat to society; and (4) the murder occurred while Duty was incarcerated.

District Attorney Jim Bob Miller said the murder of Curtis Wise was "especially heinous" because Duty talked his cellmate into acting like he was the defendant's hostage "by having Wise lay on his stomach on the cell floor, by tying the hands and feet of Wise behind his back, by strangling him until he was dead, and then by writing a letter to Wise's mother bragging about how Wise struggled for his life throughout the conscious torture."[4]

He was sentenced to death after he pled guilty—against the advice of counsel—to murder. He waived the presentation of mitigating evidence at sentencing, again against the advice of counsel. Duty made it clear he would murder again, and even requested to be sentenced to death, saying that he would rather die than spend the rest of his life in prison.

* * *

Sodium thiopental is one of three drugs used for executions by lethal injection. The drug became difficult to obtain during the second half of 2010. Hospira, Inc., the only U.S. manufacturer of sodium thiopental, originally said new batches of the drug would be available in January 2011. The company later discontinued the manufacture of sodium thiopental citing concerns with overseas partners who were opposed to the drug being used for executions.

Executions had been delayed in California, Arkansas, Tennessee and Maryland as a result of changes in those state's respective execution protocols and the consideration of different execution drugs. Ohio and Washington changed their execution protocols to allow for the use of a single dose of sodium thiopental.

The Oklahoma Department of Corrections ran out of sodium thiopental prior to Duty's scheduled execution. Oklahoma's protocol called for the use of a fast-acting barbiturate, not actually sodium thiopental, which gave the state the flexibility to use pentobarbital, an anesthetic used in animal euthanasia and assisted suicide.

Duty and two other death row inmates challenged the use of the new drug. According to court records,[5] they cited testimony of a medical doctor who is a professor of anesthesia at Harvard Medical School. This doctor contended that using pentobarbital as an anesthetic might not work to prevent "severe, excruciating pain" from the subsequent drugs.

What is the difference between sodium thiopental and pentobarbital? The media has made a big deal about the change. Experts do not seem to share the alarm sounded by defense attorneys or news reporters. In the spring of 2011, the *New York Times*[6] provided a comprehensive review of the two execution drugs and how they work.

The two drugs come from the same family: barbiturates, drugs that depress the central nervous system. Dr. John Dombrowski, director of the Washington Pain Center and a board member of the American Society of Anesthesiologists told the *New York Times*, "It's like if you ask me what's the difference between Johnnie Walker Blue, Black and Red—they're all scotch."

When injected into the bloodstream, both drugs "cross the blood-brain barrier very efficiently," Dr. Scott Segal, chairman of the department of anesthesiology at Tufts Medical Center in Boston told the *New York Times*. "They get into brain tissue itself."

"All barbiturates put the brain to sleep by slowing down brain function," Dr. Mark A. Warner, president of the American Society of Anesthesiologists told the *New York Times*. "The brain cells that drive the desire to breathe are also suppressed." Warner continued, "So any barbiturate, if you give enough of it, somebody quits breathing. Also, if you give enough of it the heart quits pumping as hard and that can cause decreased blood pressure."

Pentobarbital is used in hospitals in certain circumstances, like inducing a coma in brain-damaged patients because "that allows the brain to use more energy and oxygen to repair itself," Dr. Warner told the *New York Times*. Pentobarbital can be used to stop seizures in patients, has been used for physician assisted suicide in Oregon and is now being used to involuntarily terminate human life.

The court based its decision in large part on the testimony of the state's witness, a medical doctor and professor of anesthesiology at the University of Massachusetts, who disputed the testimony of defense witness and emphasized that a large dose of pentobarbital could alone cause death.[7]

The 10th U.S. Circuit Court of Appeals rejected the claim that pentobarbital could cause cruel and unusual punishment, in violation of the Eighth Amendment. The court concluded that the amount of pentobarbital prison officials planned to inject as the first of three execution drugs would by itself "likely be lethal in most, if not all, instances."[8]

The 10th Circuit got it right. Since Duty's execution using pentobarbital as one drug in a three-drug protocol, Ohio executed Johnnie Baston on March 10, 2011, using only a lethal dose of pentobarbital as part of a single-drug execution protocol.

*   *   *

Duty pleaded guilty to the murder of Curtis Wise. He waived the presentation of mitigating evidence during his sentencing and even requested to be sentenced to death. Apparently he had a change of heart. Long before he challenged the method of execution, he challenged whether he should even be on death row.

He filed an appeal suggesting his attorney failed in his representation. That appeal also made its way to the 10th Circuit Court of Appeals. The 10th Circuit said that Duty's case was remarkably similar to a the U.S. Supreme Court decision in *Smith v. Spisak*.[9] Frank Spisak was executed in Ohio on February 17, 2011.

Spisak was convicted by a jury of three murders and two attempted murders. During closing argument at the penalty phase of trial, defense counsel described Spisak's killings in detail and portrayed him as "sick," "twisted," and "demented" and said he was "never going to be any different."

Spisak later argued defense counsel's closing argument during the penalty phase was "so inadequate as to violate the Sixth Amendment." The Supreme Court found counsel's performance to be deficient but nevertheless found no prejudice because there was no "'reasonable probability' that a better closing argument without these defects would have made a significant difference."

Spisak bragged about the murders, relished that he carried out his Nazi duty and said he would kill again. The 10th Circuit found no differences between Duty's case and Spisak. Like Spisak, (1) Duty admitted to murdering Wise, (2) the murder was a product of a coolly calculated plan, (3) the murder was cruelly perpetrated with apparent glee, (4) Duty showed no remorse and (5) Duty planned to kill again. Any differences between Duty and Spisak are matters of degree but neither was prejudiced by ineffective assistance of trial counsel.[10]

Duty spent his final hours adjacent to the death chamber at the state penitentiary in McAlester, the same prison he was assigned to when he killed Curtis Wise. Duty received his last meal at noon on December 16, 2010—a double-cheeseburger with mayonnaise, a foot-long cheese Coney with mustard and extra onions, cherry limeade and a banana shake. Duty then visited with his spiritual advisor, the department of corrections chaplain, his family and his lawyers.[11]

Once the execution hour neared, Duty was strapped on a gurney and two separate IVs were attached. According to the prison's assistant warden, a second IV is secured, "in the case that one [the original IV] fails." Once execution witnesses were in place, the execution director received Governor Brad Henry's order to proceed with the execution.[12]

With three media representatives, three of Duty's lawyers and Duty's brother and sister-in-law present, Duty spoke his last words just minutes before the lethal injection drugs were administered. "To the family of Curtis Wise I'd like to make my apology. I hope one day you'll be able to forgive me—not for my sake, but for your own. My family and friends are here too. Thank you, you've all been a blessing. Thank you Lord Jesus, I'm ready to go home."[13]

Curtis Wise's mother, the intended recipient of Duty's cruel letter, had asked the court to impose a sentence of life in prison for her son's killer.

The Department of Corrections' three executioners then administered the three-drug lethal injection and, as Duty began to lose consciousness, he said "Thank you Lord. Thank you Lord."[14]

Duty was pronounced dead at 6:18 p.m. the first inmate in the country to be put to death using pentobarbital. The prison spokesman said, "There were no apparent issues" with the new drug.[15]

Duty was the 46th and final condemned prisoner executed in 2010.

Conclusion

What can be gleaned from an exhaustive examination of every execution in a single calendar year? A journey with death that chronicled 63 murders, 44 trials, countless appeals, 41 last meals, 33 finals statements and 46 executions.

It is incontrovertible that the depravity, the callousness, the defiance, and the silence juxtaposed with the spirituality, the contrition and the anguish—have left an indelible mark on all who have been touched by the 46 haunting stories of death and human destruction.

Public opinion polls have, in the past, supported the proposition that the more one knows about a specific murder or murderer, the more likely that person will support the death penalty. Saddam Hussein and Terry McVeigh are examples that even those who otherwise oppose the death penalty can support an execution if they are intimately familiar with the heinousness of the crime, the violent history of the killer or the vulnerability of the victim. In 2001, when 67 percent of people said they supported the death penalty, 81 percent supported the execution of McVeigh. In 2006, when 65 percent of people said they supported the death penalty, 82 percent supported the execution of Hussein.[1]

The mother of Curtis Wise who asked the court to impose a sentence of life in prison for her son's killer, John David Duty, was an anomaly. The mother of one of Darick Walker's victims, Clarence Threat, said she did not support the death penalty, but she did not wish to stop Walker's execution. Her response, though not vengeful, starts in the direction of the most common response from victim's families; lethal injection was too easy. Not only did some families want retribution, they wanted revenge—a painful sort of revenge.

Ohio, a northern state with strong Midwestern values, stands out as an interesting bundle of contradictions when it comes to the death penalty. In 2009, Ohio was the only state north of the Mason-Dixon Line to carry out an execution.

In 2010, Ohio literally set the standard for capital punishment nationwide. First, Ohio took the bold step of changing its execution protocol. All 32 states with capital punishment used a three-drug protocol that, in 2008, the U.S. Supreme Court found did not violate the Eighth Amendment ban against cruel and unusual punishment.[2]

A year later, Ohio moved from a three-drug protocol to a single-drug protocol. Ohio used a single lethal dose of sodium thiopental for executions throughout 2010. By 2013, 11 states had adopted a single drug protocol for executions.

In 2010, Ohio carried out more executions than any other state, with the exception of Texas. The eight executions were the most in any year since Ohio reinstated the death penalty in 1999. Ohio has 157 offenders on death row.

In 2010, a shortage of sodium thiopental developed when the drug's only U.S. manufacturer announced that it would no longer produce the drug. In January 2011, the Ohio Department of Rehabilitation and Corrections announced that the state would substitute pentobarbital for sodium thiopental in its execution protocol. Two months later, Ohio became the first state to use pentobarbital in its single drug execution protocol.

Most of this occurred while Ted Strickland, a Democrat, was governor of Ohio. GOP governors have typically set the pace on executions. By the end of 2013, Texas Governor Rick Perry, a Republican, was responsible for more than 270 executions during his 13 years as governor. Those executions are not only more than any other governor; they are more than any other state during the modern era of the death penalty.

After Ohio set a new standard for executions among northern states, the state's top judge publicly announced his opposition to the death penalty. Ohio Supreme Court Justice Paul Pfeifer asked Governor John Kasich and the Ohio legislature to end capital punishment. In 1981, when Justice Pfeifer was in the state senate, he helped write Ohio's death penalty statute.

Justice Pfeifer wrote an op-ed for the *Cleveland Plain Dealer*, calling for an end to the death penalty. "We set out to enact a law that would give prosecutors the capability to seek capital punishment for the absolute worst offenders." Justice Pfeifer further wrote, "The law was meant to be employed only when a certain set of aggravating circumstances warranted execution. But over the years, the death penalty has come to be applied more pervasively than we ever intended."

After years of reviewing death penalty verdicts rendered through a statute he helped write, Justice Pfeifer wrote, "I have come to the conclusion that we are not well served by our ongoing attachment to capital punishment."

Justice Pfeifer's position is reminiscent of U.S. Supreme Court Justice Harry Blackmun and Justice John Paul Stevens. Justice Blackmun wrote before his retirement in 1994, renouncing his career-long acceptance of capital punishment, "The death-penalty experiment has failed. I no longer shall tinker with the machinery of death."

Justice Stevens was one of the co-authors of *Gregg v. Georgia*,[3] the U.S. Supreme Court's 1976 decision that reinstated the death penalty. However, in 2008, Justice Stevens wrote, "The imposition of the death penalty represents the pointless and needless extinction of life with only marginal contributions to any discernible social or public purposes. A penalty with such negligible returns to the state [is] patently excessive and cruel and unusual punishment volatile of the Eighth Amendment."

Justice Pfeifer premised his new opposition to capital punishment on the idea that life without parole is a suitable alternative sentence to the death penalty. In 2005, the Ohio legislature authorized prosecutors to seek the penalty of life without the possibility of parole as an alternative to the death penalty.

Justice Pfeifer argued as a result of the new law, "We have seen the number of death sentences drop precipitously. Prosecutors and jurors have told us—by their actions—that life without the possibility of parole is a more desirable outcome to a murder trial than a death sentence."

During Justice Pfeifer's 2011 swearing-in, he urged Governor Kasich to commute all death row sentences to life without parole. There was little chance of that happening. Governor Kasich had made clear his support for the death penalty.

Does Justice Pfeifer's position hold water? A reduction in death sentences is more than just a preference for life without the possibility of parole over the death penalty. There are fewer murders in America. In fact, violent crime has decreased dramatically over the last two decades. In 2009, the rate of murder was five per 100,000 Americans, down from 9.8 in 1991. In 1991, there were 24,700 murders in the U.S.; in 2009 there were 15,241. Overall, the rate of violent crime fell more than a third during that time, from a rate of 758 violent crimes per 100,000 in 1991 to 429 in 2009. The violent crime number includes homicides, rapes, robberies and assaults.[4]

While I may not agree with Justice Pfeifer's reasoning, I do not necessarily disagree with his conclusion.

The news media regularly provides a glimpse into the untenable posture of the death penalty in America. Today's death penalty is more of a political prop than a legitimate form of punishment within the criminal justice system.

There were only 46 executions in 2010. The average length of time between murder and execution for those 46 condemned killers was 16.7 years. In 1994, about 16 years before 2010, 328 men and women were sentenced to death nationwide. That was the highest number since the death penalty was reinstated in 1976. In 2010, there were far fewer offenders sentenced to death, 112, still more than twice the number executed.

Some suggest that the death penalty has become a symbolic form of punishment. Tell that to the families of the 45 men and one woman executed in 2010, and that is precisely the problem with the death penalty. Few believe that the approximately 3,400 men and women on the nation's death rows at the end of 2010 will ultimately face execution.

Let's say that death penalty verdicts continue at 2010's pace of 112 per year for the next ten years. There would be approximately 4,500 men and women on death row. Let's say that all 32 states with the death penalty executed one offender a month for the next ten years; these occurrences are not completely realistic since only eight states have more than 120 offenders on death row. After ten years at that frantic, and frankly impossible, pace, there would be 4,300 executions, still leaving about 200 people on death row.

My point is, since the reinstatement of the death penalty in 1976, the likelihood that an offender sentenced to death will ultimately be executed is about one in seven. Yet, governors and legislators, prosecutors and defense attorneys, wardens and corrections officials consume a great deal of their time "tinkering" with the death penalty. Lawyers and prison officials have to deal with the death penalty—politicians want to manipulate the death penalty.

During a single week in early 2011, the news media reported three very different scenarios involving the death penalty. In Illinois, the legislature voted to abolish the death penalty. The bill was sitting on Governor Pat Quinn's desk, when, according to *Gatehouse News Service*, two Republican legislators had introduced bills that would seek to reinstate the death penalty if Governor Quinn signed a bill abolishing it.[5]

Illinois House Bill 1520 would ask voters at the November 2012 election whether or not they want the state to have capital punishment. The referendum would be non-binding.

House Bill 1519 would reduce the number of aggravating factors for which the death penalty could be imposed. And Senate Bill 2277 creates a panel that would have to pre-approve cases in which prosecutors seek the death penalty.

The two House bills would go into effect only if Governor Quinn signed the bill to abolish the death penalty sitting on his desk. The legislature was poised to undo a bill before it even became law.

In West Virginia, the death penalty was repealed in 1965. In January 2011, that state's House Judiciary Committee held a public hearing considering whether to reinstate the death penalty, according to the *Charleston Daily Mail*.[6] The hearing lasted about 90 minutes. Ten people spoke in favor of reinstatement, while 13 spoke against. Nearly 20 lawmakers have signed on as co-sponsors of the death penalty measure. There are two bills and one proposed constitutional amendment which would have to be approved by voters statewide.

In Montana, the state Senate sent a bill to repeal Montana's death penalty to the House, where the plan failed in 2009, according to the *Billings Gazette*.[7]

Senate Bill 185 passed the senate with a 26–24 vote. The bill had the support of all the chamber's Democrats and four Republicans.

The bill would immediately replace the death penalty with life in prison without parole and could change the sentences of Montana's two death row inmates. A similar measure passed the Senate in 2009 but failed to make it out of a House committee.

New Mexico's newly elected GOP governor proposed a measure, soon after taking office in January 2011, to reinstate the death penalty. Former Governor Bill Richardson signed a bill to outlaw the death penalty in 2009. In New Jersey, a legislator who sponsored the bill that abolished the death penalty in New Jersey came forward in early 2011 to say he would support the death penalty under limited circumstances.

Does this all sound crazy? Well it is crazy. The death penalty has more to do with political posturing, "I'm a tough, law and order guy," than holding killers accountable and deterring future murders. The death penalty has lost its way in the muddled political rhetoric of 21st century governance.

What influence can proponents of the death penalty claim of a punishment that will be impossible to carry out for the thousands of offenders already sentenced to death and have very little likelihood of being carried out for those yet to be sentenced?

I am not suggesting that the death penalty is unfairly imposed, or that it is racially biased, or that innocent men or women have been executed. In fact, no one can point to a single factually innocent offender who has been executed in the modern era of the death penalty.

The death penalty is the most accurately imposed sanction in the American criminal justice system. The underpinnings of the criminal justice system have always been that the accused be afforded due process. The Fifth Amendment guarantees that the government cannot take away a person's basic rights to "life, liberty or property, without due process of law." The Fourteenth Amendment extended the protection of due process to all the states.

The U.S. Supreme Court has, through a series of decisions, established what some would call "super due process" when pursuing and imposing the death penalty. The concept of super due process, while worthy of a punishment as final as death, has bogged down appellate review to the point that the death penalty is rarely carried out.

The death penalty is a duly enacted and appropriate sentence in 32 states and the federal government. I am not arguing that the laws used to impose the death penalty are unconstitutional. I am simply suggesting, if there are about 3,400 offenders on death row, and every year another 100 are added and only about 50 are executed, do those states with the death penalty have a punishment that is constitutional in the manner that it is imposed but arbitrary in the manner it is carried out? Eight-four percent of offenders sentenced to death will die by means other than execution. Should America continue to impose a sentence that has so little chance of being carried out?

The death penalty has become random in the way that it is carried out. In 1972, the concern was randomness in the way the death penalty was imposed, and as a result, the U.S. Supreme Court struck it down.

In *Furman v. Georgia*,[8] the 1972 decision that struck down the death penalty, Justice Potter Stewart wrote, "These death sentences are cruel and unusual in the same way that being struck by lightning is cruel and unusual." Justice Stewart further noted, "I simply conclude that the Eighth and Fourteenth Amendments cannot tolerate the infliction of a sentence of death under legal systems that permit this unique penalty to be so wantonly and so freakishly imposed."

Carrying out an execution today is as freakishly arbitrary as imposing the death penalty was in 1972. If you are one of 697 inmates on California's death row in 2013, a state that has not carried out an execution in five years, and suddenly you are scheduled for execution— that is a lot like being struck by lightning.

The modern trend with regard to carrying out the death penalty is even more dismal— only eight percent of condemned inmates were executed within the last ten years, a little less than one in ten.

Pennsylvania has had the death penalty since 1977. There are 222 killers on the state's death row. Yet Pennsylvania has executed just three men. All three waived their appeal rights and asked to be executed. Year after year, men and women in Pennsylvania are tried, convicted and sentenced to death with literally no chance of being executed.

Each of 2010's executions revealed often less than sympathetic figures, men and a single woman, whose conduct was downright frightening. Each displayed callousness toward other human beings that makes one relieved that the death penalty exists. There is no doubt that some members of society are so anti-social that they present a clear and present danger to law abiding citizens. We are, however, fooling ourselves if we believe that the 46 offenders executed in 2010 were America's "most dangerous" citizens and that the rest of the "most dangerous" are all confined to death row awaiting an unlikely execution.

Who wouldn't want to flip the switch that started the flow of lethal drugs through Cal Coburn Brown's veins? He killed a woman he abducted and tortured and then within a few days tried to kill a second woman. He complained that his imminent execution was unjust because, "I only killed one person."

When Brown was executed there were eight other killers on Washington's death row. Why was Brown executed and not Jonathan Lee Gentry? Gentry had been on death row since 1991, two years before Brown. Gentry's murder was equally ruthless.

*   *   *

In early June 1988, 12-year-old Cassie Holden was visiting her mother for the summer near Bremerton, Washington. On June 13, 1988, at approximately 4:30 p.m. Cassie went for a walk. She did not return home for dinner and was never seen alive again.

According to court records,[9] her body was found early June 15, behind a large log at the bottom of a path running adjacent to a golf course, near Bremerton. The victim's eyeglasses, earring and a bouquet of flowers were found approximately 148 feet away along the footpath.

The victim appeared to have been sexually assaulted, as her jeans and underpants were pulled down and her T-shirt and bra pulled up. Her blue sweatshirt had been removed from one arm and pulled up, partially covering her face. She had been struck in the head approximately 15 times, suffering 10 "significant" injuries.

Gentry was convicted of killing Cassie in order to cover up the sexual assault. He had a criminal record that included first degree rape, manslaughter and two burglaries. He still sits on death row.

All things being equal, lightning struck Cal Coburn Brown.

* * *

The future of the death penalty is in question. Not because some who kill deserve to die, but rather because the act of execution has become so rare as to indicate the presence of caprice if an offender is executed or fortuity if an offender is not. Neither caprice nor fortuity has a place in the criminal justice system.

Chapter Notes

Preface

1. 553 U.S. 35 (2008).

Introduction

1. "The innocent and the death penalty," Innocence Project, http://www.innocenceproject.org/Content/The_Innocent_and_the_Death_Penalty.php.

Chapter 1

1. State V. Smith, 89 ohiost.3d 323, 731 N.E.2d 645 (Oh 2005).
2. Ibid.
3. Mhadi v. Bagley, 522 F3d 631 (6th Cr. 2000).
4. Blake, E., "Pending execution stirs pain anew," *Toledo Blade*, January 6, 2010.
5. Ibid.
6. Ibid.
7. Hayes, A., "Ohio executes second man using single drug method," CNN, January 6, 2010.
8. Nash, J., "Toledo killer executed," *Columbus Dispatch*, January 7, 2010.
9. Ibid.
10. *Toledo Blade*, January 6, 2010.
11. Ibid.
12. Smith, J., "Man who killed Toledo store owner in 1993 scheduled to be executed," Associated Press, January 7, 2010.
13. Ibid.
14. *Toledo Blade*, January 6, 2010.
15. Ibid.
16. Ibid.
17. Ibid.
18. Provance, J., "Toledoan Smith was put to death under new death house protocol," *Toledo Blade*, January 8, 2010.
19. *Columbus Dispatch*, January 7, 2010.
20. Ibid.

Chapter 2

1. Jacobson, S., "Garland officer's killer executed in Huntsville," *Dallas Morning News*, January 8, 2010.
2. Graczyk, M., "Dallas-area officer's killer put to death," Associated Press, January 7, 2010.
3. Ibid.
4. Ibid.
5. Ibid.

6. Ibid.
7. "Media Advisory: Kenneth Mosley Execution," Texas Office of Attorney General Greg Abbott, January 4, 2010.
8. Ibid.
9. Ibid.
10. Jacobson, S., "Garland officer's widow struggles as killer's execution nears," *Dallas Morning News*, September 15, 2009.
11. Attorney General, January 4, 2010.
12. *Dallas Morning News*, January 8, 2010.
13. Ibid.
14. Mosley v. Quarterman, 306 Fed.Appx. 40 (5th Cir. 2008).
15. Attorney General, January 4, 2010.
16. Ibid.
17. *Dallas Morning News*, January 8, 2010.
18. Ibid.
19. Ibid.
20. *Dallas Morning News*, September 15, 2009.
21. Ibid.
22. Ibid.
23. Ibid.
24. Ibid.
25. Ibid.
26. Associated Press, January 7, 2010.
27. *Dallas Morning News*, January 8, 2010.
28. *Dallas Morning News*, September 15, 2009.
29. Ibid.
30. Ibid.
31. *Dallas Morning News*, January 8, 2010.
32. *Dallas Morning News*, September 15, 2009.

Chapter 3

1. State v. Bordelon, 2009 WL 3321481, October 16, 2009.
2. Deslatte, M., "La. man executed for 2002 murder," *Shreveport Times*, January 8, 2010.
3. Texas Department of Criminal Justice, http://www.tdcj.state.tx.us/stat/drowfacts.htm; Florida Department of Corrections, http://www.dc.state.fl.us/oth/deathrow/.
4. Minton, J., "Child killer voices remorse, executed," *Baton Rouge Advocate*, January 8, 2010.
5. Ibid.
6. State v. Bordelon, 2009 WL 3321481, October 16, 2009.
7. Ibid.

8. WAFB-TV, January 8, 2010.

9. *Shreveport Times*, January 8, 2010.

10. Ibid.

11. Ibid.

12. Ibid.

13. Minton, J., "Bordelon remorseful before execution," *Baton Rouge Advocate*, January 7, 2010.

14. Minton, J., "Lawyer: Bordelon admitted crimes," *Baton Rouge Advocate*, January 9, 2010.

15. Ibid.

16. "Murderer apologizes before his execution at Louisiana State Penitentiary," *New Orleans Times-Picayune*, January 7, 2010.

17. *Baton Rouge Advocate*, January 8, 2010.

Chapter 4

1. Rainwater, M., "Man executed for ranch murder," *Huntsville Item*, January 12, 2010.

2. Johnson V. State, 853 S.W.2d 527 (Tx. C. App. 1992)

3. Fair, K., "Jury assesses death penalty; Huntsville panel deliberates half an hour," *Houston Chronicle*, August 20, 1988.

4. Ibid.

5. Johnson v. State, (1992).

6. Ibid.

7. *Houston Chronicle*, August 20, 1988.

8. Ibid.

9. Graczyk, M., "Former worker who shot 2 at Texas ranch executed," Associated Press, January 12, 2010.

10. Ibid.

11. Ibid.

12. Ibid.

13. Texas Department of Criminal Justice, www.tdcj.tx.us/stat/execitedoffenders.htm.

14. Associated Press, January 12, 2010.

Chapter 5

1. "Oklahoma executes man convicted of killing 2," Associated Press, January 15, 2010.

2. Hampton, D., "Man executed for '93 slayings," *Tulsa World*, January 15, 2010.

3. Young v. State, 992 P.2d 332 (Okla.Crim.App. 1988).

4. Juozapavicius, J., "Oklahoma inmate executed for 1993 Tulsa beating deaths," Associated Press, January 14, 2010.

5. Associated Press, January 15, 2010.

6. "Board denies clemency for Tulsa killer," *Norman Transcript*, December 8, 2009.

7. Associated Press, January 15, 2010.

8. *Norman Transcript*, January 8, 2009.

9. Eaton, K., "Economic recession kills death penalty in Oklahoma," *The Journal Record*, December 31, 2009.

10. Ibid.

11. Sharp, D., "Death penalty and sentencing information," Justice for All, October 1, 1997.

12. Ibid.

13. *Tulsa World*, January 15, 2010.

14. Ibid.

15. Associated Press, January 15, 2010.

16. *Tulsa World*, January 15, 2010.

17. Associated Press, January 15, 2010.

Chapter 6

1. Johnson, A., "Convenience-store killer executed by lethal injection," *The Columbus Dispatch*, February 4, 2010.

2. State v. Brown, 100 Ohio St. 3d 51 (Ohio App. 2003).

3. Frazier V. Cupp, 394 U.S. 731 (1969).

4. Ibid.

5. Lowenstien, T., "Use of video to end false confessions," *The Times-Picayune*, November 6, 2009.

6. Ibid.

7. State v. Brown (2003).

8. 451 U.S. 477 (1981).

9. Davis v. U.S., 512 U.S. 452 (1994).

10. State v. Brown.

11. "Mark Aaron Brown executed, offered no final statement," *Youngstown Vindicator*, February 4, 2010.

12. Welsh-Huggins, A., "Ohio executes man who murdered shopkeeper, clerk," Associated Press, February 4, 2010.

13. Kovac, M., "Family: Justice Served to Killer," Associated Press, February 5, 2010.

14. Ibid.

15. Associated Press, February 4, 2010.

16. *Columbus Dispatch*, February 4, 2010.

Chapter 7

1. Solomant, E.B., "U.S. Jews rush to stay execution," *Jerusalem Post*, February 16, 2010.

2. Grossman v. State, 525 So.2d 833 (Fla. 1988).

3. 391 U.S. 123 (1968).

4. Crabbe, N., "Grossman executed for killing wildlife officer," *Gainesville Sun*, February 2, 2010.

5. Douglas, M., "Grossman executed; last words are of heartfelt remorse," *Tampa Tribune*, February 16, 2010.

6. Ibid.

7. *Tampa Tribune*, February 16, 2010.

8. *Gainesville Sun*, February 16, 2010.

9. *Jerusalem Post*, February 16, 2010.

10. Ibid.

11. Ibid.

12. *Gainesville Sun*, February 16, 2010

13. Ibid.

14. Ibid.

15. *Tampa Tribune*, February 16, 2010.

16. Ibid.

Chapter 8

1. "Texas man who murdered Brazilian couple set to die," Associated Press-Fox News, March 1, 2010.

2. Lozano, J., "Dallas man executed in killing of Brazilian engineer," Associated Press, March 3, 2010.

3. Sigala v. State, 2004 WL 231326 (Tx.Cr.App. 2004).

4. Associated Press-FoxNews, March 1, 2010.

5. Associated Press-FoxNews, March 1, 2010.

6. "Michael Sigala scheduled for execution," Press

Release, Texas Office of Attorney General, February 23, 2010.

7. Ibid.

8. Associated Press, March 2, 2010.

9. Ibid.

Chapter 9

1. Maxwell v. State, 2004 WL 3094649 (Tex.Cr. App. 2004).

2. Ibid.

3. Ibid.

4. Mondo, M., "Lawman's killer put to death," *San Antonio Express News*, March 12, 2010.

5. "Joshua Maxwell scheduled for execution," Media Advisory, Texas Office of Attorney, March 5, 2010.

6. "Indiana man who murdered 2 in San Antonio set to die," Associated Press, March 11, 2010.

7. Maxwell v. State.

8. Ibid.

9. Keith, K., "Indiana native to be executed in Texas tonight," WIBC, March 11, 2010.

10. Associated Press, March 11, 2010.

11. Graczyk, M., "Man executed for 2000 crime spree," Associated Press, March 11, 2010.

12. Ibid.

13. *San Antonio Express News*, March 12, 2010.

14. Graczyk, March 11, 2010.

15. Carson, D., "Joshua Maxwell," Texas Execution Information Center, March 15, 2010.

16. Graczyk, March 11, 2010.

Chapter 10

1. State v. Reynolds, 80 Ohio st.3d 670 (Ohio 1998).

2. Ibid.

3. Ibid.

4. Ibid.

5. Ibid.

6. Leingang, M., "Death row inmate overdose delays lethal injection," Associated Press, March 8, 2010.

7. Johnson, A., "Killer executed one week after suicide attempt," *Columbus Dispatch*, March 16, 2010.

8. Leingang, M., "Ohio executes inmate who killed neighbor," Associated Press, March 16, 2010.

9. Johnson, A., "Murderer's last word: 'Stop the madness,'" *Columbus Dispatch*, March 17, 2010.

10. "Cuyahoga Falls woman's killer executed," *Norwalk Reflector*, March 12, 2010.

11. Associated Press, March 17, 2010.

12. *Norwalk Reflector*, March 12, 2010.

13. *Columbus Dispatch*, March 17, 2010.

Chapter 11

1. Green, F. "Powell executed for teen's 1999 murder in Manassas," *Richmond Post-Dispatch*, March 19, 2010.

2. White, J., "Virginia executes man in 1999 murder of woman, rape of her sister," *Washington Post*, March 19, 2010.

3. Ibid.

4. Powell v. Commonwealth, 552 S.E.2d 244 (Va. 2001).

5. *Washington Post*, March 19, 2010.

6. Powell v. Commonwealth, (Va. 2001).

7. Powell v. Commonwealth, 590 S.E.2d 537 (Va. 2004).

8. Ibid.

9. *Richmond Post-Dispatch*, March 19, 2010.

10. *Washington Post*, March 19, 2010.

11. *Richmond Post-Dispatch*, March 19, 2010.

12. *Washington Post*, March 19, 2010.

13. Ibid.

14. *Richmond Post-Dispatch*, March 19, 2010.

15. *Washington Post*, March 19, 2010.

16. Ibid.

17. Ibid.

Chapter 12

1. "Man executed in slaying of Houston man during 1998 robbery," Associated Press, March 31, 2010.

2. Carson, D., "Franklin Alix," Texas Execution Information Center, April 4, 2010.

3. Canadian Coalition Against the Death Penalty, http://www.ccadp.org/franklinalix.htm.

4. Turner, A., "Houston man executed in 1998 slaying," *Houston Chronicle*, March 31, 2010.

5. Ex Parte Alix, 2006 WL 2766361 (Tex.Cr.App. 2006).

6. "Franklin Alix Scheduled for Execution," Media Advisory, Texas Office of Attorney General, March 25, 2010.

7. "Appeal Denied for Alix," Associated Press, February 10, 2009.

8. Texas Execution Information Center, April 4, 2010.

9. Associated Press, February 10, 2009.

10. Ibid.

11. Ibid.

12. Ibid.

13. Texas Execution Information Center, April 4, 2010.

14. Ibid.

15. Texas Execution Information Center, April 4, 2010.

16. Rainwater, M., "Man executed for '98 Houston murder," *Huntsville Item*, March 31, 2010.

17. Ibid.

18. Ibid.

19. Texas Execution Information Center, April 4, 2010.

Chapter 13

1. "April 2010 executions—Darryl Durr," Prodeathpenalty.com, http://www.prodeathpenalty.com/Pending/10/apr10.htm.

2. State v. Durr, 58 Ohio st.3d 86 (Ohio 1991).

3. Ibid.

4. McNiff, E., "Death row allergy claim fails to delay Darryl Durr's execution," ABC News, April 21, 2010.

5. Guillen, J., "State executes Darryl Durr for 1988 murder of teenage girl," *Cleveland Plain Dealer*, April 20, 2010.

6. Ibid.
7. Associated Press, April 21, 2010.
8. ABC News, April 21, 2010.
9. Ibid.
10. Ibid.
11. Ibid.
12. Associated Press, April 21, 2010.
13. ABC News, April 21, 2010.
14. *Cleveland Plain Dealer*, April 20, 2010.
15. Johnson, A., "Killer provides no comfort at execution," *Columbus Dispatch*, April 21, 2010.
16. Ibid.
17. Ibid.
18. *Cleveland Plain Dealer*, April 20, 2010.

Chapter 14

1. "Texas executes man convicted of killing student," Associated Press, April 22, 2010.
2. Berkley v. State, 74, 336 (Tx.Crim.App. April 6, 2005).
3. "April 2010 executions—William Berkley," Pro deathpenalty.com, http://www.prodeathpenalty.com/Pending/10/apr10.htm.
4. Ibid.
5. "William Berkley scheduled for execution," Media Advisory, Texas Office of Attorney General, April 15, 2010.
6. Ibid.
7. Ibid.
8. "William Berkley scheduled for execution," Media Advisory, Texas Office of Attorney General, April 15, 2010.
9. Carson, D., "William Berkley," Texas Execution Information Center, April 26, 2010.
10. Associated Press, April 22, 2010.
11. Texas Execution Information Center, April 26, 2010.
12. Ibid.
13. Chavez, A., "William Josef Berkley is executed, did not address Martinez family," *El Paso Times*, April 22, 2010.
14. Ibid.
15. Ibid.
16. Ibid.
17. Lozano, A., "Inmate executed for killing and raping El Paso teen," *Houston Chronicle*, April 22, 2010.
18. *El Paso Times*, April 22, 2010.
19. *El Paso Times*, April 22, 2010.

Chapter 15

1. Bustamante v. State, 106 S.W.3d 738, 742 (Tex. Crim.App.2003).
2. Carson, D., "Samuel Bustamante," Texas Execution Information Center, April 28, 2010.
3. Bustamante v. State (2003).
4. Raindeer, M., "Man executed for 1998 stabbing," *Huntsville Item*, April 27, 2010.
5. Texas Execution Information Center, April 28, 2010.
6. Ibid.
7. *Huntsville Item*, April 27, 2010.

8. Bustamante v. State.
9. Texas Execution Information Center, April 28, 2010.
10. Turner, A., "Killer in 1998 Rosenberg robbery very quiet at execution," *Houston Chronicle*, April 27, 2010.
11. 536 U.S. 304 (2002).
12. 492 U.S. 302 (1989).
13. Ibid.
14. Texas Execution Information Center, April 28, 2010.
15. *Houston Chronicle*, April 27, 2010.
16. Ibid.
17. *Huntsville Item*, April 27, 2010.
18. *Houston Chronicle*, April 27, 2010.
19. Graczyk, M., "Killer of immigrant executed," Associated Press, April 27, 2010.

Chapter 16

1. Graczyk, M., "South Dakota ex-con executed," Associated Press, May 12, 2010.
2. Ibid.
3. Varga v. State, 2003 WL 21466926 (Tx.Crim. App. 2003)
4. Associated Press, May 12, 2010.
5. Galloway v. State, 2003 WL 1712559 (Tx.Crim. App. 2003).
6. Carson, D., "Billy Galloway," Texas Execution Information Center, May 14, 2010.
7. Associated Press, May 12, 2010.
8. Rainwater, M., "Death row inmate: No justice by execution," *Rapid City Journal*, May 9, 2010.
9. Ibid.
10. Associated Press, May 12, 2010.
11. Rainwater, M., "South Dakota man executed for fatal beating," *Huntsville Item*, May 12, 2010.
12. Graczyk, M., "Killer executed for '98 robbery, slaying near Dallas," Associated Press, May 13, 2010.
13. Rainwater, M., "Second S.D. ex-con in two days executed," *Rapid City Journal*, May 13, 2010.
14. Associated Press, May 13, 2010.
15. *Huntsville Item*, May 14, 2010.
16. Rainwater, M., "Kevin Varga made religious appeal before execution," *Rapid City Journal*, May 12, 2010: "Second S.D. ex-con in two days executed in Texas," *Rapid City Journal*, May 13, 2010.
17. *Huntsville Item*, May 12, 2010.
18. *Huntsville Item*, May 14, 2010.
19. *Huntsville Item*, May 12, 2010.

Chapter 17

1. Perry, K., "Judge upset with Beuke 27 years on death row," *Cincinnati Enquirer*, April 1, 2010.
2. State v. Beuke, 38 Ohio St.3d 29 (Ohio 1986).
3. Ibid.
4. Ibid.
5. Carr, J., "Ohio executes hitchhiker who shot 3 drivers in '83," Associated Press, May 12, 2010.
6. State v. Beuke (1986).
7. Cornwell, L., "Homicidal hitchhiker faces execution," Associated Press, May 12, 2010.

8. Johnson, A., "Ohio executes homicidal hitchhiker," *Columbus Dispatch*, May 13, 2010.
9. Ibid.
10. Associated Press, May 12, 2010.
11. Craig, J. "Last statement from 'mad hitchhiker' Michael Beuke: A 17-minute prayer," *Cincinnati Enquirer*, May 13, 2010.
12. Ibid.
13. Ritz, I., "Michael Beuke executed for Ohio hitchhiker murder," *The Epoch Times*, May 13, 2010.
14. *Columbus Dispatch*, May 13, 2010.
15. *Cincinnati Enquirer*, May 13, 2010.
16. Ibid.
17. *Columbus Dispatch*, May 13, 2010.
18. *Cincinnati Enquirer*, May 12, 2010.
19. Associated Press, May 12, 2010.
20. *Cincinnati Enquirer*, May 13, 2010.

Chapter 18

1. "Rogelio Reyes Cannady scheduled for execution," Media Advisory, Texas Office of Attorney General, May 12, 2010.
2. Ryan, C., "Rogelio Cannady executed," *Valley Morning Star*, May 20, 2010.
3. Cannady v. Dretke, 173 Fed.Appx 321 (5th Cir. 2006)
4. Ibid.
5. "Rogelio Cannady scheduled for execution," Media Advisory, Texas Office of Attorney General, May 12, 2010.
6. Ibid.
7. Carson, D., "Rogelio Cannady," Texas Execution Information Center, May 20, 2010.
8. Cannady v. Dretke (5th Cir. 2006).
9. Ibid.
10. Cannady v. State, 11 S.W.3d 205 (Tex.Crim.App. 2006)
11. *Valley Morning Star*, May 20, 2010.
12. Ibid.
13. Ibid.
14. Ibid.
15. Rainwater, M., "Man executed for slaying of cellmate," *Huntsville Item*, May 19, 2010.
16. Ibid.
17. Graczyk, M. "Texas prisoner executed for killing cell mate," Associated Press, May 14, 2010.
18. *Valley Morning Star*, May 20, 2010.
19. Grann, D. "Trial by fire: Did Texas execute an innocent man?" The New Yorker. http://www.newyorker.com/reporting/2009/09/07/090907fa_fact_grann.

Chapter 19

1. Woodward v. State, 533 So.2d 418 (Miss.1988).
2. Ibid.
3. Crisp, E., "First of back-to-back executions carried out," *Jackson Clarion-Ledger*, May 20, 20010.
4. Woodward v. State (Miss. 1988).
5. Ibid.
6. Atkins v. Virginia, 536 U.S. 304 (2002), banned the execution of the mentally disabled; Roper v. Simmons, 543 U.S. 551 (2005), banned the execution of juveniles.
7. Winick, B., "The Supreme Court's evolving death penalty jurisdiction: Severe mental illness as the next frontier," 50 B.C.L. Rev 785, May 2009.
8. Ibid.
9. Ibid.
10. Ibid.
11. Ibid.
12. "Scheduled execution for Paul E. Woodward," 2 p.m. News Briefing, Mississippi Department of Corrections, May 19, 2010.
13. Ibid.
14. Elliott, J., "His last breath: Woodward executed," *Hattiesburg American*, May 20, 2010.
15. *Jackson Clarion-Ledger*, May 20, 2010.
16. Ibid.
17. "Mississippi executes Paul Everett Woodward," Associated Press, May 20, 2010.
18. *Jackson Clarion-Ledger*, May 20, 2010.
19. Ibid.
20. "Scheduled execution of Paul E. Woodward," 7 p.m. News Briefing, Mississippi Department of Corrections, May 19, 2010.
21. "Former Perry County Sheriff recalls brutal murder," WDAM-AM, May 18, 2010.

Chapter 20

1. Salter, L., "Delay looms as big issue in execution cases," DSDigitalDaily.com, May 24, 2010.
2. Holland v. State, 587 So.2d 848 (Miss. 1991).
3. Ibid.
4. Ibid.
5. Ibid.
6. Ibid.
7. Ibid.
8. Gates, J., "Second inmate in two days executed at Parchman," *Jackson Clarion-Ledger*, May 21, 2010.
9. Holland v. State (Miss. 1991)
10. Ibid.
11. *Jackson Clarion-Ledger*, May 21, 2010.
12. Ibid.
13. Ibid.
14. Ibid.
15. Elliott, J., "Another inmate put to death; Second execution this week in Mississippi," *Hattiesburg American*, May 21, 2010.
16. *Jackson Clarion-Ledger*, May 21, 2010.
17. Ibid.
18. Ibid.

Chapter 21

1. Green, F., "Walker executed for two RVA murders," *Richmond Times-Dispatch*, May 21, 2010.
2. Ibid.
3. Walker v. Commonwealth, 515 S.E.2d 565 (Va. 1999).
4. "May 2010 executions—Darick Walker," Prodeathpenalty.com, May 20, 2010, http://www.prodeathpenalty.com/Pending/10/may10.htm.
5. 536 U.S. 304 (2002).

6. Ibid.

7. Bobby v. Bies, 129 S.Ct. 2145 (2009).

8. Atkins, 536 U.S. at 317, 122 S.Ct. 2242 (quoting Ford v. Wainwright, 477 U.S. 399, 405, 106 S.Ct. 2595, 91 L.Ed.2d 335) (1986).

9. Schriro v. Smith, 546 U.S. 6, 7, 126 S.Ct. 7, 163 L.Ed.2d 6 (2005).

10. Va.Code § 19.2–264.3:1.1(C).

11. Va.Code § 8.01–654.2.

12. Walker v. Kelly, 593 F.3d 319 (4th Cir. 2010).

13. Potter, D., "Virginia executes inmate who killed two men," Associated Press, May 20, 2010.

14. *Richmond Times-Dispatch*, May 21, 2010.

15. Ibid.

16. *Richmond Times-Dispatch*, May 21, 2010.

17. Ibid.

18. Ibid.

Chapter 22

1. "John Alba scheduled for execution," Media Advisory, Texas Office of Attorney General, May 18, 2010.

2. Ibid.

3. Carson, D., "John Alba," Texas Execution Information Center, May 26, 2010.

4. Ibid.

5. Alba v. State, 905 S.W.2d 581 (TexCrim.App. 1995).

6. Texas Execution Information Center, May 26, 2010.

7. Ibid.

8. Ibid.

9. Ibid.

10. Ross, A., "Execution slated for Tuesday for Elgin native," *Bastrop Advertiser*, May 22, 2010.

11. Ibid.

12. "John Alba," Pro Death Penalty, http://off2dr.com/modules/extcal/event.php?event=332.

13. Rainwater, M., "Alba executed for wife's shooting," *Huntsville Item*, May 25, 2010.

14. Graczyk, M., "Collin County man executed in 1991 shooting death of wife," Associated Press, May 25, 2010.

15. Texas Execution Information Center, May 26, 2010.

16. Death Penalty News, http://deathpenaltynews.blogspot.com/2010/05/death-row-inmates-writing-on-death-row.html.

Chapter 23

1. Kirby, B., "Thomas Whisenhant executed for 1996 kidnapping, rape and murder," *Mobile Press-Register*, May 27, 2010.

2. Bobit, B., "Convenient excuses," *The Crime Magazine*, www.crimemagazine.com/convenient-excuses.

3. Whisenhant v. State, 370 So.2d 1080 (Ala.Cr.App. 1979).

4. "Insanity defined in the United States," Psychiatry.us, http://www.psychiatry.us/articledetail.php?ID=44&CID.

5. Whisenhant v. State (1979).

6. Whisenhant v. State (Ala.Cr.App. 1979).

7. 384 U.S. 436 (1966).

8. *Mobile Press-Register*, May 27, 2010.

9. Ibid.

10. Kirby, B. "Thomas Whisenhant's last meal: Chicken legs, chocolate pudding," *Mobile Press-Register*, May 27, 2010.

11. *Mobile Press-Register*, May 27, 2010.

12. Ibid.

13. *Mobile Press-Register*, May 27, 2010.

14. Johnson, A., "Inmate executed after 32 years on death row," Associated Press, May 28, 2010.

15. Ibid.

16. Ibid.

Chapter 24

1. "George Jones," June 2010 Executions, www.prodeathpenalty.com.

2. "George Jones scheduled for execution," Media Advisory, Texas Office of Attorney General, May 26, 2010.

3. Carson, D., "George Jones," Texas Execution Information Center, June 4, 2010.

4. Ibid.

5. Jones v. State, 982 S.W.2d 386 (Tex.Crim.App. 1998).

6. Texas Execution Information Center, June 4, 2010.

7. Rainwater, M., "Jones executed for 1993 slayings," *Huntsville Item*, June 2, 2010.

8. Texas Office of Attorney General, May 26, 2010.

9. Eskenazi, S., "Dissed robes," *Dallas Observer News*, November 18, 1999.

10. Ibid.

11. Jones V. State (1998).

12. Ibid.

13. 536 U.S. 304 (2002).

14. Pro Death Penalty, Resource Community, http://off2dr.com/smf/index.php?topic=8328.60.

15. Graczyk, M., "Dallas man executed for 1993 carjacking murder," Associated Press, June 3, 2010.

16. *Huntsville Item*, June 2, 2010.

17. Associated Press, June 3, 2010.

18. Ibid.

19. Ibid.

20. Graczyk, M., "Death row inmate maintains his innocence day before execution," Associated Press, June 1, 2010.

21. Ibid.

Chapter 25

1. Ford v. State, 360 S.E.2d 258 (Ga. 1982).

2. Cook, R., "Georgia man executed for 1986 grocery store murder," *Atlanta Journal Constitution*, June 9, 2010.

3. "Georgia man executed tonight," Associated Press, June 9, 2010.

4. Ibid.

5. 446 U.S. 668 (1984).

6. Ford v. State (Ga. 1987)

7. Pittman, A., "Melbert Ray Ford executed: No apology offered to victim's families" *Covington News*, June 9, 2010.

8. Ibid.
9. Ibid.
10. Ibid.
11. Ibid.
12. *Atlanta Journal Constitution*, June 9, 2010.
13. *Atlanta Journal Constitution*, June 9, 2010.
14. Associated Press, June 9, 2010.
15. *Covington News*, June 9, 2010.
16. Associated Press, June 9, 2010.

Chapter 26

1. Smith, T., "Parker put to death," *Times Daily*, June 11, 2010.
2. Ibid.
3. Parker v. State, 610 So.2d 171 (Ala.Cr.App. 1992).
4. "Charles Sennett: Husband, father, preacher, sociopath," *Shoalanda Speaker*, June 11, 2010, http://shoalandaspeaks.blogspot.com/search/label/Elizabeth%20Dorlene%20Sennett.
5. "Death penalty," Equal Justice Initiative, http://www.eji.org/eji/deathpenalty/override.
6. Ibid.
7. "If a jury's vote had been heeded...," Editorial Board, *Birmingham News*, June 10, 2010.
8. Stackhouse, M., "Shoals man executed Thursday night," WHNT-TV, June 10, 2010.
9. *Times Daily*, June 11, 2010.
10. Ibid.
11. Ibid.
12. Ibid.
13. *Times Daily*, June 11, 2010.
14. "State of Alabama executed John Forrest Parker," Associated Press, June 10, 2010.
15. "Alabama man executed in 1998 contract killing," Associated Press, June 10, 2010.
16. *Times Daily*, June 11, 2010.
17. *Birmingham News*, June 10, 2010.
18. Associated Press, June 10, 2010.

Chapter 27

1. Lindell, C., Plohetski, T., "Crime and Punishment: After 32 years, has Powell's execution lost its meaning?" *Austin American Statesman*, June 15, 2010.
2. Ibid.
3. Powell v. State, 742 S.W.2d 353 (Tex.Crim.App. 1987)
4. "David Powell," June 2010 executions, Prodeathpenalty.com, http://www.prodeathpenalty.com/Pending/10/jun10.htm
5. 486 U.S. 249 (1988).
6. Tex. Code Crim. Proc. Ann., Art. 37.071(b) (2)
7. Powell v. Texas, 492 U.S. 680 (1989).
8. Carson, D., "David Powell," Texas Execution Information Center, June 16, 2010.
9. Wolfson, S., "Powell executed for officer death," KXAN-TV, June 16, 2010.
10. Rainwater, M., "Drug dealer executed for 1978 slaying of Austin cop," *Huntsville Item*, June 16, 2010.
11. Texas Execution Information Center, June 16, 2010.

12. Lindell, C., Plohetski, T., "Powell executed for 1978 slaying of police officer," *Austin American Statesman*, June 16, 2010.
13. Texas Execution Information Center, June 16, 2010.
14. Ibid.
15. *Austin American-Statesman*, June 16, 2010.
16. Ibid.
17. Ibid.
18. Ibid.

Chapter 28

1. Dobner, J., "Ronnie Lee Gardner executed by firing squad," *Huffington Post*, June 18, 2010.
2. Falk, A., Morgan, E., "Ronnie Lee Gardner executed by firing squad," *Deseret News*, June 18, 2010.
3. Ibid.
4. *Huffington Post*, June 18, 2010.
5. Ibid.
6. Dobner, J., "Ronnie Lee Gardner Execution," *Christian Science Monitor*, June 16, 2010.
7. Ibid.
8. *Huffington Report*, June 18, 2010.
9. *Christian Science Monitor*, June 16, 2010.
10. Dobner, J., "Ronnie Lee Gardner Executed," *Christian Science Monitor*, June 16, 2010.
11. Ibid.
12. State v. Gardner, 789 P.2d 273 (Utah 1989).
13. Smart, C., "Gardner Executed," *Salt Lake Tribune*, June 18, 2010.
14. Ibid.
15. *Deseret News*, June 18, 2010.
16. *Huffington Post*, June 18, 2010
17. Ibid.
18. *Salt Lake Tribune*, June 18, 2010.
19. Ibid.

Chapter 29

1. Tolson, M., "Inmate execution for nurse's murder: Says he didn't kill Conroe woman," Associated Press, July 1, 2010.
2. "Michael Perry scheduled for execution," Media Advisory, Texas Office of Attorney General, June 24, 2010.
3. Perry v. State, 158 S.W.3d 438 (Tex.Crim.App. 2004)
4. Ibid.
5. Carson, D., "Michael Perry," Texas Execution Information Center, July 2, 2010.
6. Perry v. State (Tex.Crim.App. 2004).
7. Texas Execution Information Center, July 2, 2010.
8. "Michael Perry, July 2010 execution," Prodeathpenalty.com, http://www.prodeathpenalty.com/Pending/10/jul10.htm.
9. Rainwater, M., "Killer of Houston nurse executed," *Huntsville Item*, July 1, 2010.
10. Engle, S., "One of Montgomery County's worst murderers executed in Huntsville," *Montgomery County Police Reporter*, July 2, 2010.
11. Ibid.

12. *Huntsville Item*, July 1, 2010.
13. Associated Press, July 1, 2010
14. Ibid.
15. Flake, N., "Perry put to death," *Montgomery County Courier*, July 2, 2010.
16. Ibid.
17. Ibid.
18. Ibid.

Chapter 30

1. State v. Garner, 1994 WL 466508 (Ohio App. 1994).
2. Ibid.
3. Ibid.
4. Garner v. Mitchell, 557 F.2d 257 (6th Cir. 2009).
5. Viviano, J., "Ohio man executed for fire deaths of five children," Associated Press, July 13, 2010.
6. Kelly, E., "Garner goes quietly for killing 5," *Cincinnati Enquirer*, July 13, 2010.
7. Associated Press, July 13, 2010.
8. *Cincinnati Enquirer*, July 13, 2010.
9. Ibid.
10. Johnson, A., "Killer executed, but when isn't certain," *Columbus Dispatch*, July 14, 2010.
11. *Cincinnati Enquirer*, July 13, 2010.
12. Ibid.
13. *Cincinnati Enquirer*, July 13, 2010.
14. *Columbus Dispatch*, July 14, 2010.
15. Associated Press, July 13, 2010.
16. *Cincinnati Enquirer*, July 13, 2010.

Chapter 31

1. Jackson v. State, 17 S.W.3d 644 (Tex.Crim.App. 2000).
2. Carson, D., "Derrick Jackson," Texas Execution Information Center.
3. Jackson v. State (Tex.Crim.App. 2000).
4. Ibid.
5. Graczyk, M., "Man executed for death of 2 Houston opera singers," Associated Press, July 20, 2010.
6. Ibid.
7. Turner, A., "Execution set Tuesday in Houston tenors' slaying," *Houston Chronicle*, July 19, 2010.
8. Associated Press, July 20, 2010.
9. *Houston Chronicle*, July 19, 2010.
10. *Houston Chronicle*, July 19, 2010.
11. Pro Death Penalty, Resource Center, http://off2dr.com/smf/index.php?topic=3106.15
12. Associated Press, July 20, 2010.
13. Ibid.
14. Ibid.

Chapter 32

1. Crisp, E. "Killer offers apology; Court briefly stalls execution," *Jackson Clarion-Ledger*, July 22, 2010.
2. Burns v. State, 729 So.2d 203 (Miss. 1998).
3. "Criminal past & a U.S. Senator's ties to Burns," *Jackson Clarion Ledger*, July 21, 2010.
4. Solis, R., "Mississippi executes man for 1994 slaying of motel clerk," Associated Press, July 21, 2010.

5. "July 21, 2010, execution of Joseph D. Burns," News Release, Mississippi Department of Corrections, July 21, 2010.
6. Gates, J., "Man's last words: All right, devil. Let's do your work," *Jackson Clarion-Ledger*, July 21, 2010.
7. *Jackson Clarion-Ledger*, July 21, 2010.
8. Ibid.
9. Ibid.
10. Associated Press, July 21, 2010.
11. Ibid.
12. *Jackson Clarion-Ledger*, July 21, 2010.
13. "Execution of Joseph D. Burns, 7 p.m. news briefing," Mississippi Department of Corrections, July 21, 2010.

Chapter 33

1. State v. Davie, 1995 WL 870019 (Ohio App. 1995).
2. Ibid.
3. Kovac, M., "'91 killer's execution brings some closure," *Youngstown Vindicator*, August 11, 2010.
4. Ibid.
5. Ibid.
6. Nash, J. "Killer of 2 is executed at Lucasville," *Columbus Dispatch*, August 10, 2010.
7. Ibid.
8. Nuss, J. "Ohio executes man who killed 2 at warehouse in '91'" Associated Press, August 10, 2010.
9. Ibid.
10. Ibid.
11. Shank, V., "Survivor, victims families gather for death penalty," *Warren Tribune Review*, July 10, 2010.
12. Ibid.
13. Ibid.
14. Ibid.
15. Ibid.
16. Ibid.

Chapter 34

1. Johnson, A., "Inmate executed for 1992 killing," Associated Press, August 13, 2010.
2. Land v. State, 678 So.2d 224 (Ala.Cr.App. 1995).
3. Ibid.
4. Ibid.
5. Associated Press, August 13, 2010.
6. "Governor Riley issues statement on scheduled execution of Michael Land," WTVY-TV, August 11, 2010.
7. Associated Press, August 13, 2010.
8. Ibid.
9. Ibid.
10. Robinson, C., "Alabama set to execute Michael Land for murder of Candace Brown," *Birmingham News*, August 12, 2010.
11. Ibid.
12. Ibid.
13. Ibid.

Chapter 35

1. Graczyk, M., "Texas executes gang member for murder of two girls," Associated Press, August 18, 2010.

2. Cantu v. State, 939 S.W.2d 627 (Tex.Crim.App. 1997).

3. "Peter Cantu scheduled for execution," Media Advisory, Texas Office of Attorney General, August 10, 2010.

4. Associated Press, August 17, 2010.

5. Carson, D., "Peter Cantu," Texas Execution Information Center, August 18, 2010.

6. "Peter Cantu, August 2010 executions," Prodeath penalty.com, www.prodeathpenalty.com/Pending/10/aug10.htm.

7. Texas Execution Information Center, August 18, 2010.

8. 543 U.S. 551 (2005).

9. 536 U.S. 304 (2002).

10. "Adolescence, Brain Development and Legal Culpability," American Bar Association, January 2004.

11. Mangino, M., "Supreme Court strikes down mandatory life sentences for juveniles," *Pennsylvania Law Weekly*, July 10, 2012.

12. 492 U.S. 361 (1989).

13. 543 U.S. 551 (2005).

14. Volentine, J., "Peter Cantu executed," KIAH-TV, August 17, 2010.

15. Ibid.

16. Tolson, M., "Cantu executed for 1993 deaths of Houston teens," *Houston Chronicle*, August 17, 2010.

17. Ibid.

18. Associated Press, August 17, 2010.

19. *Houston Chronicle*, August 17, 2010.

20. Ibid.

21. Ibid.

Chapter 36

1. Woods v. State, 715 So.2d 812 (Ala.Cr.App. 1996).

2. Ibid

3. Ibid.

4. Duke, N., "Wood appeals to Supreme Court," *Troy Messenger*, September 9, 2010.

5. Johnson, B., "Governor rejects plea to stop Wood's execution," Associated Press, September 9, 2010.

6. 536 U.S. 304 (2002).

7. 588 U.S. ____ (2010).

8. Associated Press, September 9, 2010.

9. Ibid.

10. Sinclar, B., "The end of Holly Wood," Capitalpunishmentbook.com, http://www.capitalpunishmentbook.com/?p=485.

11. Ibid.

12. *Troy Messenger*, September 8, 2010.

Chapter 37

1. Dininny, S.; Geranios, N., "Wash. Executes man convicted of woman's murder," Associated Press, September 9, 2010.

2. State v. Brown, 940 P.2d 546 (Wash. 1997).

3. Ibid.

4. "Cal Brown, September 2010 executions," Pro deathpenalty.com, http://www.prodeathpenalty.com/Pending/10/sep10.htm.

5. Allen, M. "Final preparation underway for Cal Brown's execution," KXLY-TV, September 9, 2010.

6. Ibid.

7. Ibid.

8. Associated Press, September 9, 2010.

9. Associated Press, September 9, 2010.

10. Sullivan, J., "Washington state says new execution method carried out humanely," *Seattle Times*, September 9, 2010.

11. Sullivan, J., "Killer on death row 16½ years is executed," *Seattle Times*, September 10, 2010.

12. Associated Press, September 9, 2010.

13. KXLY-TV, September 9, 2010.

Chapter 38

1. Lewis v. Commonwealth, 593 S.E.2d 220 (Va. 2004).

2. Ibid.

3. Lewis v. Wheeler, 609 F.2d 291 (4th Cir. 2010).

4. Glod, M., "Teresa Lewis put to death for murders of husband, stepson," *Washington Post*, September 24, 2010.

5. Ibid.

6. Ibid.

7. Green, F., "Teresa Lewis executed for 2002 slayings of husband, stepson," *Richmond Times-Dispatch*, September 24, 2010.

8. Ibid.

9. Ibid.

10. De Vogue, A., James, M., "Teresa Lewis appeared fearful as she entered Virginia's death chamber," ABC News, September 24, 2010.

11. Ibid.

12. Bell, M., "Teresa Lewis's execution and the reaction to women on death row," *Washington Post*, September 23, 2010.

13. Glod, M., "Teresa Lewis to be executed tonight," *Washington Post*, September 23, 2010.

14. *Washington Post*, September 24, 2010.

15. Ibid.

16. ABC News, September 24, 2010.

17. *Richmond Times-Dispatch*, September 24, 2010.

18. *Washington Post*, September 24, 2010.

Chapter 39

1. "USA: Cruel, inhuman, degrading: 40th execution of the year approaches," Amnesty International, September 24, 2010, hptt://www.amnesty.org/en/library/info/AMR51/091/2010/en.

2. Bluestein, G., "Georgia executes inmate who had attempted suicide," Associated Press, September 27, 2010.

3. Amnesty International, September 24, 2010.

4. Rhode v. State, 552 S.E.2d 855 (2001).

5. Yimam, B., "State Board denies clemency for Jones County triple murder," WMAZ-TV, September 17, 2010.

6. Ibid.

7. Rhode v. Hall, 582 F.3d 1273 (11th Cir. 2009).

8. Associated Press, September 27, 2010.

9. WMAZ-TV, September 17, 2010.

10. Ibid.

11. "Inmate's last meal," Rhode Execution Media Advisory, Georgia Department of Corrections, September 21, 2010.

12. Associated Press, September 27, 2010.

13. Lurie-Smith, D., "Rhode finally executed," *Jones County News*, September 28, 2010.

14. "Brandon Rhode," Chamblee54, September 24, 2010, http://chamblee54.wordpress.com/2010/09/24/brandon-rhode/.

15. Newman, K., "Gerri Ann Moss: Twelve years later," *Central Georgia News*, September 20, 2010.

16. Ibid.

17. Ibid.

Chapter 40

1. Johnson, A., "Ohio executes record eighth man this year," *Columbus Dispatch*, October 6, 2010.

2. State v. Benge, 661 N.E.2d 1019 (Ohio 1995).

3. Ibid.

4. Ibid.

5. 384 U.S. 436 (1966).

6. 130 S.Ct 1213 (2010).

7. State v. Benge (Ohio 1995).

8. Ibid.

9. State v. Williams, 452 N.E.2d 1323 (Ohio 1983).

10. "Butler County Killer Put to Death," WLWT-TV, October 6, 2010.

11. *Columbus Dispatch*, October 6, 2010.

12. WLWT-TV, October 6, 2010.

13. Smyth, J., "Ohio executes man who killed lover over ATM card," *Dayton Daily News*, October 6, 2010.

14. Ibid.

15. WLWT-TV, October 6, 2010.

16. *Columbus Dispatch*, October 6, 2010.

17. Ibid.

Chapter 41

1. Wackerly v. Workman, 580 F.3d 1171 (10th Cir. 2009).

2. Ibid.

3. Ibid.

4. Ibid.

5. "Killer gets ok for post-death ritual," *Muskogee Phoenix*, October 13, 2010.

6. Murphy, S., "Oklahoma man executed for 1996 killing fisherman," *Norman Transcript*, October 15, 2010.

7. Ibid.

8. Ibid.

9. Ibid.

10. Henry, S., "Convicted murderer executed," *Sequoyah County Times*, October 15, 2010.

11. Arnold, J., "Muldron murderer executed," *Fort Smith Times Record*, October 15, 2010.

12. Krehbiel, R., "Donald Ray Wackerly executed 12 years after conviction," *Tulsa World*, October 15, 2010.

13. Baker, M., "Wackerly execution won't be delayed in Oklahoma," *Daily Oklahoman*, October 14, 2010.

Chapter 42

1. "Larry Wooten scheduled for execution," Media Advisory, Texas Office of Attorney General, October 14, 2010.

2. Carson, D., "Larry Wooten," Texas Execution Information Center, October 25, 2010.

3. Wooten v. Thaler, 598 F.3d 215 (5th Cir. 2010)

4. Texas Office of Attorney General, October 14, 2010.

5. Ibid.

6. Lozano, J., "Inmate executed for slayings of elderly Paris couple," Associated Press, October 21, 2010.

7. Davis, T., "Texas executes killer of elderly Paris couple," *Huntsville Item*, October 21, 2010.

8. 132 S.Ct. 1376 (2012).

9. 132 S.Ct. 1399 (2012).

10. Wooten v. Thaler (5th Cir. 2010).

11. Ibid.

12. Whiteley, J., "Assistant district attorney watches time run out on death penalty case," *Herald Democrat*, October 20, 2010.

13. Texas Execution Information Center, October 25, 2010.

14. Harkin, B., "Inmate appeals looming execution," *The Paris News*, October 6, 2010.

15. *Huntsville Item*, October 21, 2010.

16. Associated Press, October 21, 2010.

17. *Huntsville Item*, October 21, 2010.

18. Associated Press, October 21, 2010.

Chapter 43

1. Kiefer, M., "Arizona executes inmate after federal judge lifts stay," *Arizona Republic*, October 7, 2010.

2. State v. Landrigan, 859 P.2d 111 (Ariz. 1993).

3. Ibid.

4. Landrigan v. State, 700 P.2d 218 (Okl. Cr. 1985).

5. Kiefer, M., "Judge to question whether injection drug illegally obtained," *Arizona Republic*, October 25, 2010.

6. Ibid.

7. Ibid.

8. Ibid.

9. Ibid.

10. *Arizona Republic*, October 25, 2010.

11. Kilpatrick, J., "But the judges have changed," Lawcrossing.com, http://www.lawcrossing.com/article/2059/But-the-Judges-Have-Changed/.

12. *Arizona Republic*, October 7, 2010.

13. Ibid.

14. State v. Landrigan (Ariz. 1993).

Chapter 44

1. Elofsen, M., "Phillip Hallford executed for killing daughter's boyfriend," *Dothan Eagle*, November 5, 2010.

2. Johnson, B., "Man executed for killing of daughter's boyfriend," Associated Press, November 5, 2010.

3. Hallford v. State, 548 So.2d 526 (Ala.Cr.App. 1988).

4. Ibid.

5. Section 13A-5–45(c) and (d), Code of Alabama 1975.

6. Hallford v. State (Ala.Cr.App. 1988).

7. Associated Press, November 5, 2010.

8. Ibid.

9. Ibid.

10. *Dothan Eagle*, November 5, 2010.

11. Ibid.

12. Ibid.

13. Ibid.

14. Ibid.

15. Ibid.

Chapter 45

1. Duty v. Workman, 366 Fed.Appx. 863 (10th Cir. 2010).

2. Ibid.

3. Ibid.

4. Petersen, R., "Oklahoma death row inmate John David Duty has been executed," *McAlester News*, December 16, 2010.

5. Duty v. Workman (10th Cir. 2010).

6. Belluck, P., "What's in a lethal injection 'cocktail?'" *New York Times*, April 9, 2011.

7. Plummer, S., "Oklahoma death row inmate executed with different mix of drugs," *Tulsa World*, December 17, 2010.

8. Duty v. Workman (10th Cir. 2010).

9. 558 U.S. ___ (2010).

10. Duty v. Workman (10th Cir. 2010).

11. *McAlester News*, December 16, 2010.

12. Ibid.

13. Fenick, B., "Oklahoma uses animal euthanasia drug in execution," Reuters, December 16, 2010.

14. Ibid.

15. Ibid.

Conclusion

1. Gallup, http://www.gallup.com/poll/1606/death-penalty.aspx.

2. Baze v. Rees, 553 U.S. 35 (2008).

3. Gregg v. Georgia, 428 U.S. 153 (1976).

4. Savage, D., "FBI reports 5% drop in crime rate," *Los Angeles Times*, September 14, 2010.

5. Wetterich, C., "Bill would reinstate death penalty in Illinois," GateHouse News Service, February 15, 2011.

6. Hunt, J., "Emotions run high at death penalty debate," *Charleston Daily Mail*, February 16, 2011.

7. "Montana Senate endorses death penalty repeal," *Billings Gazette*, February 14, 2011.

8. 408 U.S. 238 (1972).

9. Washington v. Gentry, 888 P.2d 1105 (Wash. 1995).

Bibliography

"Alabama man executed in 1988 contract killing." (2010, June 10). Associated Press. Retrieved from www.ap.org.

Allen, M. (2010, September 9). "Final preparation underway for Cal Brown's execution." KXLY-TV. Retrieved from www.kxly.com.

"Appeal denied for Alix." (2009, February 10). Associated Press. Retrieved from www.ap.org.

"April 2010 Executions—Darryl Durr." Prodeathpenalty.com. Retrieved from www.prodeathpenalty.com/pending/10/apr10.htm.

"April 2010 Executions—William Berkley." Prodeathpenalty.com. Retrieved from www.prodeathpenalty.com/pending/10/apr10.htm.

Arnold, J. (2010, October 15). "Muldron murderer executed." *Fort Smith Times Record*. Retrieved from www.swtimes.com.

"August 2010 Executions—Peter Cantu." Prodeathpenalty.com. Retrieved from www.prodeathpenalty.com/pending/10/aug10.htm.

Baker, M. (2010, October 14). "Wackerly execution won't be delayed in Oklahoma." *Daily Oklahoman*. Retrieved from www.oklahoman.com.

Bell, M. (2010, September 23). "Teresa Lewis's execution and the reaction to women on death row." *Washington Post*. Retrieved from www.washingtonpost.com.

Belluck, P. (2011, April 9). "What's in a lethal injection 'cocktail'?" *New York Times*. Retrieved from www.nytimes.com.

Blake, E. (2010, January 6). "Pending execution stirs pain anew." *Toledo Blade*. Retrieved from www.toledoblade.com.

Bluestein, G. (2010, September 27). "Georgia executes inmate who had attempted suicide." Associated Press. Retrieved from www.ap.org.

"Board denies clemency for Tulsa killer." (2009, December 8). *Norman Transcript*. www.normantranscript.com.

Bobit, B. "Convenient Excuses." *The Crime Magazine*. Retrieved from www.crimemagazine.com/convenient-excuses.

"Brandon Rhode." (2010, September 24). Chamblee 54. [Web log comment]. Retrieved from http://chamblee54.wordpress.com/2010/0/24/brandon-rhode/.

"Butler County killer put to death." (2010, October 6). WLWT-TV.

Canadian Coalition Against the Death Penalty. Retrieved from www.ccadp.org/franlinalix.htm.

Carr, J. (2010, May 12). "Ohio executes hitchhiker who shot 3 drivers in '83." Associated Press. Retrieved from www.ap.org.

Carson, D. (2010, March 15). "Joshua Maxwell." Texas Execution Information Center. Retrieved from www.txexecutions.org.

Carson, D. (2010, April 4). "Franklin Alix." Texas Execution Information Center. Retrieved from www.www.txexecutions.org.

Carson, D. (2010, April 26). "William Berkley." Texas Execution Information Center. Retrieved from www.txexecutions.org.

Carson, D. (2010, April 28). "Samuel Bustamante." Texas Execution Information Center. Retrieved from www.txexecutions.org.

Carson, D. (2010, May 14). "Bill Galloway." Texas Execution Information Center. Retrieved from www.txexecutions.org.

Carson, D. (2010, May 20). "Rogelio Cannady." Texas Execution Information Center. Retrieved from www. www.txexecutions.org.

Carson, D. (2010, May 26). "George Jones." Texas Execution Information Center. Retrieved from www.txexecutions.org.

Carson, D. (2010, June 4). "George Jones." Texas Execution Information Center. Retrieved from www.txexecutions.org.

Carson, D. (2010, June 16). "David Powell." Texas Execution Information Center. Retrieved from www.txexecutions.org.

Carson, D. (2010, July 2). "Michael Perry." Texas Execution Information Center. Retrieved from www.txexecutions.org.

Carson, D. (2010, August 18). "Peter Cantu." Texas Execution Information Center. Retrieved from www. www.txexecutions.org.

"Charles Sennett: Husband, father, preacher, sociopath." (2010, June 11). Shoalanda Speaker. [Web log comment]. Retrieved from http://shoalandaspeaks.blogspot.com/search/label/Elizabeth%20Dorlene%20Sennett.

Chavez, A. (2010, April 22). "William Josef Berkley

is executed, did not address Martinez family." *El Paso Times*. Retrieved from www.elpasotimes.com.

Cook, R. (2010, June 9). "Georgia man executed for 1986 grocery store murder." *Atlanta Journal Constitution*. Retrieved from www.ajc.com.

Cornwell, L. (2010, May 12). "Homicidal hitchhiker faces execution." *Cincinnati Enquirer*. Retrieved from www.cincinatti.com.

Crabbe, N. (2010, February 2). "Grossman executed for killing wildlife officer." *Gainesville Sun*. Retrieved from www.gainesville.com.

Craig, J. (2010, May 13). "Last statement from 'mad hitchiker' Michael Beuke: A 17-minute prayer." *Cincinnati Enquirer*. Retrieved from www.news.cincinnati.com.

Crisp, E. (2010, May 20). "First of back-to-back executions carried out." *Jackson Clarion-Ledger*. Retrieved from www.clarionledger.com.

Crisp, E. (2010, July 21). "Burns doesn't want anything special for last meal." *Jackson Clarion-Ledger*. Retrieved from www.clarionledger.com.

Crisp, E. (2010, July 21). "Criminal past & a U.S. Senator's ties to Burns." *Jackson Clarion-Ledger*. Retrieved from www.clarionledger.com.

Crisp, E. (2010, July 22). "Killer offers apology: Court briefly stalls execution." *Jackson Clarion-Ledger*. Retrieved from www.clarionledger.com.

"Cuyahoga Falls woman's killer executed." (2010, March 12). *Norwalk Reflector*. Retrieved from www.norwalkreflector.com.

"Death penalty." Equal Justice Initiative. Retrieved from www.eji.org/eji/deathpenalty/override.

Death penalty news. (2010, May 22). [Web log comment]. Retrieved from http://deathpenaltynews.blogspot.com/2010/05/death-row-inmates-writing-on-death-row.html.

Deslatte, M. (2010, January 8). "La. man executed for 2002 murder." *Shreveport Times*. Retrieved from www.shreveporttimes.com.

DeVogue, A. & James, M. (2010, September 24). "Teresa Lewis appeared fearful as she entered Virginia's death chamber." ABC News. Retrieved from www.abcnews.com.

Dininny, S. & Geranios, N. (2010, September 9). "Wash. executes man convicted of woman's murder." Associated Press. Retrieved from www.ap.org.

"DNA could play major role in Bordelon case." (2010, January 8). WAFB-TV. Retrieved from www.wafb.com.

Dobner, J. (2010, June 16). "Ronnie Lee Gardner execution: Firing squads are humane say some experts." *Christian Science Monitor*. Retrieved from www.csmonitor.com.

Dobner, J. (2010, June 18). "Ronnie Lee Gardner executed by firing squad." *Huffington Post*. Retrieved from www.huffingtonpost.com.

Douglas, M. (2010, February 16). "Grossman executed: Last words are of heartfelt remorse." *Tampa Tribune*. Retrieved from www.tbo.com.

Duke, N. (2010, September 8). "Wood appeals to Supreme Court. *Troy Messenger*." Retrieved from www.troymessenger.

Eaton, K. (2009, December 31). "Economic recession kills death penalty in Oklahoma." *The Journal Record*. Retrieved from www.journalrecord.com.

Elliott, J. (2010, May 20). "His last breath: Woodward executed." *Hattiesburg American*. Retrieved from www.hattiesburgamerican.com.

Elliott, J. (2010, May 21). "Another inmate put to death; second execution this week in Mississippi." *Hattiesburg American*. www.hattiesburgamerican.com.

Elofsen, M. (2010, November 5). "Phillip Hallford executed for killing daughter's boyfriend." *Dothan Eagle*. Retrieved from www.dothaneagle.com.

Engle, S. (2010, July 2). "One of Montgomery County's worst murderers executed in Huntsville." *Montgomery County Police Reporter*. Retrieved from www.montgomerycountypolicereporter.com.

Eskenazi, S. (1999, November 18). "Dissed Robes." *Dallas Observer News*. Retrieved from www.dallasobserver.com.

Fair, K. (1988, August 20). "Jury assesses death penalty; Huntsville panel deliberates half an hour." *Houston Chronicle*. Retrieved from www.houstonchronicle.com.

Falk, A. & Morgan, E. (2010, June 18). "Ronnie Lee Gardner executed by firing squad." *Deseret News*. Retrieved from www.deseretnews.com.

Fenick, B. (2010, December 16). "Oklahoma uses animal euthanasia drug in execution." *Reuters*. Retrieved from www.reuters.com.

Flake, N. (2010, July 2). "Perry put to death." *Montgomery County Courier*. Retrieved from www.yourhoustonnews.com/courier/news.

Florida Department of Corrections. Retrieved from http://www.dc.state.fl.us.

"Former Perry County Sherriff recalls brutal murder." (2010, May 18). *WDAM-AM*. Retrieved from www.WDAM.com.

Gates, J. (2010, May 21). "Second inmate in two days executed at Parchman." *Jackson Clarion-Ledger*. Retrieved from www.clarionledger.com.

Gates, J. (2010, July 21). "Man's last words: All right, devil. Let's do your work." *Jackson Clarion-Ledger*. Retrieved from www.clarionledger.com.

Georgia Department of Corrections. (2010, September 21). "Inmates last meal." [Media Advisory].

Glod, M. (2010, September 23). "Teresa Lewis to be executed tonight." *Washington Post*. Retrieved from www.washingtonpost.com.

Glod, M. (2010, September 24). "Teresa Lewis put to death for murders of husband, stepson." *Washington Post*. Retrieved from www.washingtonpost.com.

"Governor Riley issues statement on scheduled execution of Michael Land." (2010, August 11). WTVY-TV

Graczyk, M. (2010, January 7). "Dallas-area officer's killer put to death." Associated Press. Retrieved from www.ap.org.

Graczyk, M. (2010, January 12). "Former worker who shot 2 at Texas ranch executed." Associated Press. Retrieved from www.ap.org.

Graczyk, M. (2010, March 11). "Man executed for 2000 crime spree." Associated Press. Retrieved from www.ap.org.

Graczyk, M. (2010, April 27). "Killer of immigrant executed." Associated Press. Retrieved from www.ap.org.

Graczyk, M. (2010, May 12). "South Dakota ex-con executed." Associated Press. Retrieved from www.ap.org.

Graczyk, M. (2010, May 13). "Killer executed for '98 robbery, slaying near Dallas." Associated Press. Retrieved from www.ap.org.

Graczyk, M. (2010, May 14). "Texas prisoner executed for killing cell mate." Associated Press. Retrieved from www.ap.org.

Graczyk, M. (2010, May 25). "Collin County man executed in 1991 shooting death of wife." Associated Press. Retrieved from www.ap.org.

Graczyk, M. (2010, June 1). "Death row inmate maintains his innocence day before execution." Associated Press. Retrieved from www.ap.org.

Graczyk, M. (2010, June 3). "Dallas man executed for 1993 carjacking murder." Associated Press. Retrieved from www.ap.org.

Graczyk, M. (2010, August 17). "Texas executes gang member for murder of two girls." Associated Press. Retrieved from www.ap.org.

Grann, D. (2009, September 7). "Trial by fire: Did Texas execute an innocent man?" *The New Yorker*. Retrieved from www.newyorker.com.

Green, F. (2010, March 19). "Powell executed for teen's 1999 murder in Manassas." *Richmond Post-Dispatch*. Retrieved from www.timesdispatch.com.

Green, F. (2010, May 21). "Walker executed for two RVA murders." *Richmond Times-Dispatch*. Retrieved from www.timesdispatch.com.

Green, F. (2010, September 24). "Teresa Lewis executed for 2002 slayings of husband, stepson." *Richmond Times-Dispatch*. Retrieved from www.timesdispatch.com.

Guillen, J. (2010, April 20). "State executes Darryl Durr for 1988 murder of teenage girl." *Cleveland Plain Dealer*. Retrieved from www.cleveland.com/plaindealer.

Hampton, D. (2010, January 15). "Man executed for '93 slayings." *Tulsa World*. Retrieved from www.tulsaworld.com.

Hayes, A. (2010, January 6). "Ohio executes second man using single drug method." CNN. Retrieved www.CNN.com.

Henry, S. (2010, October 15). "Convicted murderer executed." *Sequoyah County Times*. Retrieved from www.sequoyacountytimes.com

Hunt, J. (2011, February 16). "Emotions run high at death penalty debate." *Charleston Daily Mail*. Retrieved from www.dailymail.com.

"If a jury's vote had been heeded..." (2010, June 10). Editorial Board. *Birmingham News*. Retrieved from www.al.com/birminghamnews.

"Indiana man who murdered 2 in San Antonia set to die." (2010, March 11). Associated Press. Retrieved from www.ap.org.

"The innocent and the death penalty." Innocence Project. Retrieved from http://www.innocenceproject.org.

"Insanity defense in the United States." Retrieved from www.psychiatry.us.

Jacobson, S. (2009, September 15). "Garland officer's widow struggles as killer's execution nears." *Dallas Morning News*. Retrieved from www.dallasnews.com.

Jacobson, S. (2010, January 8). "Garland officer's killer executed in Huntsville." *Dallas Morning News*. Retrieved from www.dallasnews.com.

Johnson, A. (2010, March 16). "Killer executed one week after suicide attempt." *Columbus Dispatch*. Retrieved from www.dispatch.com.

Johnson, A. (2010, March 17). "Murderer's last word: 'Stop the madness.'" *Columbus Dispatch*. Retrieved from www.dispatch.com.

Johnson, A. (2010, April 21). "Killer provides no comfort at execution." *Columbus Dispatch*. Retrieved from www.dispatch.com.

Johnson, A. (2010, May 13). "Ohio executes homicidal hitchhiker." *Columbus Dispatch*. Retrieved from www.dispatch.com.

Johnson, A. (2010, May 28). "Inmate executed after 32 years on death row." Associated Press. Retrieved from www.ap.org.

Johnson, A. (2010, August 13). "Inmate executed for 1992 killing." Associated Press. Retrieved from www.ap.org.

Johnson, A. (2010, October 6). "Ohio executes record eighth man this year." *Columbus Dispatch*. Retrieved from www.dispatch.com.

Johnson, B. (2010, September 9). "Governor rejects plea to stop Wood's execution." Associated Press. Retrieved from www.ap.org.

Johnson, B. (2010, November 5). "Man executed for killing of daughter's boyfriend." Associated Press. Retrieved from www.ap.org.

"June 2010 Executions—David Powell." Prodeath penalty.com. Retrieved from www.prodeathpenalty.com/pending/10/june10.htm.

"June 2010 Executions—George Jones." Prodeath penalty.com. Retrieved from www.prodeathpenalty.com/Pending/10/jun10.htm.

"July 2010 Executions—Michael Perry." Prodeathpenalty.com. Retrieved from www.prodeathpen alty.com/pending/10/jul10.htm.

Juozapavicius, J. (2010, January 14). Oklahoma inmate executed for 1993 Tulsa beating deaths. Associated Press. Retrieved from www.ap.org.

Keith, K. (2010, March 11). "Indiana native to be executed in Texas tonight." WIBC. Retrieved from www.wibc.com.

Kiefer, M. (2010, October 7). "Arizona executes inmate after federal judge lifts stay." *Arizona Republic.* Retrieved at www.azcentral.com.

Kiefer, M. (2010, October 25). "Judge to question whether injection drug illegally obtained." *Arizona Republic.* Retrieved at www.azcentral.com.

"Killer gets ok for post-death ritual." (2010, October 13). Associated Press. Retrieved from www.musko geephoenix.com.

Kilpatrick, J. (2006, October 19). "But the judges have changed." Retrieved from www.townhall. com.

Kirby, B. (2010, May 27). "Thomas Whisenhant executed for 1996 kidnapping, rape and murder." *Mobile Press-Register.* Retrieved from www.al. com/press-register.

Kirby, B. (2010, May 27). "Thomas Whisenhant last meal: Chicken legs, chocolate pudding." *Mobile Press-Register.* Retrieved from www.al.com/press-register.

Kovac, M. (2010, February 5). "Family: Justice served to killer." Associated Press. Retrieved from www. ap.org.

Kovac, M. (2010, August 11). "'91 killer's execution brings some closure." *Youngstown Vindicator.* Retrieved from www.vindy.com.

Krehbiel, R. (2010, October 15). "Donald Ray Wackerly executed 12 years after conviction." *Tulsa World.* Retrieved from www.tulsaworld.com.

Leingang, M. (2010, March 8). "Death row inmate overdose delays lethal injection." Associated Press. Retrieved from www.ap.org.

Leingang, M. (2010, March 16). "Ohio executes inmate who killed neighbor." Associated Press. Retrieved from www.ap.org.

Lindell, C. & Plohetski, T. (2010, June 15). "Crime and punishment: After 32 years, has Powell's execution lost its meaning?" *Austin American Statesman.* Retrieved from www.statesman.com.

Lindell, C. & Plohetski, T. (2010, June 16). "Powell executed for 1978 slaying of police officer." *Austin American Statesman.* Retrieved from www. statesman.com.

Lowenstein, T. (2009, November 6). "Use of video to end false confessions." *The Times-Picayune.* Retrieved from www.nola.com.

Lozano, J. (2010, March 3). "Dallas man executed in killing of Brazilian engineer." Associated Press. Retrieved from www.ap.org.

Lozano, J. (2010, April 22). "Inmate executed for killing and raping El Paso teen." *Houston Chronicle.* Retrieved from www.houstonchronicle.com.

Lurie-Smith, D. (2020, September 28). "Rhode finally executed." *Jones County News.* Retrieved from www.jcnews.com.

"Mark Aaron Brown executed, offered no final statement." (2010, February 4). *Youngstown Vindicator.* Retrieved from www.vindy.com.

"May 2010 Executions—Darick Walker." Prodeathpenalty.com. Retrieved from www.prodeathpenal ty.com/pending/10/may10.htm.

"May 2010 Executions—John Alba." Prodeathpenalty.com. Retrieved from www.prodeathpenal ty.com/Pending/10/may10.htm.

McNiff, E. (2010, April 21). "Death row allergy claim fails to delay Darryl Durr's execution." ABC News. Retrieved from www.abcnews.com.

Minton, J. (2010, January 7). "Bordelon remorseful before execution." *Baton Rouge Advocate.* Retrieved from www.theadvocate.com.

Minton, J. (2010, January 8). "Child killer voices remorse, executed." *Baton Rouge Advocate.* Retrieved from www.theadvocate.com.

Mississippi Department of Corrections. (2010, May 19). "Scheduled execution of Paul E. Woodward." [2 p.m. News Briefing]. Retrieved from www. mdoc.state.ms.us.

Mississippi Department of Corrections. (2010, May 19). "Scheduled execution of Paul E. Woodward." [7 p.m. News Briefing]. Retrieved from www. mdoc.state.ms.us.

Mississippi Department of Corrections. (2010, July 21). "Execution of Joseph D. Burns." [News Briefing]. Retrieved from www.mdoc.state.ms.us.

Mississippi Department of Corrections. (2010, July 21). "July 21, 2010 Execution of Joseph D. Burns." [News Release]. Retrieved from www.mdoc.state. ms.us.

"Mississippi executes Paul Everett Woodward." (2010, May 20). Associated Press. Retrieved from www.ap.org.

Mondo, M. (2010, March 12). "Lawman's killer put to death." *San Antonio Express.* Retrieved from www.mysanantonio.com.

"Montana Senate endorses death penalty repeal." (2011, February 14). *Billings Gazette.* Retrieved from www.billingsgazette.com.

"Murderer apologizes before his execution at Louisiana State Penitentiary." (2010, January 7). *New Orleans Times-Picayune.* Retrieved from www.nola.com.

Murphy, S. (2010, October 15). "Oklahoma man executed for 1996 killing of fisherman." *Norman Transcript.* Retrieved from normantranscript. com.

Nash, J. (2010, January 7). "Toledo killer executed." *Columbus Dispatch.* Retrieved from www.disp atch.com.

Nash, J. (2010, August 10). "Killer of 2 is executed

at Lucasville." *Columbus Dispatch*. Retrieved from www.dispatch.com.

Newman, K. (2010, September 20). "Gerri Ann Moss: Twelve years later." *Central Georgia News*. Retrieved from www.newscentralga.com.

Nuss, J. (2010, August 10). "Ohio executes man who killed 2 at warehouse in '91." Associated Press. Retrieved from www.ap.org.

"Oklahoma executes man convicted of killing 2." (2010, January 15). Associated Press. Retrieved from www.ap.org.

Perry, K. (2010, April 1). "Judge upset with Beuke 27 years on death row." *Cincinnati Enquirer*. Retrieved from www.news.cincinnati.com.

Petersen, R. (2010, December 16). "Oklahoma death row inmate John David Duty has been executed." *McAlister News*. Retrieved from www.mcalesternews.com.

Pittman, A. (2010, June 9). "Melbert Ray Ford executed: No apology offered to victim's families." *Covington News*. Retrieved from www.covnews.com.

Plummer, S. (2010, December 17). "Oklahoma death row inmate executed with different mix of drugs." *Tulsa World*. Retrieved from www.tulsaworld.com.

Potter, D. (2010, May 20). "Virginia executes inmate who killed two men." Associated Press. Retrieved from www.ap.org.

Pro Death Penalty, Resource Community. Retrieved from http://off2dr.com/smf/index.php?topic=8328.60.

Provance, J. (2010, January 8). "Toledoan Smith was put to death under new death house protocol." *Toledo Blade*. Retrieved from www.toledoblade.com.

Raindeer, M. (2010, April 27). "Man executed for 1998 stabbing." *Huntsville Item*. Retrieved from www.itemonline.com.

Rainwater, M. (2010, January 12). "Man executed for ranch murder." *Huntsville Item*. Retrieved from www.itemonline.com.

Rainwater, M. (2010, March 31). "Man executed for '98 Houston murder." *Huntsville Item*. Retrieved from www.itemonline.com.

Rainwater, M. (2010, May 9). "Death row inmate: No justice by execution." *Rapid City Journal*. Retrieved from www.rapidcityjournal.com.

Rainwater, M. (2010, May 12). "Kevin Varga made religious appeal before execution." *Rapid City Journal*. Retrieved from www.rapidcityjournal.com.

Rainwater, M. (2010, May 12). "South Dakota man executed for fatal beating." *Huntsville Item*. Retrieved from www.itemonline.com.

Rainwater, M. (2010, May 13). "Second S.D. ex-con in two days executed." *Rapid City Journal*. Retrieved from www.rapidcityjournal.com.

Rainwater, M. (2010, May 14). "Second S.D. ex-con in 2 days executed for 1998 murder." *Huntsville Item*. Retrieved from www.itemonline.com.

Rainwater, M. (2010, May 19). "Man executed for slaying of cellmate." *Huntsville Item*. Retrieved from www.itemonline.com.

Rainwater, M. (2010, May 25). "Alba executed for wife's shooting." *Huntsville Item*. Retrieved from www.itemonline.com.

Rainwater, M. (2010, June 2). "Jones executed for 1993 slayings." *Huntsville Item*. Retrieved from www.itemonline.com.

Rainwater, M. (2010, June 16). "Drug dealer executed for 1978 slaying of Austin cop." *Huntsville Item*. Retrieved from www.itemonline.com.

Rainwater, M. (2010, July 1). "Killer of Houston nurse executed." *Huntsville Item*. Retrieved from www.itemonline.com.

Ritz, I. (2010, May 13). "Michael Beuke executed for Ohio hitchhiker murder." *The Epoch Times*. Retrieved from www.theepochtimes.com.

Robinson, C. (2010, August 12). "Alabama set to execute Michael Land for murder of Candace Brown." *Birmingham News*. Retrieved from www.al.com/birminghamnews.

Ross, A. (2010, May 22). "Execution slated for Tuesday for Elgin native." *Bastrop Advertiser*. Retrieved from www.statesman.com.

Ryan, C. (2010, May 20). "Rogelio Cannady executed." *Valley Morning Star*. Retrieved from www.valleymorningstar.com.

Salter, L. (2010, May 24). "Delay looms as big issue in execution cases." Retrieved from wwwclarkprosecutor.org.

Savage, D. (2010, September 14). "FBI reports 5% drop in crime rate." *Los Angeles Times*.

Section 13A-5-45 (c) and (d), Code of Alabama 1975.

"September 2010 Executions—Cal Brown." Prodeathpenalty.com. Retrieved from www.prodeathpenalty.com/pending/10/sep10.htm.

Shank, V. (2010, July 10). "Survivor, victims' families gather for death penalty." *Warren Tribune Review*. Retrieved from www.tribtoday.com.

Sharp, D. (1997, October 1). "Death penalty and sentencing information." *Justice for All*. Retrieved from www.jfa.net.

Sinclair, B. (2010, September 11). "The end of Holly Wood." Capital punishmentbook.com. Retrieved from http://www.capitalpunishmentbook.com/?p=485.

Smart, C. (2010, June 18). "Gardner executed." *Salt Lake Tribune*. Retrieved from www.sltrib.com.

Smith, J. (2010, January 7). "Man who killed Toledo store owner in 1993 scheduled to be executed." Associated Press. Retrieved from www.ap.org.

Smith, T. (2010, June 11). "Parker put to death." *Times Daily*. Retrieved from www.timesdaily.com.

Solis, R. (2010, July 21). "Mississippi executes man for 1994 slaying of motel clerk." Associated Press. Retrieved from www.ap.org.

Solomant, E.B. (2010, February 16). "U.S. Jews rush to stay execution." *Jerusalem Post*. Retrieved from www.jpost.com.

Stackhouse, M. (2010, June 10). "Shoals man executed Thursday night." WHNT-TV.

"State of Alabama executed John Forrest Parker." (2010, June 10). Associated Press. Retrieved from www.ap.org.

Stevenson, B. (2011, July). "The death penalty in Alabama: Judge override." *Equal Justice Initiative*.

Sullivan, J. (2010, September 9). "Washington State says new execution method carried out humanely." *Seattle Times*. Retrieved from www.seattletimes.com.

Sullivan, J. (2010, September 10). "Killer on death row 16½ years is executed." *Seattle Times*. Retrieved from www.seattletimes.com.

Tex. Code Crim. Proc. Ann., Art. 37.071(b)2.

Texas Department of Criminal Justice, executed offenders, Gary Johnson. Retrieved from www.tdcj.tx.us.

Texas Department of Criminal Justice. Retrieved from http://www.tdcj.state.tx.us.

"Texas executes man convicted of killing student." (2010, April 22). Associated Press. Retrieved from www.ap.org.

"Texas man who murdered Brazilian couple set to die." (2010, March 1). Associated Press-FoxNews. Retrieved from www.foxsanantonio.com.

Texas Office of Attorney General. (2010, February 23). Michael Sigala scheduled for execution. [Press Release]. Retrieved from www.oag.state.tx.us.

Texas Office of Attorney General. (2010, March 5). Joshua Maxwell scheduled for execution. [Media Advisory]. Retrieved from www.oag.state.tx.us.

Texas Office of Attorney General. (2010, March 25). Franklin Alix scheduled for execution. [Media Advisory]. Retrieved from www.oag.state.tx.us.

Texas Office of Attorney General. (2010, April 15). William Berkley scheduled for execution. [Media Advisory]. Retrieved from www.oag.state.tx.us.

Texas Office of Attorney General. (2010, May 26). George Jones scheduled for execution. [Media Advisory]. Retrieved from www.oag.state.tx.us.

Texas Office of Attorney General. (2010, June 24). Michael Perry scheduled for execution. [Media Advisory]. Retrieved from www.oag.state.tx.us.

Texas Office of Attorney General. (2010, August 18). Peter Cantu scheduled for execution. [Media Advisory]. Retrieved from www.oag.state.tx.us.

Texas Office of Attorney General Greg Abbott. (2010, January 4). Kenneth Mosley Execution. [Media Advisory]. Retrieved from www.oag.state.tx.us.

Texas Office of Attorney General Greg Abbott.

(2010, May 12). Rogelio Reyes Cannady scheduled for execution. [Media Advisory]. Retrieved from www.oag.state.tx.us.

Tolson, M. (2010, July 1). "Inmate execution for nurse's murder: Says he didn't kill Conroe woman." Associated Press. Retrieved from www.ap.org.

Tolson, M. (2010, August 17). "Cantu executed for 1993 deaths of Houston teens." *Houston Chronicle*. Retrieved from www.houstonchronicle.com.

Turner, A. (2010, March 31). "Houston man executed in 1998 slaying." *Houston Chronicle*. Retrieved from www.houstonchronicle.com.

Turner, A. (2010, April 27). "Killer in 1998 Rosenberg robbery very quiet at execution." *Houston Chronicle*. Retrieved from www.houstonchronicle.com.

"USA: Cruel, inhuman, degrading: 40th execution of the year approaches." (2010, September 24). Amnesty International. Retrieved from http://www.amnesty.org/en/library/info/AMR51/091/2010/en.

Va. Code § 8.01–654.2.

Va. Code § 19.2–264.3:1.1(c).

Volentine, J. (2010, August 17). "Peter Cantu executed." KIAH-TV. Retrieved from www.newsfixnow.com.

Welsch-Huggins, A. (2010, February 4). "Ohio executes man who murdered shopkeeper, clerk." Associated Press. Retrieved from www.ap.org.

Wetterich, C. (2011, February 15). "Bill would reinstate death penalty in Illinois." GateHouse News Service. Retrieved from www.gatehousemedia.com.

White, J. (2010, March 19). "Virginia executes man in 1999 murder of woman, rape of her sister." *Washington Post*. Retrieved from www.washingtonpost.com.

Winick, B. (2009, May). "The Supreme Court's evolving death penalty jurisdiction: Severe mental illness as the next frontier." 50 *B.C.L. Rev* 785.

Wolfson, S. (2010, June 16). "Powell executed for officer death." KXAN-TV.

Yimam, B. (2010, September 17). "State board denies clemency for Jones County triple murder." WMAZ-TV. Retrieved from www.13wmaz.com.

Court Cases

Alba v. State, 905 S.W.2d 581 (TexCrim.App. 1995).

Atkins v. Virginia, 536 U.S. 304 (2002), banned the execution of the mentally disabled.

Baze v. Rees, 553 U.S. 35 (2008).

Berkley v. State, 74, 336 (Tx.Crim.App. April 6, 2005).

Bobby v. Bies, 129 S.Ct. 2145 (2009).

Bruton v. U.S., 391 U.S 123 (1968).

Burns v. State, 729 So.2d 203 (Miss. 1998).

Bustamante v. State, 106 S.W.3d 738, 742 (Tex.Crim.App.2003).

Cannady v. Dretke, 173 Fed.Appx 321 (5th Cir. 2006).

Cannady v. State, 11 S.W.3d 205 (Tex.Crim.App. 2006).

Cantu v. State, 939 S.W.2d 627 (Tex.Crim.App. 1997).

Davis v. U.S., 512 U.S. 452 (1994).

Duty v. Workman, 366 Fed. Appx. 863 (10th Cir. 2010).

Edwards v. Arizona, 451 U.S. 477 (1981).

Ex Parte Alix, 2006 WL 2766361 (Tex.Cr.App. 2006).

Ford v. State, 360 S.E.2d 258 (Ga. 1987).

Frazier v. Cupp, 394 U.S. 731 (1969).

Furman v. Georgia, 408 U.S. 238 (1972).

Galloway v. State, 2003 WL 1712559 (Tx.Crim.App. 2003).

Gregg v. Georgia, 428 U.S. 153 (1976).

Grossman v. State, 525 So.2d 833 (Fla.1988).

Hallford v. State, 548 So.2d 526 (Ala.Cr.App. 1988).

Holland v. State, 587 So.2d 848 (Miss. 1991).

Johnson v. State, 853 S.W.2d 527 (Tx. C. App. 1992).

Jones v. State, 982 S.W.2d 386 (Tex.Crim.App. 1998).

Land v. State, 678 So.2d 224 (Ala.Cr.App. 1995).

Landrigan v. State, 700 P.2d 218 (Okl. Cr. 1985).

Lewis v. Commonwealth, 593 S.E.2d 220 (Va. 2004).

Lewis v. Wheeler, 609 F.2d291 (4th Cir. 2010).

Maryland v. Shatzer, 130 S.Ct 1213 (2010).

Maxwell v. State, 2004 WL 3094649 (Tex.Cr.App. 2004).

Mhadi v. Bagley, 522 Fd 631 (6th Cr. 2000).

Miranda v. Arizona, 384 U.S. 436 (1966).

Mosley v. Quarterman, 306 Fed.Appx. 40 (5th Cir. 2008).

Parker v. State, 610 So.2d 171 (Ala.Cr.App. 1992).

Perry v. Lynaugh, 492 U.S. 302 (1989).

Perry v. State, 158 S.W.3d 438 (Tex.Crim.App. 2004).

Powell v. Commonwealth, 52 S.E.2d 244 (Va. 2001).

Powell v. Commonwealth, 590 S.E.2d 537 (Va. 2004).

Powell v. State, 742 S.W.2d 353 (Tex.Crim.App. 1987).

Powell v. Texas, 492 U.S. 680 (1989).

Rhode v. Hall, 582 F.3d 1273 (11th Cir. 2009).

Rhode v. State, 552 S.E.2d 855 (2001).

Roper v. Simmons, 543 U.S. 551 (2005).

Satterwhite v. Texas, 486 U.S. 249 (1988).

Schiriro v. Smith, 546 U.S. 6, 7, 126 S.Ct. 7, 163 L.Ed.2d 6 (2005).

Sigala v. State, 2004 WL 231326 (Tx.Cr.App. 2004).

Stanford v. Kentucky, 492 U.S. 361 (1989).

State v. Benge, 661 N.E.2d 1019 (Ohio 1995).

State v. Beuke, 38 Ohio St.3d 29 (Ohio 1986).

State v. Bordelon, 2009 WL 3321481, October 16, 2009.

State v. Brown, 100 Ohio st.3d 51 (Ohio App. 2003).

State v. Brown, 940 P.2d 546 (Wash. 1997).

State v. Davie, 1995 WL 870019 (Ohio App. 1995).

State v. Durr, 58 Ohio st.3d 86 (Ohio 1991).

State v. Gardner, 789 P.2d 273 (Utah 1989).

State v. Landrigan, 859 P.2d 111 (Ariz. 1993).

State v. Reynolds, 80 Ohio st.3d 670 (Ohio 1998).

State v. Smith, 89 Ohio st.3d 323, 731 N.E.2d 645 (Oh 2005).

State v. Williams, 452 N.E.2d 1323 (Ohio 1983).

Strickland v. Washington, 466 U.S. 668 (1984).

Varga v. State, 2003 WL 21466926 (Tx.Crim.App. 2003).

Wackerly v. Workman, 580 F.3d 1171 (10th Cir. 2009).

Walker v. Commonwealth, 515 S.E.2d 565 (Va. 1999).

Walker v. Kelly, 593 F.3d 319 (4th Cir. 2010).

Washington v. Gentry, 888 P.2d 1105 (Wash. 1995).

Whisenhant v. State, 370 So.2d 1080 (Ala.Cr.App. 1979).

Woods v. State, 715 So.2d 812 (Ala.Cr.App. 1996).

Woodward v. State, 533 So.2d 418 (Miss.1988).

Young v. State, 992 P.2d 332 (Okla.Crim.App. 1988).

Index